Writing Men

·

Literary Masculinities from Frankenstein *to the New Man*

·

Berthold Schoene-Harwood

Edinburgh University Press

Edinburgh University Press Ltd
22 George Square, Edinburgh

Typeset in Baskerville
by J&L Composition Ltd, Filey, North Yorkshire, and
printed and bound in Great Britain by
MPG Books Ltd, Bodmin

A CIP Record for this book is available from the British Library

ISBN 0 7486 1000 6 (paperback)

Books are to be returned on or before
the last date below.

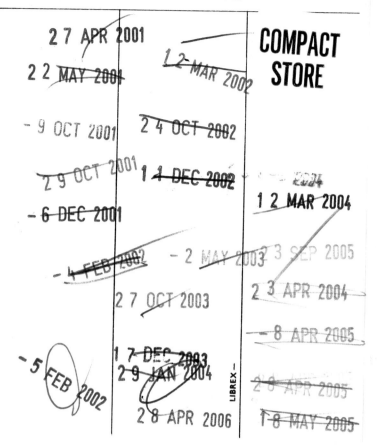

27 APR 2001

22 MAY 2001

12 MAR 2002

COMPACT
STORE

- 9 OCT 2001   2 4 OCT 2002

2 9 OCT 2001   1 1 DEC 2002

- 6 DEC 2001

12 MAR 2004

- 4 FEB 2002   - 2 MAY 2003   3 SEP 2005

27 OCT 2003   2 3 APR 2004

- 8 APR 2005

- 5 FEB 2002   1 7 DEC 2003
2 9 JAN 2004   2 8 APR 2005

LIBREX —

2 8 APR 2006   1 8 MAY 2005

This book is dedicated to the memory of
Ken Harwood
(15.9.1927–15.1.1999)
and ·
Anni Schöne
(28.11.1925–24.12.1980)

Contents

Contents

'I dare do all that may become a man;
Who dares do more, is none.'

Macbeth

'Be the Best!'

British Army advertising slogan

Preface

OVER THE PAST TWENTY years or so, many men have won considerable expertise at speaking for and even facilitating women's particular needs and 'differences'. Male-authored works on women writers
proliferate; nor is it entirely unheard-of for men to teach courses on
feminist theory. Ask any discerning male student to write an essay on
Jane Austen's representation of women, or the straitjacketing impact of
patriarchal gender politics on the women in Shakespeare's comedies,
and the result is often clearly and cogently argued. However, ask them to
comment on the representation of men and the response is often a
mixture of discomfort, nervous agitation and silence. Stubbornly reluctant, or perhaps genuinely unable, to identify with the often justifiably
unsympathetic representation of masculinity in feminist discourse, an
overwhelming number of contemporary men appear to find themselves
at a loss for an appropriate terminology that would enable them to speak
about themselves as men. Their conspicuous inarticulacy could in fact be
seen as symptomatic of how invisible they still are to themselves as one-
sidedly gendered beings. To compound matters further, under patriarchy a man's reticence and silence constitute insidious imperatives that
safeguard and control his masculine authenticity. For a man to speak
about his gender in a critical, self-conscious manner already indicates
that he has failed to live up to the patriarchal ideal and that, consequently, his masculinity is 'in trouble'.

According to Judith Butler, in patriarchal discourse 'the universal
person and the masculine gender are conflated, thereby defining women
in terms of their sex and extolling men as the bearers of a body-

transparent personhood' (Butler 1990: 9). Whereas this discursive disembodiment, or categorical 'unsexing', of men no doubt privileges them, it also facilitates their systemic instrumentalisation by depriving them of adequate means to give voice to their intrinsic emotional complexity. Encouraged and authorised to cultivate a gender-specific lack of self-knowledge, men find themselves systematically incapacitated to behold and scrutinise, let alone enunciate, the condition of their singularly engendered interiority. As a result, men ultimately end up disenfranchised by the same discursive mechanisms that appear to empower them. One of the main objectives of Men's Studies must therefore consist in helping men to re-equip themselves with 'the lost language of emotion' or introspection (Middleton 1990: 166–232) that alone can form an enduringly successful basis for masculine emancipation from the fraudulent master trajectories of patriarchal emplotment. No matter how well-intentioned, it does not appear to be enough for men simply to adopt and start ventriloquising feminist perspectives, aims and resolutions. In order to tackle the specific dilemma of their patriarchal condition, men must develop their own counterdiscourse against ideological remote control and systemic pressure. Feminist thought has exerted an invaluable catalytic impact on contemporary men who have begun to re-imagine and re-authenticate themselves beyond traditional gender formations; it must not now become a convenient substitute for radically self-conscious masculine change.

Sharing feminism's concern with the problematic of gendered writing and its socio-political implications, *Writing Men* is inspired by – and critically responds to – the relatively new academic discipline of Men's Studies, defined by Michael Kimmel as an attempt 'to treat masculinity not as the normative referent against which standards are assessed but as a problematic gender construct' (Kimmel 1987: 10). As Harry Brod argues, 'while *seemingly* about men, traditional scholarship's treatment of generic man as the human form in fact systematically excludes from consideration what is unique to men *qua* men' (Brod 1987a: 264). However, despite its explicit programmatic benevolence, Men's Studies remains fraught with manifold tensions between men's accustomed imaging of themselves as privileged representatives of a persistent gender hegemony and their newly emergent efforts to assist the feminist cause in demolishing their own normative status and patriarchally sanctioned superiority. Notably, both Kimmel and Brod's influential manifestoes appear to perpetuate the patriarchal and deeply hetero-sexist myths of masculine strength and plenitude in opposition to an assumed feminine incompetence and deficiency. Brod describes Men's

Studies as 'a necessary complement to women's studies, needed to bring to completion the feminist project' (Brod 1987a: 264). Similarly, while protesting that 'men's studies seeks neither to replace nor to supplant women's studies', Kimmel stresses the necessity 'to buttress, to augment women's studies, to complete the radically redrawn portrait of gender that women's studies has begun' (Kimmel 1987: 10–11). In light of this 'telling choice of metaphors . . . of a hegemonic masculinity in a scholarly guise' (Cornwall and Lindisfarne 1994: 34), it seems hardly surprising that women remain highly sceptical of the New Man's allegedly profeminist project of masculine reconstruction.

In order to save Men's Studies from being categorically disqualified and dismissed before it has even had a chance to find a suitable voice in which to argue its case, it seems important to note that not only women scholars are aware of the profoundly problematic, double-edged ambivalence of contemporary men's reconstructive endeavour. Commendably, Mark Justad introduces his enquiry into a possible 'transvaluation of phallic masculinity' with a pertinent explication of the terminological ambiguity of masculine 'reconstruction':

> The reconstruction of masculinity may be thought of as a manipulation of an identified oppressive social construct that has historical, but not essential, associations with men . . . or it may be an effort to re-establish some true or archetypal form of being and acting like men that has been obscured by a larger social or political force such as feminism, or industrialization.
>
> (Justad 1996: 355)

As David Morgan points out, Men's Studies is beset by the fundamental problem of how men can possibly take a self-conscious step back and critically assess 'a world of and for men . . . a world which allows men to disappear into an undifferentiated humanity' (Morgan 1992: 2). As complicitous keepers of the patriarchal order, men have fashioned society in their own image at the same time as society has fashioned them (and women) to suit and effect its smooth systemic perpetuation. The fallacious circumstance addressed by both Justad and Morgan is that whatever change men may eventually set in motion is at risk of becoming yet 'another construction, part of the continuous outpouring of men into a man-made world' (Morgan 1992: 2). It seems equally important not to forget that Men's Studies essentially represents a reactive, post-feminist formation necessitated by, rather than originarily instigating, societal change. As such, it invariably embodies 'some kind of readjustment by men: either a redefinition of manhood or else a reassertion of the old definition' (Schwenger 1984: 8), both of which may ultimately be motivated by an expedient politics of patriarchal accommodation and containment rather than endorsing a groundbreaking deconstruction of traditional power relations.

In response to feminism's successful explosion of the normative standard of patriarchal femininity and its subsequent pluralist diversification into a multitude of autonomous femininities, representative spokesmen of Men's Studies have been quick to claim a similar wealth of multidimensional differentiation for the masculine gender:

> we cannot study masculinity in the singular, as if the stuff of man were a homogeneous and unchanging thing. Rather, we wish to emphasize the plurality and diversity of men's experiences, attitudes, beliefs, situations, practices, and institutions, along lines of race, class, sexual orientation, religion, ethnicity, age, region, physical appearance, able-bodiedness, mental ability, and various other categories with which we describe our lives and experiences. (Brod and Kaufman 1994: 5–6)

In contrast, although its title and subtitle acknowledge that there is a great diversity of different kinds of men, *Writing Men* contests the widespread assumption that a vibrant plurality of masculinities, in the sociopolitical sense of the word, is already in existence. As a distinct social grouping of their own, heterosexual men especially have so far failed to emancipate themselves from the persistent grip of traditional masculine ideals and imperatives. There is no straight male counterdiscourse that would compare with those of the gay and feminist liberation movements which originally emerged from a communal alliance across and beyond the restrictive boundaries of race, class and nation. As Joseph Bristow writes, 'straight-identified men – one of the main objects for transformation by and through feminist and gay critique – are still largely without a vocabulary for articulating a radical difference within the sex/gender hierarchy' (Bristow 1992: 60).

However vociferous and eloquent in the articulation of their racialist or classist oppression, even black and working-class men never argue their case in terms of their gender which, even under otherwise severely unpropitious conditions, remains apt to demarcate them favourably from their female and gay counterparts. Accordingly, *Writing Men* insists on speaking of patriarchal masculinity in the singular in order to highlight the insidious impact its inherent conceptual contradictions and inconsistencies continue to exert on the individuation and self-formation of both men and their others. My usage of 'patriarchal masculinity' corresponds with R.W. Connell's designation of 'hegemonic masculinity' as 'the configuration of gender practice which embodies the currently accepted answer to the problem of the legitimacy of patriarchy, which guarantees (or is taken to guarantee) the dominant position of men and the subordination of women' (Connell 1995: 77). This hegemonic configuration of masculinity is always bound to constitute an impossible, phantasmatic ideal that ultimately no man can live up to or fulfil. As a result, all flesh-and-blood masculinities must ineluctably find themselves in a position of either complicity, marginality or subordination.

Patriarchal masculinity is characterised by an inscription of hierarchical binarisms that continue to impair present-day humanity's communal desire for authentic self-fulfilment. Traditionally thriving on an endless proliferation of oppressive violence, it consolidates its hegemony both discursively and by actual physical force in a systemic display of omnipotent power. Engaged in continuous battles for authoritative predominance, patriarchally organised societies perpetrate an irrevocable split of the dominant self from its subordinate others, a split that manifests itself in institutionalised sexism, classism and racism at one end of the spectrum and rape, torture, even full-scale, worldwide war at the other. Within such a system that reverberates with conflictual tensions between a totalitarian self and its margin of excluded others, the individual male is summoned not only to uphold but also to epitomise the normative standard. Lest his own manliness become culturally unintelligible and ambiguous, he must aim to stay uncontaminated by the alleged inferiority of (his own intrinsic) alterity. A state of acute paranoia seems inevitable, entrapping patriarchal man in a limbo of phobic self-containment compounded rather than resolved by ceaseless manoeuvres of indiscriminate shadow-bashing.

By focusing on the imperatives and normative standards of patriarchal masculinity, *Writing Men* does not seek to dispute or detract from Máirtín Mac an Ghaill's proposition that 'we need to move away from categorical theories that emphasize that gender/sexual relations are shaped by a single overarching factor' (Mac an Ghaill 1996: 1). Rather, *Writing Men* intends to contour a genealogy of progressive masculine devolution from patriarchal man's incarceration within the monolith of traditional *Bildung* to his present emancipatory re-authentication as a potential carrier of a pluralist diversity of post-patriarchal masculinities. The study's insertion of two female-authored texts into this narrative seeks to demonstrate the indispensable and integral component women's writings and life experiences constitute within male writers' current envisioning of less systemically predictable and circumscriptive modes of masculine self-representation. *Writing Men* represents an enquiry into why and to what extent 'there has been a shift to the notions of hegemonic masculinity and multiple masculinities' (Mac an Ghaill 1996: 2), not only in gender criticism but also in the works of creative men writers. Thus, while tracing and signposting the imminent emergence of a socio-political plurality of multiple masculinities, the study remains predominantly concerned with patriarchal man's troubled heritage of systemic oppression and regulatory masculine self-deformation that continues to occlude his devolutionary reconstruction.

Writing Men is subdivided into four parts. The first introductory part embarks on an excursion into the nineteenth-century pre-history of post-war and contemporary British men's writing. *Frankenstein, Heart of Darkness* and *The Turn of the Screw* are read as paradigmatic examples of gendered writing. By demonstrating how these texts are informed by a struggle for narrative supremacy between antagonistic male and female voices, the three individual readings introduce readers to literature's capacity for both – and sometimes simultaneously – consolidating and unsettling traditional conceptions of femininity and masculinity. Shelley, Conrad and James experiment with differently gendered positions of narration that interrogate their own problematic emplotment – as well as their society's ideological inscription – of a hierarchical system of gender relations. In Part II, detailed readings of literary 'classics' like *Lord of the Flies, A Clockwork Orange, Look Back in Anger* and *Room at the Top* reveal the imperative impact these gender hierarchies continue to exert on (the representation of) boys' and young men's strategies of masculine self-authentication in the 1950s and early 1960s.

The third and central section of *Writing Men* explores the influence feminist thought has had on men's writing in our immediate present. A major concern in this context is contemporary men writers' self-conscious envisioning of an *écriture masculine* that would interrogate and deconstruct their predecessors' often stereotyped and profoundly androcentric conceptions of masculinity. Importantly, all the novels discussed in Part III, including Angela Carter's *The Passion of New Eve*, tell in effect two stories at the same time, that of a man and that of a woman, thus highlighting men and women's common dilemma as oppositionally gendered beings in a world that appears to thrive on polarity and segregation. Gender is recurrently problematised as a mutually injurious construct that obstructs, rather than facilitates, the successful formation and maintenance of heterosexual relationships. Instead of revisiting the often uncompromising sex-war literature of the past, these contemporary writers seem primarily concerned with re-introducing the sexes to each other in utopian allegories of curative self-reformation.

The concluding part of *Writing Men* discusses Neil Bartlett's *Ready to*

Catch Him Should He Fall as an attempt to subvert patriarchal masculinity from a gay male perspective. Whereas any discussion of masculinity would be incomplete without addressing its dichotomous division into straight and gay identifications, the inclusion of a gay-authored text within the framework of an investigation predominantly concerned with representations of heterosexual masculinity must inevitably be at risk of instigating a binarist rhetoric of contrast. In this respect, my decision to open up a gay perspective on masculinity in a separate section at the very end of *Writing Men* may certainly – at least initially – appear dubious. All it intends to indicate, however, is the categorical exclusion of male homosexuality from the patriarchal conception of masculinity as well as the central, if passive, role homosexual men may have played in the original formation of that conception. Accordingly, the thirteenth chapter of *Writing Men* offers itself to two alternative readings as either a mere appendix or a climactic crescendo.

Writing Men developed out of two undergraduate courses I taught at the Universities of Swansea and Glamorgan in 1996–98. I would like to take this opportunity to thank all my students – if perhaps most emphatically those participating in the pilot project of 'Posting the Male' – for their inquisitiveness and unwavering enthusiasm. My gratitude also goes to Jackie Jones at Edinburgh University Press whose editorial vision helped to set this project in motion and whose patient understanding of the manifold vicissitudes of academic life continued to provide invaluable support and reassurance. *Writing Men* also owes its existence to John Mepham and Christopher Whyte who, at a very early stage in the writing of this book, had the courage of guessing at where I might want to be going. I would also like to thank Carol Duncan at Edinburgh University Press for patiently seeing me through the final stages of completing the manuscript.

Special thanks are due to my friends and colleagues for their insight, advice and invariably constructive criticism: Rhiannon Davies, Glenda Norquay, Gill Plain, Helen Rogers, Andrew Smith, Tamsin Spargo and Kati Stammwitz. I am particularly indebted to the diligence, clear-sightedness and critical imagination of Jeni Williams who read and re-read chapter after chapter. I would also like to thank Pam Morris for spotting 'Men, Sea and Moon' at the Walker Art Gallery in Liverpool and Basil Blackshaw for allowing me to use his painting as the cover illustration of *Writing Men*.

Finally – and this is where words must inevitably fail me – I am grateful to David Schoene-Harwood for all his love, patience and sanity.

Part I

Monsters, Heroes and Ghosts:
Narratives of Masculine Self-(De)Formation

TRADITIONAL GENDER NORMS SIGNIFICANTLY contribute to the constitu-
tion of a societal frame of *Bildung* under whose systemic pressure
individuals aspire to become the men and women they ought to be.
Males and females are moulded by patriarchal imperatives to suit the
configurative standards of a societally acceptable masculinity or femininity. As the cataclysmic trajectories of *Frankenstein, Heart of Darkness* and
The Turn of the Screw demonstrate, gender is a formative imposition which
individuals resist, appropriate and transgress at their own existential
peril. Coming down on offenders with the force of annihilative tragedy,
the system of nineteenth-century patriarchy is shown to be practically
impervious to deconstructive revelations of its inherent inconsistencies
and contradictions. The gender performances of overly autonomous
men, who design and direct their own heroic exploits, are doomed to
end in horror and death. Similarly, even the most tentative, often purely
accidental emergence of hitherto unprecedented, alternative femininities
– like that of Frankenstein's female monster – results in spontaneous
abortive destruction.

A late twentieth-century reading of *Frankenstein, Heart of Darkness* and
The Turn of the Screw discloses their subversive potential as narratives of
apocalyptic self-(de)formation that interrogate the societal construction
of monstrosity. Is it not 'monstrous', too – that is, does it not also deform
the self – to give in to normative gender imperatives in denial of the
intrinsically multi-gendered complexity of one's *human* disposition? In all
three works, the deviant and transgressive appear as reflective projections of a hidden regulatory agenda of systemic expediency that seeks to
naturalise and perpetuate its own monstrous formations. Against this
background, a thorough reassessment of the *doppelgänger* motif becomes
necessary, identifying not Frankenstein and his monster as doubles but
Victor and his brother Ernest, not Marlow and Kurtz, but the transgressor in his relation to the many less distinguished instruments of
patriarchal and imperial power. Correspondingly, rather than contend-
ing with a couple of uncanny, apparitional usurpers of systemic authority,
James's governess is shown to find her plight 'doubled' by little Miles, the
boy child, whose burgeoning masculinity eventually expires in the
phallogocentric grasp of her vicarious aspirations. Invariably, monstrosity outside the system is highlighted to deflect from the complicity of 'the
ordinary fellow' and – more crucially – the inherent monstrosity of
patriarchal society's own normative standards.

Harry Brod writes that 'men are generally nostalgic for a past perceived as embodying a more stable and secure masculine identity',
adding that 'identifying the historical inaccuracies of this mythologizing

[handwritten margin notes:]
other 'feminine' traits = undesirable masculine
Part One
Part in 19C so strong it couldn't be criticised
deconstruct the "self" Masc + Fem
the Book Reveals hidden monsterous formation of society
highlighted deflect from inner-corruption

3

of the past can free men's attentions to encounter present realities more directly' (Brod 1987a: 268). Accordingly, the first part of this study constitutes an attempt to reveal individual impersonations of patriarchal masculinity as precarious, tragically unstable and ultimately detrimental identity constructs that, instead of conducing to a man's quest for autonomous self-authentication, rigidly circumscribe it. Like traditional femininity, masculinity represents an imperative ideal of systemic perfection that obstructs rather than facilitates the liberation of the self.

[handwritten margin notes: "By rejecting what masculinity is you can free self identify yourself"]

[handwritten note: "Pat confines men too."]

[handwritten note: "Pat & masculinity is destructive and restrictive."]

1

.

About Man-Making

.

Mary Shelley's Frankenstein

MARY SHELLEY'S *FRANKENSTEIN* IS widely read as 'a woman's text concerned with women's issues' (Smith 1992: 284), a semi-autobiographical 'birth-myth' featuring a triad of central characters (Robert Walton, Victor Frankenstein, the Monster) who despite their explicit maleness are seen to operate as allegorical signifiers in a literary configuration of Shelley's own repressed and traumatised psyche (see Gilbert and Gubar 1979: 213–47; Johnson 1982; Moers 1977). Suggesting that even in the realm of fiction a woman's experience can never venture far from the vicarious, *Frankenstein* is interpreted as an andromorphic encapsulation of its author's own suffering, both as a daughter whose mother died giving birth to her and as a mother many of whose children were stillborn or died in early infancy. This kind of reading accentuates the novel's conceptually chaotic nature as an outpouring of long-suppressed female dream-work, detracting from its imaginative and intellectual powers as a consciously crafted work of fiction. *Frankenstein* is not the desultory product of an emotionally confused case of deep-psychological cross-gender projection. Rather, its formal peculiarities ingeniously disclose the complex gender dynamics at work within patriarchy and – in particular – the predicament of the individual male psyche under patriarchal pressure.

Initially, *Frankenstein* seems quite conventionally gendered, intent on confirming rather than criticising or even subverting traditional patriarchal structures. The novel is written in the form of an epistolary report posted by Walton at sea in the Arctic to his older married sister Margaret Saville at home in England. From the very beginning Shelley appears to distinguish clearly between masculine and feminine spheres of being, between manly adventure in the wilderness on the one hand and womanly domesticity in the maternal safety of hearth and home on the other. Masculinity and femininity reflect the allegedly natural opposition of the male and female sexes as well as their biologically determined complementarity. As Victor comments on his relationship with Elizabeth, 'the diversity and contrast that subsisted in our characters drew us nearer together'. Elizabeth is said to be 'of a calmer and more concentrated disposition' while Victor believes himself 'capable of a more intense application' and due to his maleness 'more deeply smitten with the thirst for knowledge' (p. 42). The men and women of *Frankenstein* represent the stereotypes of perfect heterosexual polarity, with the superior prowess of the male crystallising in the light of the 'shrine-dedicated lamp' (p. 43) of female receptivity. In their unwavering dutifulness Caroline Beaufort and Elizabeth Lavenza resemble picture-book caricatures of ideal woman-hood. Both are introduced into the Frankenstein family as orphaned beggars, each providing her future husband with a welcome opportunity to exhibit his aristocratic generosity and knightly stature.

However, the women's rescue from an undignified life in squalid destitution comes at the high price of total commodification. Victor is given Elizabeth as 'a pretty present' and soon comes to regard her as 'a possession of my own' (p. 41). Similarly, his father Alphonse casts himself in the role of protective gardener to Caroline's 'fair exotic' (p. 39). No matter what remarkable strength and courage Victor's mother displays in later life, it is her original weakness that is commemorated by the Frankenstein family. Alphonse has a picture painted of his young wife 'in an agony of despair, kneeling by the coffin of her dead father' (p. 74). Standing over the mantelpiece in the drawing-room, this picture gives iconic evidence of the now frail and elderly patriarch's erstwhile heroism while at the same time inscribing Caroline's definitive inferiority. Alphonse's fatherly protection effects his wife's domestic imprisonment within the framework of enduring female indebtedness and gratitude. Shelley presents both Caroline and Elizabeth's maidenly helplessness as projections of a narcissistic male desire that constructs the myth of its own monumental potency in diametric opposition to the deficiencies of an equally man-made femininity. Thus, *Frankenstein* highlights a rigid gender binarism that promotes male freedom and superiority by legit-imating women's domestic confinement and intellectual debilitation. Shelley exaggerates the corollaries of this binarism by presenting her women characters as a silent audience devotedly attentive to the narra-tion and centre-stage performances of their men. As a result, the fable of *Frankenstein* is deprived of its universally human applicability and the expressive gender-specificity of Victor's tragedy becomes apparent. The exponentially increasing destructiveness of the novel testifies to a specifically masculine propensity for excessive behaviour out of all societal control. In contrast, due to their categorical exclusion from the main action of the novel, the women have no influence whatsoever on the fateful plot developments of Shelley's tale.

Both traditional and feminist criticisms have so far overlooked the possibility of reading the novel's multi-layered narrative concentricity of story-within-story as a gradual female-authored fathoming of the male consciousness. Importantly, as Beth Newman notes, 'the novel fails to provide significant differences in tone, diction and sentence structure that alone can serve, in a written text, to represent individual human voices' (Newman 1995: 171). Shelley's three male narrators end up speaking from the common position of a specifically masculine quandary. The narratives of Walton, Victor and the Monster become variations on one and the same theme, concentrating on the gestation of something dark and apocalyptic at the core of man's psychological make-up, something self-inflicted and essentially man-made, yet something also whose original motivation escapes masculine reasoning. The three young men are preoccupied with the various processes of their coming of age. However, instead of describing their maturation as a gradual unfolding of a healthy, natural disposition, Shelley chooses to problematise it as a compulsive, potentially tragic struggle. In *Frankenstein* masculinity manifests itself as a complex syndromic condition seeking to fulfil itself in heroic acts of self-assertion like Victor's god-like creation of the Monster or Walton's groundbreaking voyage to the North Pole. Shelley identifies masculinity as a closed set of behavioural characteristics, all of which evolve out of a strict opposition to femininity and develop into a single-minded predilection for manly adventure and scientific experimentation. Shelley's male characters experience masculinity as an urgent imperative that is felt to originate at the core of their innermost selves. However, its exact source and purpose remain obscure, as Walton indicates in the second letter to his sister:

> There is something at work in my soul, *which I do not understand . . .* there is a love for the marvellous, a belief in the marvellous, intertwined in all my projects, which hurries me out of the common pathways of men, even to the wild sea and unvisited regions I am about to explore.
>
> (pp. 30–1; my emphasis)

In striking contradiction to their general scientific curiosity, Victor and Walton never turn to probe this mysterious darkness within them. It seems as if the heroic idealism of patriarchal masculinity were exempt from moral questioning or scientific analysis, as if it were simply to be taken for granted as a sublime principle of 'The Truth about Men'. According to Shelley, it is this acute lack of self-knowledge in Walton and Victor, their boyish naivety and quite astounding capacity for self-delusion, which propels them down the path of tragic self-destruction. Expert at 'penetrat[ing] into the recesses of nature [to] show how she works in her hiding places' (p. 51), they fail to explore their own interiority and remain blind to the patriarchal agenda which not only governs their everyday existence but determines their whole understanding of themselves, as well as the limits of that understanding. While scientifically scrutinising, objectifying and dissecting the world, their inquisitive male gaze never turns inwards to reflect on the nature of its own origin and motivation.

In his preface to the 1818 edition of *Frankenstein* Percy Shelley writes that his wife's novel is essentially to be understood as a commendation of 'the amiableness of domestic affection' (Shelley 1992: 25). As such, it is bound to be highly critical of a kind of masculinity that perpetuates itself out of a categorical disruption of familial harmony, a masculinity that defines itself in opposition to femininity, seeking excellence and heroic refinement in deliberate attempts 'to become different from nature, to oppose nature, to become unnatural' (Flannigan-Saint-Aubin 1994: 244). What has horrified readers of *Frankenstein* so enduringly is perhaps first and foremost Shelley's acute insight into the male psyche as formed by patriarchal conditioning. Her representation of Victor and Walton's death-bound masculinities is far from fantastic; on the contrary, it gives a realistic portrayal of the actual sentiments, values and pursuits of traditional masculinity, characterised by Arthur Flannigan-Saint-Aubin as follows:

> Masculinity is a 'becoming,' a process as opposed to a perceived feminine 'being' or state. Like 'progress' within patriarchy, it is something to be achieved and to be experienced as triumph over nature, and therefore it seeks to penetrate and appropriate virgin frontiers. It is linear in orientation and directed toward goals. (Flannigan-Saint-Aubin 1994: 241)

Despite Shelley's deliberate marginalisation of the feminine in *Frankenstein*, it never vanishes from the narrative altogether but remains to embrace the three male heroes' disastrous escapades. The novel's narrative structure exposes the men's agency and their ambitious aspirations at least potentially to the judgement of a female gaze, which belongs to both the fictional reader Margaret Saville and the writer Mary Shelley, as the two women's common 'M.S.' signature suggests. 'Will you smile at the enthusiasm I express concerning this divine wanderer?' (p. 36), Walton asks his sister when writing about his first encounter with Victor Frankenstein. In Walton's imagination whatever he does, feels or declares is at risk of being fondly indulged and hence belittled by a woman. Rather than serving the traditional purpose of reflecting and consolidating men's heroic superiority, in *Frankenstein* the enduring passivity of receptive womanhood becomes a site of masculine self-doubt and insecurity.

Walton's paranoia finds a fitting mirror image in Victor's conviction that his whole life is framed by the 'innumerable laws' of malevolent female deities like Destiny, Despair and Nature who 'had decreed my utter and terrible destruction' (p. 46). Victor blames his tragic deterioration on a whimsical conspiracy of metaphysical matriarchs rather than the influence of any real-life, structural coercion. Thus projecting a phantasmatic sisterhood of female adversaries, his own systemic subjection remains invisible to him. His faith in himself as a hero – albeit a thwarted one – stays intact. Shelley exposes this fateful manly unselfconsciousness, directing her narrative spotlight on masculinity's every move, searching the routine of its deceptively familiar behavioural patterns for deconstructive inconsistencies and contradictions. As a result of Shelley's probing, masculinity – gender's normative standard – is forced to emerge from its tradition of representational transparency. Shelley's narration causes men to fall out of their carefully contrived framework of human universality. They become visible as gendered beings. As Bette London writes, Shelley manoeuvres her male protagonists into 'the position of spectacle', animating the masculinities of Walton, Victor and the Monster 'to reveal the condition of their articulation' (London 1993: 265).

Contrary to its initial appearance as a text that confirms patriarchal gender roles, *Frankenstein* turns out to be in fact profoundly subversive as Shelley engages in a complex project of cross-writing. The representation of gender in *Frankenstein* is imbued with deliberate ambivalence, emanating from the novel's unique quality as a woman writer's ventriloquial adaptation of a chorus of imposing male voices, not only Walton's but also Victor's and the Monster's. As Devon Hodges has pointed out, 'in adopting a male voice, the woman writer is given the opportunity to intervene from within, to become an alien presence that undermines the stability of the male voice' (Hodges 1983: 157). Intricately entwining the differently gendered primary and secondary voices of female author and male characters, Shelley's novel comes to resemble a cross-written 'drag narrative' within which female-authored men are presented as the mere impersonators of a supposedly authentic masculinity. The voices of the Monster, Victor and Walton are not male, but 'male'. Their masculinity must be regarded as a highly gender-conscious imitation, a parody oscillating between representation and ironic critique. As Judith Butler's explication of gender parody indicates, Shelley's cross-writing device in *Frankenstein* is possibly the most effectively subversive vehicle in her exposure of traditional conceptions of gender identity:

> The notion of gender parody . . . does not assume that there is an original which such parodic identities imitate. Indeed, the parody is *of* the very notion of an original; just as the psychoanalytic notion of gender identification is constituted by a fantasy of a fantasy, the transfiguration of an Other who is always already a 'figure' in that double sense, so gender parody reveals that the original identity after which gender fashions itself is an imitation without an origin. (Butler 1990: 138)

Gender is marked by flux and indeterminacy. Neither masculinity nor femininity exists naturally; both are created *ex nihilo* to meet and, ironically, to necessitate certain systemic requirements in connection with the societal distribution and organisation of power. In *Frankenstein*, as in real life, both genders are constantly destabilised by their own internal ambiguity. They are always already inhabited by the presence of their other(s) or – to employ the imagery of *Frankenstein* – their *doppelgänger*, at once intimately familiar and monstrously alien. An idealised, strictly segregated man-made world composed of pure masculinity and pure femininity (like that portrayed in Shelley's novel) is bound either to suffer an irreparable split or to cancel itself out.

True to his irresolvably ambivalent identity as Victor's *doppelgänger*, the Monster's murderous rampage not only illustrates the consequences of Victor's emulation of the patriarchal ideal of masculinity but also his fateful repression of the female and feminine. According to Burton Hatlen, 'the most significant similarity between God and Victor Frankenstein is their common status as "male mothers"' (Hatlen 1983: 32). Like God with Adam and Eve, Victor fails to love his child unconditionally, nurture it, and forgive it all its shortcomings, a failure that unleashes violence and destruction upon society. Although born out of Victor's most radically masculinist eclipse of what is the most prominent prerogative of the female, the gender identity of the Monster is initially far from unequivocal. Made up of incongruent body parts, the Monster learns to recognise and engender himself as male only after several painful confrontations with society's symbolic perception of him.

Initially, in what is probably the most frequently cited passage of the novel, the newborn Monster steps forth into the precarious, highly contestable sphere of both its maker's bride and mother:

> I thought I saw Elizabeth, in the bloom of health, walking in the streets of Ingolstadt. Delighted and surprised, I embraced her; but as I imprinted the first kiss on her lips, they became livid with the hue of death; her features appeared to change, and I thought that I held the corpse of my dead mother in my arms; a shroud enveloped her form, and I saw the graveworms crawling in the folds of the flannel. I started from my sleep with horror . . . when . . . I beheld the wretch – the miserable monster whom I had created . . . He might have spoken, but I did not hear; one hand was stretched out, seemingly to detain me, but I escaped, and rushed down stairs. (p. 58)

Victor flees from the horror vision of threefold domestic entrapment by the familial obligations of marital, filial and parental love. Instead of affirming his manly integrity and independence from the realm of domesticity, Victor's most heroic deed – the creation of the Monster – locates him within a complex web of emasculating family relationships. The Monster is his child but also – due to its unnatural conception and birth – an unwelcome reminder of the wife and mother Victor sought to omit from the procreative equation. The Monster thus comes to stand for both Victor's masculine self and its other: the feminine and the maternal. Gradually Victor disintegrates, caught up in what is an impossible double bind of feeling compelled simultaneously to pursue and escape the Monster. Victor's efforts to prove himself as an unequivocally masculine subject elicit a monstrous *doppelgänger* symbolic of the inherent self-and-otherness of all gender identities. The Monster embodies the grotesque, loosely pieced together by-product of Victor's idealisation of a sharply contoured, pure masculinity. Victor's crisis appears as a direct corollary of his inability to identify himself as more-than-one, to resist the discrepancies and inconsistencies not of chaotic/female, but of monolithic/masculine identification. His internal split represents a case of Kristevan abjection produced by 'what disturbs identity, system, order. What does not respect borders, positions, rules. The in-between, the ambiguous, the composite' (Kristeva 1982: 4). Significantly, Elizabeth Grosz defines abjection as 'the expression of a contradictory self-conception, one in which the subject is unable to reconcile its (imaginary, felt, fragmented) experience of itself with its idealized image' (Grosz 1990: 94).

Victor's intense paranoia is caused by what Thomas Byers has identified as traditional masculinity's 'extreme concern with the defense of the (illusory) unity, integrity, and significance of the subject' (Byers 1995: 12). Both the male hero's abjection and his paranoia derive from his attempt to embody the masculine self in its perfect, uncontaminated individuality, his adamant refusal to admit a presence of the other into his self-representations. Ironically, it is Victor's need for demonstrative acts of pure self-idealisation – motivated by a fear of the disorderly, chaotic and ambiguous – which produces the Monster. In *Frankenstein*, a man's emulation of the masculine ideal is thwarted by the very impurities and contradictions he seeks to expunge from the image he has cultivated of himself. In rendering himself a god-like, hypermasculine transgressor free of all domestic obligations and encumbrances, Victor evokes the most irresistibly iconic image of feminine domesticity: the bond between a mother and her child. While the usurpation of maternity presents itself as the ultimate feat of masculine self-assertion, it also erases traditional gender distinctions and thus compromises the usurper's manliness. At the same time, most importantly perhaps, it definitively demonstrates to which sex (pro)creative superiority comes 'naturally' and to which it is a strenuous, 'unnatural' act.

A further important aspect of Shelley's cross-writing technique resides with the way in which Frankenstein and Walton's quests for public recognition reflect the specific conditions of Shelley's own creative struggle with *Frankenstein*. Like her central characters Shelley, too, felt she had to prove herself worthy of public (that is, male) acknowledgement. As Shelley explains in the 1831 introduction to her novel, the tale of Frankenstein was originally conceived as her contribution to a story-telling competition between herself, her husband, Lord Byron and his companion Polidori. '*Have you thought of a story?* I was asked each morning, and each morning I was forced to reply with a mortifying negative', Shelley writes (p. 23). The production of *Frankenstein* was induced by incessant male prompting. Memorably referring to the novel as 'my hideous progeny', Shelley likens her composition of the text to Victor's creation of the Monster as well as Walton's voyage to the North Pole, which after the duration of nine laborious months (from 11th December to 17th September) is abruptly aborted for a safe journey home. While the men's projects are shown to be subject to unpredictable risks comparable to the manifold hazards accompanying pregnancy and childbirth, Shelley's female authorship is suggested to share the anxieties typical of masculine self-assertions in the realms of science and adventure. In the production of *Frankenstein* maleness and femaleness are released from the traditional predictability of gender and shown to subvert behavioural certainties by freely intersecting and interpermeating. Gender roles are revealed to signify little more than a particular social *situatedness* that is in effect experientially open to members of both sexes. Accordingly, within the context of *Frankenstein*, a male scientist and a male explorer come to share their specifically masculine dilemma with an inexperienced young woman writer. Shelley is keen to rival her male companions' ghostly tales to prove a woman can tell as exquisitely horrific a story as any man. In this respect, her authorial trepidations emanate from the same pressures that manifest themselves in Victor and Walton's endeavours to comply with masculine imperatives and fulfil the allegedly natural destiny of their sex.

Both Victor and Walton's quests could be interpreted as motivated by male womb envy. As Judith Spector writes, 'Freud enables us to see the creation of culture and art as a masculine compensatory activity in lieu of woman's physical procreative function' (Spector 1981: 22). Principally, womb envy denotes a man's acknowledgement of the awesome super-iority of female (and especially maternal) power, triggering his urge to emulate woman's natural creativity by dint of his imagination and intellect. In Shelley's novel, it is womb envy that triggers the compulsive urge in young men to distance themselves from the domestic sphere of their boyhood in order to explore what is as yet unknown, even – or especially – if this involves a deliberate seeking out of danger. Embarking on projects at once self-effacing and monumentally self-aggrandising, Victor and Walton launch themselves into explorations of geographical and scientific *terrae incognitae* whose conquests are expected to result in epoch-making, universally beneficial contributions to human progress. At the same time, the relatively minor biological differences between female and male freeze into the absolutist hierarchical oppositions of the private/domestic on the one hand and the public on the other. Conse-quently, femaleness suffers an ideological transmogrification into femi-ninity, causing it to become associated with weakness and debility instead of generative resourcefulness or creative empowerment. Womb envy results in misogyny, inducing men to denigrate and systematically infan-tilise women in order to usurp their reproductive faculties and subject them to the authority of patriarchal law.

In *Frankenstein* the female monster, whom Victor destroys halfway through her creation, embodies the originary female powers which inculcate in men the mixed emotions of admiration, envy, fear and loathing. The female monster is not allowed to live because there is no warranty that she will voluntarily bow to the yoke of femininity, or tolerate the domestic confinement and marital subjugation both her maker and her mate intend to impose upon her. Physically powerful, she might choose to resist the straitjacketing grasp of gender. She might also choose to become a mother on her own terms, impervious to the customary patriarchal policing of female sexuality. Most threateningly, however, she might 'become a thinking and reasoning animal' (p. 140), boldly reaching out for the traditional privileges of masculinity rather than yielding without demur to the feminine imperative of unconditional subordination. Within patriarchy woman is defined as body without mind. Hence, to achieve proper manliness a man must acquire and cultivate knowledge and intellectual sophistication. Woman's physical nature is spurned as inferior to the metaphysical cogency of man. Entrapped by birth in the sphere of maternal domesticity, every boy 'has to "grow out of" and "away from" his first encounter with mother's female body and feminine qualities' (Flannigan-Saint-Aubin 1994: 244) in order to find acceptance as a man within the symbolic order of patriarchy.

Walton's Arctic expedition is modelled after a long-cherished boyhood fantasy of leaving home in the company of other males. He begins his journey full of 'the joy a child feels when he embarks in a little boat, with his holiday mates, on an expedition of discovery up his native river' (p. 26). Deprived of suitable male role models or peers (his father is said to have died when he was still a young boy), Walton spent his youth under his sister's 'gentle and feminine fosterage' which 'so refined the groundwork of my character that I cannot overcome an intense distaste to the usual brutality on board ship' (p. 29). His expedition to the North Pole is shown to be a self-inflicted ordeal, designed not only to bring him fame but also to make him 'a real man'. However, while trying hard to live up to the rough, potently heroic masculinity of a seafaring life, Walton evidently finds it extremely difficult to abandon the strongly feminised sphere of his boyhood. Strengthening the impression of *Frankenstein* as a parodic 'drag narrative', Walton's whole story is couched in confidential private letters addressed to a female confidante, his sister, thus mimicking a mode of writing traditionally associated with the plights of a feminine subject struggling for clarity and a sense of self in generally unpropitious circumstances.

Like Walton, Victor feels 'cooped up' at home and longs 'to enter the world' (p. 49). He is keen to prove himself as a man amongst men, something he cannot accomplish at home, which has been an exclusively private, domestic domain ever since his father 'relinquished all his public functions' (p. 39) to marry Victor's mother. Like Walton's Arctic expedition, Victor's struggle for initiation is to compensate for his boyish lack of masculine stature and his familial exclusion from the organisation of life in public. Both young men's departures from home are perhaps best described as *domophobic* escape routes, within the context of which where they go is far less important than what they leave behind: the feminine, the domestic, the maternal. As Walton says goodbye to his motherly sister, Victor extricates himself from the overly solicitous embrace of his family and most saliently his mother, whose death significantly coincides with her eldest son's departure to university. Both young men must abandon and purposely alienate themselves from what has hitherto nurtured and sustained them. The femininity of their loved ones is a stigma to be resolutely scrubbed off if they want to succeed in asserting themselves as men.

Due to their familial circumstances, Walton and Victor feel particularly insecure about what they perceive as their conspicuous lack of masculinity. This sense of inadequacy engenders in them a special susceptibility to patriarchal pressure, a susceptibility that will eventually manifest itself in acts of reckless, overcompensatory heroism. However, the tragedy of *Frankenstein* is not solely triggered by the young men's urge to prove themselves as 'real' men, defying death to create 'inestimable benefit [for] all mankind to the last generation' (p. 26), but also by their zealous single-mindedness, which causes them to overshoot the mark. Walton and Victor are overreachers. In pursuing their ambitions on their own and in opposition to paternal advice, both of them become tragically oblivious to the patriarchal commandments of filial obedience and absolute communal servitude. Walton goes against his 'father's dying injunction [that] had forbidden [his] uncle to allow [him] to embark on a seafaring life' (p. 27). Similarly, Victor is repeatedly warned by Alphonse of the detrimental impact excessive non-conformist behaviour may have on 'the discharge of daily usefulness, without which no man is fit for society' (p. 83). Victor ends up destroyed by the very ideal of masculinity he is trying to epitomise. The problem is that he becomes so inebriated with hopes for personal glory that he fails to submit to the wider design of patriarchal expediency which reserves the award of heroic status exclusively for exemplary feats of obedient servitude. Heroic masculinity represents a contradiction in terms, unhealthily conflating a man's desire for outstanding individual autonomy with the emasculating imperative to succumb without objection to the remote control of patriarchal law.

Shelley contrasts Walton and Victor with a number of other male figures, some of whom perish as a result of Victor's monstrous creation, while a couple manage to resist being drawn into the destructive vortex of complicitous narrative concentricity and emplotment in *Frankenstein*.

Alphonse is said to have 'passed his younger days perpetually occupied by the affairs of his country' (p. 38). Similarly, Henry Clerval intends to employ his resolution 'to pursue no inglorious career' (p. 67) as 'the means of materially assisting the progress of European colonisation and trade' (p. 135). Neither Victor's father nor his best friend ever confuses masculine heroism with personal self-aggrandisement or total individual independence. Notably, Henry seems prepared to abandon 'the plan of life he had marked out for himself' (p. 67) when his father initially withholds permission to let him attend university. There are men in *Frankenstein* who, unlike Walton and Victor, dare not do anything without prior patriarchal sanction. Strangely, these are the men who feel secure enough in their masculinity to display feelings of domestic affection, who patiently and without any apparent loss of face nurse Victor back to health, who seem perfectly balanced in their manliness which incorporates rather than categorically excludes the feminine. These men's main concerns are of a social rather than scientific nature, to do 'with the moral relations of things' rather than 'the secrets of heaven and earth' (p. 43).

Alphonse and Henry's alternative realisation of the masculine ideal is complemented by the seemingly gratuitous presence of another two figures whom Shelley precariously retains on the outermost margin of her narrative. There is the lieutenant on board Walton's ship, whose intrinsic nobility of mind is illustrated in what at first appears a desultory digression relating how he not only released his much-loved fiancée from their engagement but also gave her the money to be able to marry someone else. Pertinently, the lieutenant is described by Walton as 'madly desirous of glory: or rather, to word my phrase more characteristically, of advancement in his profession' (p. 29). Like those of Alphonse and Henry, the lieutenant's masculine ambitions are realised within the legitimate, patriarchally sanctioned confines of service, either to another man or to society at large, and are therefore in no danger of going wildly astray like Victor's or – to a lesser degree – Walton's. Another most intriguing presence in Shelley's novel is that of Ernest Frankenstein, Victor's younger brother, who finds brief, if detailed mention in Elizabeth's letter to Victor shortly before the murder of William, the youngest of the brothers Frankenstein:

> How pleased you would be to remark the improvement of our Ernest. He is now sixteen and full of activity and spirit. He is desirous to be a true Swiss, and to enter into foreign service; but we cannot part with him, at least until his elder brother return to us. My uncle is not pleased with the idea of a military career in a distant country; but Ernest never had your powers of

application. He looks upon study as an odious fetter; – his time is spent in the open air, climbing the hills or rowing on the lake. I fear that he will become an idler, unless we yield the point, and permit him to enter on the profession which he has selected. (p. 63)

Ernest Frankenstein is such a dull character most readers will have completely forgotten about him by the time they reach the end of Elizabeth's letter. Nevertheless, his presence in the novel serves an obvious function, his soldierly dedication and filial obedience clashing markedly with Victor's resolute severance of all familial and communal ties for the sake of science. Ernest's mediocrity and willing instrumentality within the wider patriarchal framework is contrasted to the untrammelled intellectual freedom of Victor's anarchic project of making himself the god-like father of a new species who 'would bless [him] as its creator and source' (p. 55).

The crucial question is which brother Shelley herself prefers. The high-flying transgressor who comes to a tragic end? Or the reliable patriarchal helpmate and functionary who is the sole member of his family to survive the novel? Is it legitimate to assume that Shelley's own favourites are the characters whom she allows to live? If so, her representation of patriarchy would be conservative rather than subversive. Shelley would ultimately seem to approve of traditional masculinity, at least as long as it is exercised in moderation and with societal sanction, that is, as long as a man's heroism is held in check by his self-effacing docility and subservience to patriarchal law. Accordingly, it is neither the lieutenant nor Ernest who find themselves on the margins, but Walton and Victor, whose disobedience catapults them out of the system to the uninhabitable Arctic periphery of human society. Although pursuing glory within patriarchally sanctioned limits, Alphonse and Henry must perish because their close relationship with Victor exposes them too intimately to the destructive blast of his monstrous deviance, his illicit departure from the norm of masculinity as heroism-cum-servitude. Notably, instead of celebrating the rebellious transgressor's heroic exploits and commending his enactment of a radical counterdiscourse to systemic normality – as her husband and his fellow Romantics would have been prone to do – Shelley appears to blame excessive male heroism outside societally approved limits for everything that ever went wrong in history:

A human being in perfection ought always to preserve a calm and peaceful mind, and never to allow passion or a transitory desire to disturb his tranquillity. I do not think that the pursuit of knowledge is an exception to this rule. If the study to which you apply yourself has a tendency to weaken your affections, and to destroy your taste for those simple pleasures in which no alloy can possibly mix, then that study is certainly *unlawful*, that is to say, not befitting the human mind. If this rule were always observed; if no man allowed any pursuit whatsoever to interfere with the tranquillity of his domestic affections, Greece had not been enslaved; Caesar would have spared his country; America would have been discovered more gradually; and the empires of Mexico and Peru had not been destroyed. (p. 57; my emphasis)

This passage, one of the rare instances in *Frankenstein* where the author's own voice appears to surface, constitutes Shelley's anti-patriarchal (wo)manifesto, condemning men's compulsive, domophobic search for heroism while recommending the pleasures of domesticity. At first it seems as if Shelley accuses only exceptionally gifted men (like Caesar) of at times 'unlawfully' suspending even the most basic rules of human civility and manipulating others into following their example. But then, only little damage is done unless the born leader's desire for heroic achievement is complemented by the ready subservience of a multitude of others. The ideal of masculinity as heroism-cum-servitude creates a solid basis for successful military action, ensuring that a man – any man – can find glory in the most menial tasks, tasks so degrading they would normally be considered emasculating. As expressed in the Monster's perplexed incredulity at man's being 'at once so powerful, so virtuous, and magnificent, yet so vicious and base' (p. 105), within patriarchy masculinity remains an essentially self-contradictory, even schizophrenic phenomenon, both heroic and monstrous, compelling and compulsive, free and conscripted.

With great psychological insight Shelley delineates the emotional turmoil the patriarchal condition inflicts even on a man as intelligent and gifted as Frankenstein. On the one hand, Victor seems eager to learn from the failed experiment his life has become. On the other, he cannot let go of the promise masculinity and heroism appeared to hold in store for him before it all started to go so disastrously wrong. Victor repeatedly warns Walton not to make the same mistake, proffering the story of his life as a didactic example. 'Unhappy man!' he exclaims. 'Do you share my madness? Have you drank [sic] also from the intoxicating draft? Hear me – let me reveal my tale, and you will dash the cup from your lips!' (pp. 35–6). However, when eventually Walton's crew – 'unsupported by ideas of glory and honour' (p. 179) – urge their captain to abandon his impossible project and return home, neither Walton nor Victor seems capable of breaking with what they themselves identify as the madness of heroism. Although he finds it 'terrible to reflect that the lives of all these men are endangered through me. If we are lost, my mad schemes are the cause' (p. 177), Walton declares that he 'had rather die than return shamefully – my purpose unfulfilled' (p. 179). And Victor? Instead of supporting the crew, he turns to taunt them in a speech of great heroic fervour, testifying to how irrevocably he has internalised patriarchy's inexorable gender imperatives:

> Turning towards the men, he said –
> 'What do you mean? What do you demand of your captain? Are you then so easily turned from your design? Did you not call this a glorious expedition? And wherefore was it glorious? . . . You were hereafter to be hailed as the benefactors of your species; your names adored, as belonging to brave men who encountered death for honour, and the benefit of mankind. And now, behold, with the first imagination of danger . . . you shrink away . . . and so, poor souls, they were chilly, and returned to their warm firesides. Why, that requires not this preparation; ye need not have come this far, and dragged your captain to the shame of a defeat, merely to prove yourselves cowards. Oh! be men, or be more than men. Be steady to your purposes, and firm as a rock . . . Do not return to your families with the stigma of disgrace marked on your brows. Return as heroes who have fought and conquered, and who know not what it is to turn their backs on the foe.' (p. 178)

The dilemma of masculinity within patriarchy seems irremediable, always one whole U-turn removed from thorough self-reflection and a successful liberation of the self from oppressive gender norms. Even towards the very end, when he yet again advises Walton to 'seek happiness in tranquillity, and avoid ambition' (p. 181), Victor concludes with a contradiction, paying homage to patriarchy's endlessly deferred projection of an infallible hypermasculinity, conjured out of every individual male's deep-rooted sense of lack and inadequacy. 'I have myself been blasted in these hopes', Victor says, *yet another may succeed* (p. 181; my emphasis).

Frankenstein is not only geared towards, but driven by the delusive fantasy of an all-powerful, supermanly *alter ego* which will compensate for the self's congenital inability to live up to its own impossible ideal. According to Bette London, *Frankenstein* is a novel about man-making in two closely interrelated respects, as Victor seeks to make 'a man' out of himself by creating a man, 'opening to view the inevitable gap between image and ideal that structures male self-representations' (London 1993: 264). Since patriarchal masculinity requires boys to fashion themselves into something larger than life, it is not so much Victor's own megalomaniacal narcissism that is accountable for his creature's gross gigantism as the phantasmatic ideal after which it has been moulded. As the Monster later complains, 'God, in pity, made man beautiful and alluring, after his own image; but my form is a filthy type of yours, more horrid even from the very resemblance' (p. 113). Victor's man-making is an act of ugly self-distortion. Marked by precipitation, a lack of care and self-awareness, it results in large-scale horror rather than progressive, superhuman refinement. Born out of a denial of the female, the Monster is also born out of a denial of the self which – 'emaciated with confinement' (p. 55) – gradually disintegrates at the same time as the ideal assumes its monstrous, outsize shape.

In the attempt to bridge the insurmountable gap between his own fallible self and the infallible normative standard, Victor creates the hypermasculine 'not-me' as representative evidence of his heroic potential. However, what begins its existence as something man-made and dependent soon develops into a powerful force enslaving, haunting and destroying its maker while fundamentally re-emplotting the intended course of his life. 'You are my creator', the Monster tells Victor, 'but I am your master – obey!' (p. 142). The masculine ideal has turned into an inexorable imperative perpetuating itself beyond all human control. The Monster comes to embody the ubiquitous and omnipotent, often deadly influence patriarchal law exerts on the lives of both men and women. As innocent Justine's trial and execution signal, its compelling voice quickly proceeds to pervade and corrupt the practices and discourses of both justice and common sense (see Newman 1995: 175). Only once this epitome of patriarchal oppression has been recognised for what it is and how it operates, does it become possible to resist the allure of its power. What ultimately saves Walton from being taken in by the creature's persuasive rhetoric, and hence from following Victor into despair and self-destruction, is his very simple insight that 'such a monster has then really existence!' (p. 174).

2

.

Kurtz's Curse

.

Joseph Conrad's Heart of Darkness

CHRIS BALDICK HAS DESCRIBED *Heart of Darkness* as 'a novella which bears a number of uncanny resemblances to the design of *Frankenstein*' (Baldick 1987: 165). Baldick points at conspicuous structural correspondences between the two narratives, most overtly revealing themselves in the parallel relationships of Walton/Frankenstein and Marlow/Kurtz. *Heart of Darkness* also resembles Shelley's novel in that it is a profoundly gendered text, informed by the same behavioural norms and conventions, inhabited by similar men and haunted by equally destructive monsters of individual and communal apocalypse. Once again, patriarchal imperatives both encourage and frustrate male confidence in the feasibility of progress against nature. Like *Frankenstein, Heart of Darkness* illuminates the predicament of the individual male psyche as it falls prey to the delusive, intrinsically contradictory implications of heroic achievement and fatefully entraps itself in a dark continent of its own making. Yet another man's quest for spectacular self-fulfilment results in his annihilative confrontation with abject horror.

Conrad's tale of masculine adventure can easily be read as an inspired world-political rewrite of Shelley's private vision of a male-authored cataclysm. Contrary to Chinua Achebe's accusation, *Heart of Darkness* does not perversely indulge in the detailed depiction of 'the breakup of one petty European mind' (Achebe 1977: 788). As the character of Marlow insists, he does not 'want to bother [us] much with what happened to [him] personally' (p. 21). Although initially *Heart of Darkness* appears to focus on the fate of just one individual transgressor, overreaching and thus monstrously disfiguring the patriarchal ideal of heroic masculinity, what Conrad's novella ultimately exposes – by 'bringing the

Heart of Empire into correspondence, complicity, even equivalence, with the Heart of Darkness' (Baldick 1987: 165) – is the immediate and inextricable involvement of the whole of European civilisation in the remote-controlled rampage of its self-expansive, monstrous *doppelgänger*: imperialism.

No longer confined to the intimately personal sphere of Marlow's identification with Kurtz, the motif of the *doppelgänger* becomes an apt historical metaphor. Africa, as a 'dark continent', is created by the Europeans. At about the end of the nineteenth century, Africa ceases 'to be a blank space of delightful mystery – a white patch for a boy to dream gloriously over' (p. 22) and becomes Europe's tortured, demonically enigmatic other, casting a haunting shadow on the white man's adventurous spirit and missionary zeal, a self-inflicted, man-made shadow that endures into our own immediate present. As *Heart of Darkness* makes explicit, 'all Europe contributed to the making of Kurtz' (p. 66). Africa is rife with men from Denmark, Sweden, Germany, France, England, Belgium and Russia. Like Shelley's, Conrad's monster is an incongruously patched-together composite, created out of many bodies. Moreover, similar to the ugly aspect and unlawful agency of Frankenstein's monster, it is crucial for the perpetuation of imperialist practices that their true nature remain hidden from the sensitive, easily repulsed eyes of those who have stayed at home. Essentially, the exploits and barbarous *modi operandi* of imperialism are anathema to the civilised principles of European modernity. To secure its ongoing success, effective strategies of obfuscation are required, an intricate manipulation of truth perpetrated by the fraudulent rhetoric of authoritative male voices.

Conrad reveals the implicit genderedness of imperialism's ideological doubling of secret male homosocial knowledge with domestic ignorance. In *Heart of Darkness*, it is women like Marlow's Aunt and Kurtz's Intended under whose veiled gaze male corruption crystallises into glorious heroism. The Intended's unconditional enthusiasm for her lover's enterprise is typical of the European public's blind support for their men's 'real work' (p. 24) in the colonies, a support without which the idealistic make-up needed to conceal imperialism's monstrously exploitative aspects would rapidly disintegrate. The Intended's credo is vital for both the construction and maintenance of her man's heroic status: 'Ah, but I believed in him more than any one on earth – more than his own mother, more than – himself. He needed me! Me!' (p. 94). In Africa itself the men find precious little to back them up. Their unsolicited presence is shown to be a precarious pretence permanently at risk of caving in on itself. As Marlow realises in a sudden panic, 'there was nothing behind me! There was nothing but that wretched, old, mangled steamboat I was leaning against . . .' (p. 43).

The men of *Heart of Darkness* undergo an identity crisis of existential destabilisation that greatly increases their need for a polar opposite onto whom they are able to project their unmanly fears, weaknesses and inadequacies. It is essential to realise in this context that Marlow's infamous, starkly misogynous remark on the world of women – suggesting that 'it is too beautiful altogether, and if they were to set it up it would go to pieces before the first sunset' (p. 27) – provides us in fact with an accurate description of his own dilemma. Marlow's narrative is marked by the striking paradox of including women by expressly excluding them, thereby ironically causing the latter's alleged insignificance to become an issue of considerable narrative import. Women's categorical absence appears as the last stronghold of masculine integrity; it is women's faith and credulity in which men's phantasmatic credibility is anchored. As Marlow exclaims, 'they – the women I mean – are out of it – *should* be out of it. We must help them to stay in that beautiful world of their own, *lest ours gets worse*' (p. 64; my emphasis). According to Bette London, this ultimately signifies that 'women's expulsion from the world of dark truths does not so much protect women's position as preserve masculine constructs; for women's absence constitutes . . . the foundation of masculine authority' (London 1989: 238).

Far from endorsing misogynous prejudice, Conrad highlights and criticises the insidious functionality of gender binarisms in patriarchal discourse. Equally manifest is his sensitive alertness to imperialism's racialist strategies of ideological legitimation. What has too often been ignored by critics is Conrad's own marginality as a Polish exile writing in a foreign (his third!) language. It is crucial to note that there are no Poles amongst the men in Conrad's Africa. At the time Conrad wrote his novella, there had not been an independent Poland for over a hundred years. Widely branded as a morally flawed, disingenuous commentary from the centre, *Heart of Darkness* may be far more significantly informed by the literary imagination of Poland than hitherto acknowledged. During his early formative years, Conrad shared in the history of a country and people traumatised by repeated territorial carve-ups, centuries of imperialist exploitation, and more than one premeditated attempt at genocidal extirpation. If a categorisation must be made, Conrad ought perhaps to be regarded as a postcolonial rather than colonial writer, as a spokesman and representative not of the imperial centre but of the oppressed, dislocated other. In this light, it may be a justified critical manoeuvre to view his complex, often difficult style as aiming at a deliberate counterdiscursive decentring of both imperialist and patriarchal myths of truth and cultural superiority.

In his critique of traditionally masculine behaviour Conrad follows in the footsteps of Shelley. Discerning readers of *Heart of Darkness* will find the novella reverberating with Shelley's anti-imperialist (wo)manifesto that 'if no man allowed any pursuit whatsoever to interfere with the tranquillity of domestic affection . . . America would have been discovered more gradually; and the empires of Mexico and Peru had not been destroyed' (Shelley 1992: 57). Also, significantly, Marlow's motivation to embark on an expedition to the Congo is identical with Walton's urge to explore a route to the North Pole. Both quests derive from the same, seemingly irresistible young male desire to venture beyond the *domus* to prove one's heroic stature in a wilderness of seemingly limitless opportunities for successful exotic self-expansion:

> Now when I was a little chap I had a passion for maps. I would look for hours at South America, or Africa, or Australia, and lose myself in all the glories of exploration. At that time there were many blank spaces on the earth, and when I saw one that looked particularly inviting on a map (but they all look that) I would put my finger on it and say, When I grow up I will go there. The North Pole was one of these places, I remember. Well, I haven't been there yet, and shall not try now. The glamour's off. (p. 22)

However, Marlow's narrative is emphatically not that of an excited, inexperienced youth full of zest and naive enthusiasm, but that of a sadder and perhaps wiser man markedly shaken by his past encounter with an unspeakable monstrosity. The narrative of *Heart of Darkness* is one of exponential disintegration, triggered by the impact of abject horror, which not only 'draws attention to the fragility of the law' (Kristeva 1982: 4) but in fact ruptures the processes and means of traditional phallogocentric coherency beyond all hope of repair.

The heroic self-fashioning of Kurtz incorporates a forceful deconstructive subversion of the neatly ordered stability of patriarchal law. Baldick has described Kurtz as 'both an ungodly-godlike transgressor and a factitious and miscreated agent of civilised trade who runs destructively out of his masters' control' (Baldick 1987: 166). Kurtz's defiant appropriation of the normative ideal of heroism-cum-servitude in pursuit of his own personal agenda renders visible patriarchy's inherently contradictory organisation. Even before meeting Kurtz, Marlow catches 'a distinct glimpse [of] the lone white man turning his back suddenly on the headquarters, on relief, on thoughts of home' (p. 47). Kurtz has successfully escaped from the clutches of the imperialist monster whose atrocities appear to have full patriarchal sanction. However, taking 'his unlawful soul beyond the bounds of permitted aspirations' (p. 83), Kurtz's domain replicates the system that engendered, shaped and promoted him. Kurtz poses such a great threat to patriarchal imperialism precisely because he emulates and thus challenges the latter's systemic claim to absolutist legislative omnipotence. As Marlow observes, 'there was nothing either above or below [Kurtz], and I knew it. He had kicked himself loose of the earth. Confound the man! He had kicked the very earth to pieces' (p. 83). Ultimately, however, the Law cannot tolerate such disobedience and individual independence. Viewing any proliferative growth beyond its own limits as an abominable, abject aberration, the system refuses to stomach the existence of a self-professed other who is at once different from and identical with itself.

Due to its tenebrous ambiguity, which disperses all palpable distinctions between the civilised and the savage, Kurtz's story must forever elude Marlow's narrative grasp. Like Walton, Marlow returns home after conversing *tête-à-tête* with the Monster. As he says, 'it is [Kurtz's] extremity that I seem to have lived through. True, he had made that last stride, he had stepped over the edge, while I had been permitted to draw back my hesitating foot' (p. 87). However, by allowing himself to become Kurtz's confidant, Marlow travels to the limits of conceivability, the very edge where the speakable gives way to the unsignified, finally arriving at Kurtz's Inner Station which reaches beyond or, rather, burrows ever more deeply into the Central Station of common symbolic referentiality. Marlow's narrative is a result of the European male gaze growing vertiginous at discovering an irremediable rupture within its hitherto uncontested, definitive core, at coming face to face with an unrestrained, lawless darkness beyond the reach of its comprehension. Marlow finds himself driven towards an existential showdown both Frankenstein and Walton managed to avoid by subscribing to knowledge and science without much self-consciousness. It is introspection that has caused Kurtz's heroic manliness to disintegrate and now threatens Marlow's own self-containment. 'Being alone in the wilderness, [Kurtz's soul] had looked within itself, and, by Heavens! I tell you, it had gone mad. I had – for my sins, I suppose, to go through the ordeal of looking into it myself!' (p. 83). Unlike Frankenstein, Kurtz opens up to the dark other within himself and eventually becomes one with his shadowy *doppelgänger*. As they merge, the strictly expedient economy of the masculine ideal implodes, disclosing once and for all the pre-programmed hegemony of the monstrous over the manly. Kurtz never shares Frankenstein's didactic zest but appears to have withdrawn into an almost autistic solipsism beyond the ability to give advice or feel compassion. When Marlow first lays eyes on Kurtz, he has already metamorphosed into outsize, self and world-annihilating horror, cultivated – yet quite obviously never fully contained – by the administrations of European imperialist ideology: 'He looked at least seven feet long I saw him open his mouth wide – it gave him a weirdly voracious aspect, as though he had wanted to swallow all the air, all the earth, all the men before him' (p. 76).

How exactly are we to understand Kurtz's deformation from a noble-spirited idealist, cherished by his fiancée at home, into the legendary epitome of monstrous European greed and savagery? Perhaps we could liken his tragedy to that of Frankenstein, who only on animating his creation, when it is already too late, realises that his well-intentioned ambitions have made him not a hero, but a loathsome perpetrator of horror and destruction. In *Frankenstein* as in *Heart of Darkness*, processes of heroic man-making seem precariously at risk of producing monsters rather than men. Promising youths follow the guidelines of patriarchal heroism in a dedicated, self-disciplined manner only to find themselves horrifically alienated, disfigured and corrupted by the implemented ideal. The magical blueprint, after which they are induced to fashion themselves, is a treacherous design, concealing its callous expediency behind a beautiful rhetoric of noble man(ner)liness and altruistic missionary zeal. Both Frankenstein and Kurtz end up disastrously dis-illusioned. Yet only Kurtz appears to see through the fraudulent design that lured him to believe in himself as 'a remarkable man' (p. 79), when in fact he was never intended to be anything but a remote-controlled instrument furthering the project of ivory-grubbing exploitation. As Frankenstein rushes off to hide from the Monster's gaze, Kurtz turns to face the spectacle of horror that has started to emerge with terrifying clarity from the debris of the man he thought he ought to be. As a result, all his arduous commitment to civilisational progress is reduced to just one violently unequivocal imperative: 'Exterminate all the brutes!' (p. 66).

It is the patriarchal system as a whole that gives birth to Frankenstein's monster, not just Victor himself as an individual. Equally, Kurtz must be viewed as both a perpetrator and a victim, if not of actual oppression, then of ideological manipulation. In recent years scholars committed to a feminist critique of patriarchy have begun to realise 'that not only does systemic male dominance oppress women, it deforms men' (Cockburn 1991: 222). Sadly, men are highly susceptible to total identification with an ideology that promises them power, privilege and heroic status. Only much too late – when they have already violated, pillaged and killed in the name of 'just causes' such as progress, freedom, patriotism, and so on – do some of them recognise how expertly they have been brainwashed into collusion with a system interested only in their success as unconditionally obedient instruments of oppression and exploitation. Commendably, Conrad never allows either Marlow or Kurtz to refer to the systemic manipulation of their fates as a valid excuse for their complicity. As Conrad indicates, both should have known better. Significantly, Marlow has a drink with a young chap in Brussels who, on being asked if he has ever been tempted to enter imperial service, replies in a rather unequivocal manner: 'I'm not such a fool as I look, quoth Plato to his disciples' (p. 26). If this youth has seen through the false rhetoric of imperial heroism, why not Marlow or Kurtz? Be this as it may, it should be noted that ultimately, in both Shelley and Conrad's novels, the true stalwarts of patriarchy are not the men of outstanding talent and intelligence, who combine with their heroic manliness an almost feminine kind of introvert sensibility, but the entirely unspectacular functionaries of little individual distinction, let alone tragic potential. It is the latter, as represented by one of the managers Marlow encounters in the Congo, whom the system depends on for its successful perpetuation:

> He was commonplace in complexion, in feature, in manners, and in voice. He was of middle size and of ordinary build. His eyes, of the usual blue, were perhaps remarkably cold, and he certainly could make his glance fall on one as trenchant and as heavy as an axe. (p. 36)

As Marlow remarks, 'what redeems [a project like "the conquest of the earth"] is the idea only' (p. 21). What happens to Kurtz is that the beautiful idea of altruistic imperial heroism falls off the ugly, naked truth like a brittle shell, entailing a profoundly traumatic experience comparable perhaps only to that suffered by soldiers in a war, when the apocalyptic monsters of nationalist violence and greed are abruptly stripped of their patriotic apparel and display their ignominious, murderous disposition. Understandably, Kurtz is desperate to resuscitate the noble idea, 'to hide in the magnificent folds of eloquence the barren darkness of his heart', to conjure and reinstate 'the original Kurtz [who] frequented the bedside of the hollow sham' (p. 85). Yet, tragically, the ideal heroic man has dissipated beyond recall. What remains is too monstrous for words: 'The horror! The horror!' (p. 86), leaving Conrad's readers to contemplate Marlow's final disturbing question of 'what else had been there' (p. 87).

Marlow is the protagonist against whose progress we are asked to imagine the genesis of Kurtz's total disillusionment with European civilisation. Perhaps not quite as naively idealistic as Kurtz may have been on first arriving in Africa, Marlow is nevertheless 'horror-struck' (p. 32) on beholding the full extent and relentlessness of the continent's exploitation. As it gradually smells out 'all the dead cats of civilisation' (p. 67), Marlow's narrative traces the reasons for Kurtz's demise while highlighting – often sarcastically – the egregious fraudulence of imperialist rhetoric. Under Marlow's scrutiny, heroic explorers are unmasked as despicable criminals: 'To tear treasure out of the bowels of the land was their desire, with no more moral purpose at the back of it than there is in burglars breaking into a safe' (p. 46). Marlow's experience of the imperial enterprise is one of anticlimactic tristesse. About halfway through his journey to Kurtz, he suffers 'a sense of extreme disappointment, as though I had found out I had been striving after something altogether without a substance'. However, although he feels as if he had been 'robbed of a belief or had missed [his] destiny in life', his frustration is not quite as acute as Kurtz's, perhaps because as a greater realist than his predecessor, he never truly imagined the ideal hero of imperialism 'as doing, you know, but as discoursing' (p. 63).

Conrad's representation of Africa subverts the symbolic solidity of European discourse whose 'baseless fabric' is shown to unravel on confrontation with the overwhelming preverbal self-referentiality, the textual *jouissance*, of the jungle. Conrad's Africa tolerates neither definitive abstraction nor conclusive narrative encapsulation. The white man struggles through an impenetrable thicket of hitherto unprecedented information that renders traditional strategies of comprehension futile. The wilderness that was meant to serve as a mere backdrop to his heroic self-authentication unexpectedly begins to exuberate, thus creating a sense of existential bewilderment impervious to discursive penetration. Africa preserves its indigenity as an ultimately absent cause that even words as vague as 'dark', 'mysterious' or 'inscrutable' fail to adumbrate. *Heart of Darkness* records the capitulation of masculinist, phallogocentric language before its essentially chaotic extra-linguistic other. As the fate of Kurtz the idealist indicates, the primordial integrity of Africa quickly reduces imperialism's 'magic current of phrases' (p. 66) to a feeble rivulet petering out long before it has got anywhere near its practical consummation. Consequently, in order to avoid a similarly premature termination, readings of Conrad's text must learn to follow, rather than aim to overtake, Marlow's hazardous journey on his rickety steamboat up an unknown river in a dark and uncharted land. Like him, readers will instinctively look for as smooth a passage as possible, constantly tempted to reshape the text in accordance with what they already know. Clearly, going by plane would be easier, or regulating the flow of the river, or deforesting the jungle and thus ridding ourselves of its uncanny inter-rogation of our 'monkey tricks' (p. 50) at absolute, comprehensive mas-tery. But then we too would become imperialists, colonising both the text and its referent instead of giving in and fruitfully exposing ourselves to its obscurity and radical alterity.

F.R. Leavis has accused Conrad of gratuitous indeterminacy, of con-juring aporetic inconclusiveness out of 'an emotional insistence on the presence of what he can't produce'. Leavis deplores Conrad's irritating tendency of 'making a virtue out of not knowing what he means' (Leavis 1963: 180). At the other extreme end of the critical spectrum, Achebe attacks Conrad for the binarist unequivocality and racialist crassness of his representation, suggesting that '*Heart of Darkness* projects the image of Africa as "the other world," the antithesis of Europe and therefore of civilization' (Achebe 1977: 783). What makes Conrad's novella so offen-sive to Africans is what Achebe erroneously identifies as its intrinsically imperialist rhetoric of black/bad versus white/good. Contrary to Leavis, Achebe finds that 'for Conrad, things (and persons) being in their place is of the utmost importance' (Achebe 1977: 785). Ironically, whereas Leavis criticises Conrad for his lack of manly determination, clarity and expres-sive rigour – his almost 'effeminate' tendencies to dither and digress – Achebe finds Conrad's style too inexorably monolithic, a characteristic typical of masculinist, phallogocentric representation. Leavis totally fails to appreciate the subversive potential of Conrad's decentred style while Achebe, impatient with Europe's ostentatiously apolitical aestheticism, finds it exasperating that Conrad should refrain from hinting 'however subtly or tentatively at an alternative frame of reference by which we may judge the actions and opinions of his characters' (Achebe 1977: 787). The critical problem is that Conrad deliberately abstains from providing his readers with a climactic focus where all the different strands of the narrative would converge and resolve themselves. Instead, Conrad suggests that Marlow does not know any more what he thought he knew for certain. The narrative peculiarities of *Heart of Darkness* reflect a man's desperate attempt at making sense of his past experiences and thereby regaining control of his life. Marlow's com-pulsive repetition of his tale is to compensate for his loss of meaning, in itself probably one of the most traumatically emasculating experiences there is.

Marlow struggles to put himself back together again, yet his desire for traditional masculine integrity proves irreconcilable with the decentred recalcitrance of the tale he has to tell. Already, his difference from other, 'ordinary' men is conspicuous. He has become incapable of telling a tale of 'direct simplicity, the whole meaning of which lies within the shell of a cracked nut'. Instead, he finds his voice invariably on the outside, 'enveloping the tale which brought it out only as a glow brings out a haze' (p. 20). For the duration of *Heart of Darkness*, Conrad suspends the realist principles of narrative clarity and coherence, intimating the existence of a mode of writing that operates in opposition to what Hélène Cixous has called 'the old Apartheid routine' (Cixous 1976: 877) of phallogocentric expression. As Bette London argues, 'woman's unauthorized presence at the center of the text threatens narrative itself: it collapses inside and outside, story and frame, speech and silence, past and present' (London 1989: 238). Boldly positioning the disconcerting gaze of a superb, perhaps superior other at the uncharted core of his narrative, Conrad effects a radical interrogation of eurocentric certainties. The central encounter in *Heart of Darkness* between white man and black woman bristles with subversive potential, threatening to fracture European myths once and for all by dint of what Cixous has envisaged as an explosive 'Laugh of the Medusa'.

Unlike the Intended, the Black African woman – Kurtz's mistress – bears no resemblance to a Victorian lady with her sexuality policed and held in check by the normative standards of patriarchal femininity. 'Savage and superb, wild-eyed and magnificent' (p. 77), she embodies a wilderness beyond the white man's definitional reach. Being both black and female, she ought to be the most inferior presence in the text, yet she holds the position of utmost centrality. The Black African woman incorporates a radical otherness beyond mere binarist oppositioning, an otherness that cannot be annihilated or contained, that is not man-made. She stands for a human potential that survives outside of the conceptual boundaries of oppressive discourse, that predates and will outlast the dominance of man. And yet, she clearly senses that her autonomy, dignity and 'stately progress' depend for their continuation on her intrepid resistance to being objectified, gendered, raced. Resolutely and defiantly, she exposes herself to Europe's male gaze. As Marlow reports, 'she looked at us all as if her life had depended upon the unswerving steadiness of her glance' (p. 78). Her powerful unruliness strikingly resembles that of the female monster torn asunder by Frankenstein soon after her conception. Significantly, what Marlow says about the jungle applies to the African woman with equal validity: 'We are accustomed to look upon the shackled form of a conquered monster, but there – there you could look at a thing monstrous and free' (p. 51). Moreover, the life she has lived with Kurtz in the jungle is curiously reminiscent of the blissful existence Frankenstein's monster envisages for himself and his mate in South America, only in this case it appears to be the female who is in charge of the outlawed partnership or who is, at least, her lover's equal. At the centre of *Heart of Darkness* we find an astonishingly elaborate, anti-patriarchal vision of the other coming to power and asserting herself against the threat of restrictive determination from outwith her own sphere.

Nina Straus's speculation that 'the peculiar density and inaccessibility of *Heart of Darkness* may be the result of its extremely masculine historical referentiality' (Straus 1987: 124) is clearly misleading. Conrad shrewdly pits Marlow's traditional desire for closure against his own powerfully subversive experimentation with indeterminacy. The apparent obscurity of Conrad's novella derives from its counterdiscursive struggle to give voice to something as yet unsaid or hitherto silenced; it is thus far removed from the claustrophobic paranoia of male homosocial secrecy detected by Straus. *Heart of Darkness* takes the narrative mode of *Frankenstein*, often criticised for being chaotic and dream-like, a crucial step further. As Donald Spence has observed, 'this story is so murky and ambiguous that it has neither beginning nor end; thus it is hard to tell when we move back into the outer boxes [of narration]' (Spence 1987: 194). In contrast to much traditional men's writing, *Heart of Darkness* is informed by Conrad's radically anti-phallogocentric endeavour *not* 'to appropriate the world', *not* 'to dominate it through verbal mastery' (Jones 1986: 362). In fact, Conrad's narration seems intent on not only interrogating but subverting the discursive means 'through which man objectifies the world, reduces it to his terms, speaks in place of everything and everyone else' (Jones 1986: 362).

Struggling for his experience to shape itself out of darkness, silence, nothingness, Marlow becomes a stunned spectator to the genesis of his own tale. Unable to bring about the illusion of comprehensive, self-contained emplotment he resorts to loosely adumbrative evocation. Driven by an unrelenting inward gaze, his voice appears to emanate from a site of utmost self-reflection, precariously anchored in an improvised cultural in-between, 'the pose of a Buddha preaching in European clothes and without a lotus-flower' (p. 21). His is the disembodied, oracular voice of an apocalyptic past that refuses to be laid to rest. Both the content and mode of his narration illustrate how, on confrontation with radical alterity, imperial Europe's phallogocentric 'world of straightforward facts' (p. 28) becomes a perilous balancing act, requiring almost impossible concentration, a single-minded steering against unpredictable nature:

I had to keep guessing at the channel; I had to discern, mostly by inspiration, the signs of hidden banks; I watched for sunken stones; I was learning to clap my teeth smartly before my heart flew out, when I shaved by a fluke some infernal sly old snag that would have ripped the life out of the tin-pot steamboat and drowned all the pilgrims . . . (pp. 49–50)

It seems tempting to identify Marlow as English literature's first male Kristevan *sujet en procès*, although clearly he does not volunteer for the part. Marlow has marginality thrust upon him, a marginality that places him potentially, if involuntarily, 'on the side of the explosion of social codes: with revolutionary moments' (Kristeva 1981: 166). Confronted with counterdiscursive powers that 'reject everything finite, definite, structured, loaded with meaning, in the existing state of society' (Kristeva 1981: 166), he becomes 'something else' to what he strives to be, namely 'a subject-in-the-making, a subject on trial' (Kristeva 1981: 167).

However, Marlow's position of marginality is prone to compromise his masculine integrity whose successful reconstruction constitutes the chief *telos* of his narration. If he wants to be a 'real' man, Marlow must relinquish the chance of constructively re-inventing himself out of the chaos of his life experiences. He must cling to the familiar, what he refers to as the 'real', and forever refrain from seriously contemplating any manifestations of alterity. Once allowed access, the African jungle may turn to permeate its penetrator, swallow him up, and totally annihilate his attempt at heroic self-authentication. Therefore, on leaping ashore for the first time, Marlow is markedly relieved to come across a reassuring sample of European discourse, Towser or Towson's *Enquiry into Some Points of Seamanship*, 'not a very enthralling book', yet a text which makes him 'forget the jungle' and fills him with 'a delicious sensation of having come upon something unmistakably real' (p. 53). As he assures his listeners, 'to leave off reading was like tearing myself away from the shelter of an old and solid friendship' (p. 54). Ineptly, if no doubt deliberately, Marlow never stops referring to Africa in terms of a domesticated patriarchal femininity, a tendency that bears blatant rhetorical and conceptual inconsistencies. According to Marlow's own description, it is 'the virgin forest [that] like a rioting invasion of soundless life [seemed ready] to sweep every little man of us out of his little existence' (p. 45). Clearly, Africa makes no easy conquest. Despite its apparent immobility, it does not hold still but awesomely obstructs European progress.

Throughout *Heart of Darkness* Marlow resorts to projection to salvage what little sense of masculine integrity he has left. Most pronounced in this respect is certainly his general denigration of women. And yet, while

insisting on their ineffectual passivity, he also shares Frankenstein's paranoia concerning a female conspiracy that authors and directs the tragic
downfall of men. Confronting Kurtz in the jungle, Marlow is haunted by
his memory of two women whom he first met at the office in Brussels and
already then imagined as a witch-like pair of fateful sisters, 'knitt[ing]
black wool feverishly [and] guarding the door of Darkness' (p. 25).
Marlow's encounter with the Intended is equally fraught with paranoia.
Kurtz's fiancée attracts Marlow's anger as she thwarts his hope of finding
a representative of perfect femininity against whose contrastive presence
he could reconstruct his badly damaged masculinity. To Marlow's utmost
consternation, the Intended rivals his authority on the matter of Kurtz's
memory by orchestrating his speech, even finishing his sentences for him,
and thus 'silencing [him] into an appalled dumbness' (p. 92). Prepared to
dedicate her life to Kurtz even beyond his death, the Intended never
defers to Marlow whom she evidently considers a man of lesser import
and generally inferior status. In a fit of jealousy, rather than out of
gentlemanly tact or genuine pity, Marlow lies to the Intended about
her lover's last words, replacing Kurtz's dying invocation of apocalyptic
horror with a melodramatic whisper of his beloved's name. In an effort
to assert himself as a carrier of exclusive knowledge, Marlow condemns
the Intended to spend the rest of her life devoutly cherishing not the
memory of her beloved Kurtz but a corrupt artifice of selfish masculine
mendacity. Up to the very end of *Heart of Darkness*, Conrad misses no
opportunity to demonstrate how nothing of what imperialism may originally have *intended* escapes being sacrificed sooner or later to the
expedient vanities of the masculine self.

As Bette London observes, to maintain their masculinity in a time of
crisis, men like Marlow are prepared even to turn against their own kind.
Like Frankenstein on board Walton's ship, accusing his friend's crew of
shameful cowardice, Marlow positions a group of other men 'in woman's
place: excluded from knowledge, truth, and adventure – excluded from
even imaginative entry into man's terrain' (London 1989: 248). Marlow
perceives his audience of men as 'intruders whose knowledge of life was
to me an irritating pretence, because I felt so sure they could not possibly
know the things I knew' (p. 88). With all his certainties crushed, Marlow
implements phallogocentric strategies of hierarchical oppositioning to
reconsolidate his superiority. At the same time, against gross inconsistencies and contradictions, he elevates Kurtz to the sublime status of an
infallible model of superheroic masculinity. According to Marlow –
whose own deficit in masculine stature benefits greatly from his intimate
knowledge of the man himself – 'Kurtz was able to face the darkness; he

was *man enough* to be damned' (p. 95; my emphasis). To affirm his hero's masculine integrity, Marlow must insist on definitive, triumphant closure unaffected by the diffusive impact of horror and darkness.

At the end of *Heart of Darkness*, Marlow stands as a man who has forfeited the chance of re-imagining himself as a subject-in-the-making, of exploring and negotiating his own intrinsic alterity. Instead, he has re-erected the self and – in Madeleine Gagnon's words – 'set up the mirror, projected the fantasm . . . to become his own representative, his own reference point . . . to become Master of others' (Gagnon 1981: 180).

34

3

·

Grasping the Boy

·

Henry James's The Turn of the Screw

L IKE *FRANKENSTEIN* AND *HEART OF DARKNESS*, Henry James's *The Turn of the Screw* illustrates the deformative impact patriarchal gender norms exert even, or especially, on enthusiastic individuals eager to conform and comply with what is expected of them. James's governess finds herself under extreme pressure to perform. Her particular quandary appears considerably compounded by the fact that she is required to negotiate and, if at all feasible, reconcile traditional feminine virtues with the responsibilities of masculine authority. Yet how can anyone be convincingly passive and active at the same time, innocent and knowledgeable, maternal and authoritarian, featuring at once as a damsel in distress and as a saviour or infallible supersleuth?

The governess's self becomes the site of a highly problematic collision of two diametrically opposed sets of behavioural imperatives, prompting a dilemma that quickly results in the development of a serious nervous condition. The 'fluttered anxious girl out of a Hampshire vicarage' (p. 25), trained in – and no doubt excelling at – the impersonation of impeccable feminine decorum, is corrupted by having 'supreme authority' (p. 26) thrust upon her. Due to the master's absence from his country estate at Bly, as well as his categorical refusal to let her contact him whatever happens, the governess becomes head of the household, as highly regarded by the other servants 'as if [she] had been the mistress or a distinguished visitor' (p. 28). However, her position of authority is far from secure and is soon contested by other aspirants, most notably Peter Quint, the male ghost and former headservant, and 'little Miles', the master's orphaned nephew and heir to the estate. As Edwin Fussell remarks, the governess is only 'a little governor' (Fussell 1980: 124), a diminutive, provisional substitute. Her space is that of a conflictually gendered in-between fraught with manifold irresolvable tensions between masculine privileges on the one hand and feminine constraints on the other. Instead of coming to enjoy a man's prerogatives of authority and personal autonomy, the governess ends up in a high-pressure zone, doubly straitjacketed by the incompatible imperatives of both genders:

> It was the first time, in a manner, that I had known space and air and freedom, all the music of summer and all the mystery of nature. And then there was consideration – and consideration was sweet. *Oh it was a trap* – not designed but deep – to my imagination, to my delicacy, perhaps to my vanity; to whatever in me was most excitable. The best way to picture it all is to say that I was off my guard. (p. 36; my emphasis)

Albeit firmly anchored within the confines of a domestic setting, the course taken by the governess's story clearly resembles that of Walton and Marlow's voyages into unknown territory. Finding herself 'strangely at the helm' (p. 31), the governess sets out to prove herself against her feminine upbringing. She quickly develops manly ambitions and behavioural characteristics that bring about her resolute self-transformation into a resilient explorer and detective, a fierce rival to Quint, and a fatherly/authoritarian rather than maternal/affectionate presence in the lives of the two children in her care. She even encounters her own monstrous *doppelgänger* in Miss Jessel, her predecessor, who descended into moral depravity on entering into an illicit affair with the infamous Peter Quint.

Significantly, all the governess's thoughts and actions seem motivated by her desire to please the children's uncle, her master, with whom she has become infatuated despite – or perhaps because of – his absence. Devoutly internalising the patriarchal ethos of heroism-cum-servitude, the governess begins to emulate masculine ideals with astonishing fervour and skill. As her attempt at manly self-fashioning illustrates, social role-play and situatedness determine an individual's gender-specific development at least as significantly as any innate biological disposition. Patriarchal masculinity inspires and deludes, pressurises and entraps, individuals entirely irrespective of their sex:

> I was in these days literally able to find a joy in the extraordinary flight of heroism the occasions demanded of me. I now saw that I had been asked for a service admirable and difficult; and there would be greatness in letting it be seen – oh in the right quarter! – that I could succeed where another girl might have failed. (p. 51)

However, the governess fails, inadvertently causing Miles's death and badly traumatising Flora, his younger sister. Her tragic dilemma ensues from the same frustrated yearning for the phallic perfection of patriarchy's heroic ideal that motivates Shelley and Conrad's protagonists. Like the men's, her tragedy is not totally inevitable either. There are opportunities for escape and, as the governess herself admits, 'there was no one to stop me; I could give the whole thing up – turn my back and bolt' (p. 84). Curiously, like the men also, she eventually comes to regard her ever less redeemable descent into horror as the only possible, dignified route out of it, her 'own interest . . . violently tak[ing] the form of a search for the way to escape from it' (p. 58). Once again revealing the paradoxical inextricability of heroic manliness and destructive monstrosity, the allure of the ideal seems irresistible, insidiously presenting itself as the remedy rather than the disease.

Like Marlow's, the governess's tale is told in retrospect after her encounter with a fatal horror that appears to be as much of her own making as the result of systemic coercion. Interestingly, however, the coercive aspect of her gradual transmogrification from an enthusiastic idealist into an agent of violent destruction seems more apparent to the governess than her male counterparts. On looking back, she describes her experience in terms of a sexual assault, a subtle yet invasive corruption of her innocence. 'I continued unmolested', she writes, 'if unmolested one could call a young woman whose sensibility had, in the most extraordinary fashion, not declined but deepened' (p. 77). Her state of highly strung nervous agitation, most commonly interpreted as an instance of hysteria, does not derive from an allegedly natural female propensity for psychic disintegration but constitutes in fact an ineluctable corollary of her efforts at masculine 'depth' and competency. Rather than the putative congenital frailties of the female sex, it is the pressures that inform the masculine gender role which manifest themselves in an 'excess of sensitiveness', as Frankenstein's temporary madness after his creation of the monster demonstrates: 'I was unable to remain for a single instant in the same place; I jumped over chairs, clapped my hands, and laughed aloud' (Shelley 1992: 61).

By focusing on a woman's assumption of masculine agency, James is not only able to highlight the independence of social gender assignments from biological determination. He also reveals how our desires are shaped in perfect compliance with systemic requirements, so that who we strive to become is identical with who we ought to be. The governess is culturally preconditioned to confuse the intimately personal dynamics of heterosexual love with societal structures that traditionally regulate the public organisation of power. The country estate at Bly, securely grounded by the absent master's business interests in a wider national and imperial framework, strikes her at first sight as 'a castle of romance' (p. 31). On yielding to the picture-book charms of the children's uncle – 'a bachelor in the prime of life, such a figure as had never risen [before her], save in a dream or an old novel' (p. 25) – the governess's romantic involvement becomes indistinguishable from her employment in patriarchal service. Her desires thus channelled and manipulated, she becomes a willingly remote-controlled pawn, driven by the need to earn her master's approval and terrified of 'his derision, his amusement, his contempt' (p. 75) should she for some reason fail to implement his orders. Thriving within the confines of a patriarchal frame, the governess finds heroic self-fulfilment in a posture of deliberate subservience:

> by my discretion, my quiet good sense and general high propriety, I was giving pleasure – if he ever thought of it! – to the person to whose pressure I had yielded. What I was doing was what he had earnestly hoped and directly asked of me, and that I *could*, after all, do it proved even a greater joy than I had expected. (p. 37)

The absent master's powerful remote control of his subservient proxy is analogous to the omnipotent impact gender imperatives exerted on nineteenth-century men and women's every move, desire, thought or sentiment. The structures of systemic oppression are internalised, allowing one's obedience to patriarchal jurisdiction – the governess's compliance with 'the sacred laws of [her master's] comfort' (p. 79) – to be construed as a manifestation of personal accomplishment. To break out of her master's domain and deny him any further directive control of her authority at Bly – the way Kurtz did with his masters in Conrad's novella – is quite evidently inconceivable to the governess. Nevertheless, her personal tragedy seems triggered by 'a bewilderment of vision' (p. 38) equivalent to Kurtz's fatal insight into the essential fraudulence of imperialist idealism. Uncannily, the governess sees through the uncle's desirable appearance to the apparitional horror beneath it. Her attempt to conjure an image of his paternal guardianship over her presence at Bly evokes the manifestation of a totally different, unexpected aspect of his masterly prowess. The ghost of Peter Quint – 'very erect, as it struck me' (p. 39) – makes its first appearance 'at the very top of the tower' (p. 37). The governess's fervent belief in the Law's paternal benignity gives way to a sudden unveiling of its phallic principle, testifying to all desire's unholy alignment with the interests and ambitions of power.

Quint makes a habit of wearing his master's waistcoats and in his lifetime 'had everything to say' (p. 51). Yet the governess refuses to recognise him as the uncle's representative at Bly, as some kind of depraved Mr Hyde to the latter's distinguished Dr Jekyll. Instead, due to his illicit sexuality, low servant status and obtrusive desire for upward social mobility, she identifies him as 'a horror' (p. 45): 'He's tall, active, erect . . . but never – no, never! – a gentleman' (p. 47). Intent on defending the uncle's aristocratic interests, his superior position within the patriarchal order, as well as his traditional heritage dependent on the children's unharmed survival, the governess – according to Bruce Robbins – 'conflat[es] supernatural evil with social anomaly' (Robbins 1984: 196). There are several conspicuous resemblances between the ghosts on the one hand and servants exceeding their station on the other. For example, in altogether three encounters the governess's narrative introduces the ghosts of Quint and Jessel '"below" her on the staircase, that ready-made icon of the vertical difference between masters and servants' (Robbins 1984: 196). As Graham McMaster explains, the uncanny social turmoil portrayed in *The Turn of the Screw* reflects real political anxieties in late nineteenth-century Britain, with Bly being 'at once the product and mirror of the imperial situation' (McMaster 1988: 32). Significantly, Miles and Flora are introduced as Indian orphans. Hence, the name *Bly* could be construed as an abbreviation of 'Blighty', a term popular amongst British servicemen abroad and originally derived from the Hindi word *Bilayati* meaning 'foreign land' or 'England'. Accordingly, 'the struggle for Bly is a struggle for England and for governorship' (McMaster 1988: 30), indicating how traditional patriarchal structures of class and gender are in the process of being challenged, destabilised and possibly overthrown. Robbins aptly describes *The Turn of the Screw* as a story about 'love that triumphs over class in a house without a master' (Robbins 1984: 197), a subversive kind of love across class boundaries and directed towards greater democratic equality – like that between Quint and Jessel, or between Quint, Jessel and the children – in contrast to the governess's love for the master, which affirms and consolidates the traditional hegemony.

With respect to Miles, it clearly is a major concern of the governess and her confidante Mrs Grose, the housekeeper, that 'young gentlemen [do] not forget their station' (p. 60) and socialise too intimately with 'a base menial' (p. 61) like Quint. However, the main thrust of the battle for the children seems informed by the ghosts' menace of sexual rather than hierarchical, class-related corruption. Quint and Jessel are demons of illicit desire, personifying not only the outrage of their own scandalous alliance but also the governess's sexual fascination with the children's uncle, a desire equally pursued in breach of patriarchal proprieties. The governess projects her repressed desire for unseemly intercourse across class boundaries – as well as her fear of corruption and its possible consequences – onto the children in her care. Clearly, Flora's presence in *The Turn of the Screw* accentuates the governess's anxieties about the preservation of her own feminine properties which seem seriously under threat due to the circumstance that most of her energies are invested in a masculine vying for power and control on behalf of the uncle, and against Quint and Miles. Thus we witness how, on allegedly conspiring with Miss Jessel, beautiful, innocent Flora is transformed into 'a vulgarly pert little girl in the street . . . common and almost ugly' (p. 99). Similarly, whenever Miles displays 'bad' behaviour, the governess suspects him of secretly communing with the ghost of Quint.

In the governess's account, the children assume an allegorical significance declared by their names which pertinently encapsulate the Victorian ideals of masculinity and femininity. *Flora* ('flower') stands for decorative beauty and innocence while *Miles* ('soldier') incorporates military valour and heroic servitude. It is these stalwarts of systemic solidity that are at stake in *The Turn of the Screw*, embattled by the antagonistic forces of subversive societal change on the one hand and a residual possessive conservatism on the other. Ironically, in James's novella the absent patriarch asks to be represented not only by a woman, but a woman at risk of marring her immaculate femininity with improper sexual yearnings. Thus, the system initially appears to disregard one of its own most fundamental principles which is the categorical exclusion of women from power due to both their alleged inadequacy and potentially subversive alterity. However, as *The Turn of the Screw* illustrates, femaleness alone is never enough to unsettle the system, even if it finds itself in a position of authority. Patriarchy perpetuates itself on the basis of its subjects' obedient realisation of the gender roles allocated to them and, in this respect, the governess's conduct is impeccable. She never rebels but seems at great pains always to heed and act on her master's commands.

The general critical neglect of the psychology of both children, and Miles especially, is astonishing, considering that *The Turn of the Screw* comprises an account of their personal tragedy. It is Miles with whose death the novella concludes, and it is crucial to realise that he is rather more than a mere theatrical prop designed to stress the governess's ultimate failure. Marked throughout by great mutual affection and an atmosphere of loving intimacy, the relationship between the boy and the young woman also becomes a site of fierce rivalry and contention. Ever

40

more preoccupied with asserting her authority, the governess denies Miles any acknowledgement of his gender difference, his boyishness and burgeoning masculinity. Instead, she renders him as 'incredibly beautiful' as Flora, as exuding 'the same positive fragrance of purity, in which I had from the first moment seen his little sister' (p. 35). The governess seems entirely oblivious to the unwholesome impact this kind of treatment and representation is likely to exert on the mental disposition of a prepubescent boy like Miles. Significantly, she agrees with Mrs Grose that 'a boy who never is [bad] . . . is no boy for *me*!' (p. 33). She even finds it necessary to declare that his gentleness and cherubic appearance 'never made Miles a muff' (p. 41). And yet, virtually from their first encounter, the governess cramps Miles's development into an unequivocally gendered being by recurrently undermining his incipient cultivation of a superior masculine pose and self-image. One only has to remind oneself of the boy's many defiantly domophobic protestations of his essential difference to comprehend that his eventual demise is far from sudden. On at least one occasion Miles leaves the house at midnight 'just to show you I could!' and 'I can again' (p. 81). His suffocation in the governess's domestic embrace is a gradual delirious process fuelled by her adamant refusal to 'think [him] – for a change – *bad*!' (p. 72). As Flannigan-Saint-Aubin's general theorisation of masculinity suggests, rather than uniquely mysterious, Miles's dilemma is in fact typical and paradigmatic:

> For the little boy, masculinity is experienced as a constant insecurity in face of the threat 'of feminine absorption; the ubiquitous fear that one's sense of maleness and masculinity are in danger . . . When compared to girls, boys, therefore, appear to experience more stress as they develop and mature.
> (Flannigan-Saint-Aubin 1994: 245)

Like Victor and Walton in Shelley's novel, Miles finds himself 'cooped up' in a domestic environment inhabited almost exclusively by females. The boy should be at school and definitely not in the care of his younger sister's governess. Repeatedly, Miles demands to be sent away, calling on his absent uncle's authority to induce the governess to take the appropriate action. With ever greater urgency the boy emphasises the very unnaturalness of the domestic set-up at Bly which seriously occludes his masculine individuation:

> 'You know, my dear, that for a fellow to be with a lady *always* – ! . . . Ah of course she's a jolly perfect lady; but after all I'm a fellow, don't you see? Who's – well, getting on.' (p. 81)

'Well – I want to see more life . . . I want my own sort! . . . You really compare me to a baby girl? . . . Does my uncle think what *you* think?' (p. 82)

'Well, I think also, you know, of this queer business of ours . . . Why the way you bring me up. And all the rest!' (p. 89)

   'Oh *you* know what a boy wants!' . . .
'If we do [settle things],' [the governess] returned with some spirit, 'you may be sure it will be to take you quite away.'

'Well, don't you understand that's exactly what I'm working for? You'll have to *tell* [my uncle] – about the way you've let it all drop; you'll have to tell him a tremendous lot!' (p. 90)

Unlike Quint, Miles is entitled to challenge the governess's authority. He is the legitimate future master of Bly while she is only a servant, temporarily in charge yet ultimately little more than a means to an end. The governess is forced to realise that, having 'all but pinned the boy to my shawl', she acts 'like a gaoler' (p. 80), expecting Miles to lead an existence 'that's so unnatural for a boy' (p. 84). And yet, she continues to control him 'to provide against some danger of rebellion' (p. 80). All her effort and concentration seem focused on debarring Miles from becoming what he already is:

Turned out for Sunday by his uncle's tailor, who had had a free hand and a notion of pretty waistcoats and of his grand little air, Miles's whole title to independence, the rights of his sex and situation, were so stamped upon him that if he had suddenly struck for freedom I should have had nothing to say.
(p. 80)

In *The Turn of the Screw* we witness a tragic struggle between two individuals longing for a kind of personal autonomy that is traditionally the prerogative of the masculine gender. While the behavioural constraints of Victorian femininity stop the governess ever definitively asserting her supremacy, Miles is held back by the fact that his masculinity has only just begun to emerge from the nebulous sphere of prepubescent, 'angelic' gender neutrality. Due to unfortunate circumstances that are entirely to blame on the arbitrary dictum of the children's uncle as chief representative of the patriarchal order, the boundaries between what is appropriate behaviour and what is not, between what is 'natural' and 'unnatural', are in total confusion at Bly. Both Miles and the governess's claims for predominance, freedom and authority are legitimate. Whereas Miles's rank as heir to the estate seems naturally superior to that of the governess, the latter's supremacy is justified by explicit patriarchal sanction. Systemic indifference creates a monstrous deformation of social relations and traditional hierarchies at Bly. With the master removed, the system threatens to deconstruct itself, throwing its subjects into existential turmoil and instigating a process of cataclysmic destabilisation. Eventually, the *bli*ghted erupts from the *bli*the, revealing the precarious ambiguity of a coercive communal order that, in time, must inevitably give birth to a spec(tac)ular set of doubles, monsters and ghosts.

The governess and Miles imagine themselves in ways that mutually exclude each other, a dilemma further exacerbated by the urgency of their desire to have their new identities – as female 'governor' and boy/young man respectively – publicly acknowledged and validated. As Graham Dawson explains in *Soldier Heroes*, the dynamic interplay between processes of individual self-imagining and social recognition:

> is deeply bound up with power – to elicit recognition or to refuse it, to impose or to contest it. It is therefore shaped by the relations of power that constitute the social divisions and conflicts of the wider hegemonic order. Children, while peculiarly dependent upon affirmative recognition, are relatively powerless to determine its conditions or forms. (Dawson 1994: 262)

To consolidate her own position, the governess aims at keeping Miles 'little'. Since Miles's 'natural' manliness would seriously challenge hers, which is obviously an artifice maintained entirely by proxy, she seeks to pre-empt, or at least procrastinate, his ultimately inevitable masculine self-assertion. Her problem becomes evident when she admits 'that there was something I was much afraid of, and that [Miles] should probably be able to make use of my fear to gain, for his own purpose, more freedom' (p. 83). The governess's liaison with patriarchal authority is revocable. Unlikely ever to become the uncle's wife, she turns to focus her desire on Miles with whom at one point she curiously fancies herself 'as some young couple who, on their wedding-journey, at the inn, feel shy in the presence of the waiter' (p. 109). In her eyes, Miles comes to symbolise the phallus of supreme masculine power, and the desire to seize 'the chance of possessing him' (p. 91) begins totally to consume her. This may be the reason why she does not simply send the boy back to school which would – at least for the time being – resolve the tension between them. She finds herself compelled to be near him, grasp him, make him her instrument and, if at all possible, become one with him.

The governess's transformation from a sisterly guardian into a deadly oppressor is caused by patriarchal coercion. Like Shelley and Conrad's protagonists, she strives to prove herself by unselfconsciously steering towards a supposedly heroic destination that only in retrospect reveals itself as a site of horror and death. The performative pressure becomes so unbearable that eventually the governess starts prosecuting herself, as Shoshona Felman's reading of the novella suggests. 'In James's text as well as in [*Oedipus Rex*]', Felman writes, 'the self-proclaimed detective ends up discovering that he himself is the author of the crime he is investigating: that the crime is his, that he is, himself, the criminal he seeks' (Felman 1995: 204). No sooner does the governess adopt the masculine role and embark on her ill-omened investigation than the pristine harmony between her and the children deteriorates into a possessive relationship marred by the interests of knowledge and power. Unconditional maternal affection and 'the possibilities of beautiful inter-course' (p. 112) are superseded by an inexorable imposition of the Law so calculated that it fills even the perpetrator with 'a perverse horror of what I was doing' (p. 111). It is almost as if the governess had started to colonise the children, turning their blissful innocence into a 'dark con-tinent' in need of rigorous exploration. However, her attempt at grasping the boy, who not only by name represents the promise and allure of patriarchal masculinity, finally leaves her devastated, face to face with her own deathly monstrosity.

As in *Frankenstein* and *Heart of Darkness*, in *The Turn of the Screw* the central protagonist – although biologically female – ends up haunted by a phantasmatic standard of impossible heroic achievement, conjuring a horror considerably exacerbated by her own deep-seated sense of lack, inadequacy and pre-programmed failure. The governess's quest for knowledge and triumphant self-authentication results in tragedy, with the relationship dearest to her consumed (rather than consummated) in a final apocalyptic challenge of the phallus.

Part II

Masks of Savagery and Acts of Anger:
Perspectives on Patriarchal Conditioning

E VER SINCE *LORD OF THE FLIES* became a best-selling modern classic in the early 1960s, it has been read as a fable on the eternal vying for predominance between the moral absolutes of 'good' and 'evil'. Patrick Reilly's comment is typical of the humanist consensus on the moral significance of the text. 'Here, thinly disguised as a boy's adventure story', Reilly writes, 'is a searching analysis of the human situation, a profound parable of man's condition' (Reilly 1992: 7). Indeed, *Lord of the Flies* is a *boy's* adventure story shedding light on *man's* condition; it is a male-authored text employing male characters in the rendition of a typically male genre. However, although Reilly himself implicitly stresses the gendered bias of Golding's point of view, his reading fails to discuss the novel's gender-specificity which seems strategically obscured by the tendency of traditional scholarship to generalise:

> from male to generic human experience [which] not only distorts our understanding of what, if anything, is truly generic, [but also] misdirects attention away from the study of masculinity as a *specifically male* experience, seeing it instead solely as a universal paradigm for *human* experience.
>
> (Brod 1987a: 264)

Lord of the Flies focuses on a group of children exclusively composed of boys. There are no girls on the island, presumably in order not to distract the reader by any irrelevant complications, ensuring that 'sex is no problem' (O'Hara 1966: 411). However, it seems crucial to speculate how a group of girls would have fared on Golding's island. Is what the boys experience markedly dissimilar to the experiences a group of girls might conceivably have undergone in similarly extreme circumstances? Would girls have continued to subsist on mangoes and bananas, or would they – like the boys – have started to hunt down the pigs on the island and eventually the 'piggies' amongst themselves? Another question is if, immersed in the straitjacketing gender ideology of post-war Britain, Golding could at all have dared to imagine girls behaving like boys even in a state of exceptional emergency. What seems certain is that, had Golding in fact written about girls, the novel would probably never have gained its current status as a literary classic widely held to be illustrative of a profound human truth. Only male experience is commonly granted a universal truth-claim in generic terms. Representations of female experience, on the other hand, are invariably viewed as 'a case of special pleading' (Culler 1983: 55), as gender-specific and hence devoid of the same universal applicability.

William Golding and Anthony Burgess's dystopian portrayals of boyhood masculinities are typical of pre-feminist male writing in the 1950s and 1960s, a time when the normative pressure exerted by patriarchal imperatives on men and women alike went largely unnoticed and was identified only very inchoately and misleadingly as a general *conditio humana* or 'human predicament'. As a closer, gender-specific and historical analysis of classics like *Lord of the Flies* and *A Clockwork Orange* brings to light, human identity cannot ever adequately be dealt with in such universalist terms since it is never inevitable or 'natural' but always discursively constructed. In his postmodern interrogation of traditional masculinity, David Gutterman writes that 'as member of any particular culture, community, or group, individuals are given a vast array of scripts that together constitute them as social subjects'. Importantly, he adds that 'some scripts are branded onto individuals more emphatically than others' (Gutterman 1994: 223). Within patriarchy, masculinity is probably the most compelling and imperative script there is, crucially determining and directing the behaviour of everyone, be it directly or indirectly.

The conflicts at work in Golding and Burgess's novels do not mirror a universal human dilemma but express boyhood's particular struggle with masculine imperatives and ideals. The boys' problematic condition is considerably compounded by the fact that masculinity ultimately represents a normative fantasy whose superheroic aspects condemn boys and men to live in a permanent state of paranoid uncertainty about their personal adequacy and competence. To exacerbate matters further, male aggression can be viewed as both 'good' and 'evil', depending on whether it is legitimately employed in patriarchally sanctioned causes or practised in the absence of official authorisation as a cause in itself.

The second part of this study aims to re-historicise *Lord of the Flies* and *A Clockwork Orange* against the rise and astonishing popularity of so-called Angry Young Male writing in the 1950s, of which John Osborne's *Look Back in Anger* and John Braine's *Room at the Top* represent two well-known examples. What Golding, Burgess, Osborne and Braine have in common is that they all write in the aftermath of two devastating world wars which significantly contributed to Britain's gradual loss of imperial supremacy. While Golding and Burgess confront the trauma of worldwide horror, violence and aggressive complicity by encapsulating it in neat universal allegories of tragic or 'natural' inevitability, Osborne and Braine – as members of a new generation of men – give voice to the later-born's despair for an effective return of the heroic. Symptomatically, much of the critical acclaim that accompanied the emergence of the Angry Young Man smacked of a celebratory resuscitation of the hoary strategies of manly self-assertion that had once made Britain great.

And yet, despite his apparent promise to reinvigorate post-war culture by strutting the national stage with an air of reckless self-confidence and potent anger, the new hero ultimately heralded no fresh beginning or inspirited reawakening. Rather, the Angry Young Man turned out to be a wistful chimera willed into existence by theatrical artifice subsequently validated by media publicity. Far from effecting revolutionary change, both his popular and critical success signalled little more than the persistence in the national imagination of an already hopelessly obsolescent masculine ideal.

4
·

Boys Armed with Sticks
·

William Golding's Lord of the Flies

H UMANIST READINGS OF *Lord of the Flies* as an allegory of the intrinsic depravity of human nature are built on the premise that the disastrous emergency landing of their plane has transported Golding's boys into a virginal *terra incognita* beyond the reach of any intelligible cultural or historical parameters. Such an exotic no man's land seems ideal for the production of a modern morality play, featuring fair-haired, golden-bodied everyman (Ralph) in a heroic contest against the ugly, red-haired villain (Jack) and his sadistic, Satan-like companion (Roger). This basic constellation of antagonistic figures is complemented by several equally typified extras: the very fat, effeminate, bespectacled and asthma-ridden intellectual (Piggy), the queer prophet or seer prone to epileptic fits (Simon) and the vaguely freakish fairground attraction of two-boys-in-one ('Samneric', the twins). The ensuing drama unfolds before a largely anonymous crowd whose individual constituents never crystallise and are eventually, without exception, assimilated into a uniform tribe of evil savages. The universal truth-claim of the parable is finally driven home by a sketchy subplot in which a selection of 'littluns' (Henry, Johnny, Percival) echo in their seemingly innocuous boyishness the more fundamental conflicts that are consuming the only slightly more mature 'biguns'.

As a closer analysis reveals, such allegorical readings fail to acknowledge the very specificity of Golding's point of departure. The boys are by no means untouched by the values and actualities of the world from which they originate and which still palpably surrounds them. Most of them are identifiable as coming from an English, middle-class, public-school background. The island itself is engulfed by a world at war, and the mores and behavioural practices, which motivate and sustain that war, almost instantly inscribe themselves on the island. Erstwhile perhaps an idyllic *tabula rasa*, it becomes abruptly implicated in English military and colonial history by 'the long scar smashed into the jungle' (p. 7) at the boys' arrival. Before the end of the first chapter the boys are shown to re-enact the violence that catapulted them onto the island, signalling their alignment with the destructive forces from which they have ostensibly escaped. Out of pure fun they launch their own bomb:

> 'Heave!'
> The great rock loitered, poised on one toe, decided not to return, moved through the air, fell, struck, turned over, leapt droning through the air and smashed a deep hole in the canopy of the forest. Echoes and birds flew, white and pink dust floated, the forest further down shook as with the passage of an enraged monster: and then the island was still.
> 'Wacco!'
> 'Like a bomb!'
> 'Whee-aa-oo!' (p. 30)

The infliction of yet another, third scar on the pristine body of nature is only narrowly escaped when Jack hesitates to kill a stray piglet 'because of the enormity of the knife descending and cutting into living flesh' (p. 34). However, one cannot fail to register Jack's ominous apology for his lack of courage: '"I was going to . . . I was choosing a place. Next time!"' (p. 34). At this point a discerning reader may already guess which course the novel is going to take. As they follow the 'enraged monster' they have set in motion, the boys' attempt at organising their life on the island seems already doomed by what appears to be wild, boyish fun gone out of its perpetrators' control. Crucially, however, as Jack's embarrassment at failing to kill the piglet and his apologetic promise to do better next time indicate, boyishness is not 'wild' or 'out of control' at all. Rather, it is subject to a rigid script of tough, competitive rules by which a boy's performance is assessed as either successful and triumphant or as disappointing and shameful.

Golding's novel reveals the ambiguity of the behavioural norms that govern the boys' existence on the island. There is the law of civilised, domestic society, which says 'Thou Shalt Not Kill', and there is the law of heroic masculinity, which describes the exertion of violence as a challenge and a skill, a crucial test of manly courage, as the ultimate act of self-assertion. In the absence of any clear ideological guidance the boys are bewildered by the disturbing inextricability of masculine heroism and destructive monstrosity. Far from constituting an allegory of the human condition in general, *Lord of the Flies* problematises the irresolvable contradictoriness of two different traditional ideals of masculinity, one marked by stoical self-restraint, the other maintained by means of self-aggrandising violence. The novel testifies to the arbitrary, if invariably functional, ideological malleability of definitions of 'good' and 'evil', masculine heroism and brutal barbarity, organised warfare in compliance with internationally sanctioned, 'fair' rules on the one hand and gratuitous sadism or tyrannical destruction on the other. Patriarchal masculinity appears to promote mutually exclusive, even inimical patterns of behaviour, and the boys on Golding's island find themselves exposed to both: Jack's 'brilliant world of hunting, tactics, fierce exhilaration, skill' and Ralph's 'world of longing and baffled common-sense' (p. 77).

While Ralph and Jack are worlds apart – 'two continents of experience and feeling, unable to communicate' (p. 60) – they also never cease to haunt each other. As Ralph realises, 'there was that indefinable connection between himself and Jack; who therefore would never let him alone, never' (p. 203). Golding's creation of Ralph and Jack as antithetical archetypes belies the complementarity of their psychological dispositions. One only has to consider contemporary advertising strategies for the recruitment of young men into the armed forces to realise that, rolled into one, Jack and Ralph would make the perfect soldier. Army authorities all over the world promise young men legitimate means and opportunities to assuage their burgeoning masculine desire for freedom and heroic independence. At the same time, quite paradoxically, they expect them to submit unconditionally to patriarchal military law. With respect to *Lord of the Flies*, it is hence difficult to decide who is the glamorous hero and who his antithetical *doppelgänger*. The most fundamental difference between Jack and Ralph is that Jack dares to take the initiative, making himself his own anarchic legislator and commander-in-chief, whereas Ralph is clearly of a more subservient disposition. Jack is a born military leader; Ralph would make a good soldier. As Golding puts it, 'Ralph *might* make a boxer, as far as width and heaviness of shoulders went, but there was a mildness about his mouth and eyes that proclaimed no devil' (p. 10–11; my emphasis). While Golding stresses Ralph's incorruptible goodness, he keeps quiet about the easy exploitability of his heroic integrity, for example, within the framework of a devastating war just like the one that is being fought while the boys are on the island. One cannot help getting the impression that if Ralph had been a little older, he could easily have become the 'beast from air', that is, the parachutist whose corpse is swept onto the island and who appears to Simon as 'the picture of a human at once heroic and sick' (p. 113).

Presented with a legitimate and just (that is, a patriarchally sanctioned) cause, neatly packaged as 'manly duty' in conjunction with 'heroic adventure', would Ralph have been able to resist?

Ralph's susceptibility to boyhood fantasies of masculine freedom and adventure is patent from the beginning. When Ralph first finds himself marooned on the island, he can hardly contain his joy at the prospect that 'here at last was the imagined but never fully realised place leaping into real life' (p. 16). Ironically, it is Jack's first appearance – vaulting like a comic-book superhero onto the platform 'with his cloak flying' (p. 21) – which indicates that the fantasy has indeed come true. Like many a young soldier, Ralph realises too late that the fantasy of heroic masculinity serves to cover up a nightmare of manly self-destruction. About half way through the novel Golding writes that 'the world, that understandable and lawful world, was slipping away' (p. 99). In fact, it only reveals the expedient functionality of its constructed nature. The boys aim 'to do the right things' (p. 47), yet 'right' and 'wrong' turn out not to be infallible, solid values but terms open to discursive redefinition. Civilisation is 'in ruins' (p. 67) because what is ordinarily designated as taboo behaviour can under certain circumstances become legitimate, even strongly recommended and compulsory practice. Ultimately, the insidious group dynamics, which affect the boys' existence on the island and seem responsible for their deterioration into savagery, are determined by the man-making imperatives of patriarchal masculinity. According to Lynne Segal, the specific problematic of this particular kind of masculinity is grounded in the fact that its most powerful axiomatic constitutes at once also its most fundamental dilemma. Masculinity is traditionally defined in exclusive, negative terms as what it is not; what it is in itself appears to go without saying. With respect to Ernest Hemingway, whose work celebrates virile manliness at its purest and most excessive, Segal writes that 'masculinity cannot be asserted *except* in relation to what is defined as its opposite. It depends upon the perpetual renunciation of "femininity"' (Segal 1990: 114).

Immediately after their arrival on the island the boys embark on a dramatic assertion of their masculinity in contradistinction to what they perceive as its 'other'. In the absence of girls or women, nature itself – announcing its untamed difference 'with a *witch*-like cry' (p. 7; my emphasis) – provides the otherness over which the boys attempt to gain control and establish their superiority. They set out to map the wilderness, casting themselves in the role of heroic explorers who confidently inscribe their presence on the island. In this context, Golding suggests that the urge to dominate and the excitement derived from finding oneself in a position of power is innate to the boys, as his description of Henry, one of the younger children, demonstrates:

> Henry became absorbed beyond mere happiness as he felt himself exercising control over living things. He talked to them, urging them, ordering them. Driven back by the tide, his footprints became bays in which [the little sea creatures] were trapped and gave him the illusion of mastery. (p. 66)

The boys' tendency to set themselves off as controlling agents against an objectified, 'othered' world is not simply a gratuitous pleasure, but a highly functional (if catastrophic) element in a vicious circle of hierarchical self-assertion. While Henry is rejoicing in his rule over 'tiny transparencies' (p. 66), Roger starts throwing stones at him. Both boys are desperate to distract from their own helplessness and do so by projecting their fear of subjection onto an even weaker other. While bullying appears as a reliable strategy of expressing one's superior masculine composure, a self-conscious admission of fear would threaten their integrity as boys. As Peter Lewis writes in an account of his past as a public schoolboy, 'teasing illustrates, and tests, an important feature of masculinity. You push someone till they lose control, break down, cry or lash out in anger. Then *you* have won and *they* have lost' (Lewis 1991: 181).

As the boys' sense of forlornness steadily increases, so does their need for 'others' to testify to their masterful superiority. Their hunting of the pigs, for example, is clearly motivated by a desire for manly autonomy. The act of killing provides relief from their quintessentially 'feminine' and hence shameful feelings of fear and disempowerment, endowing them with the 'knowledge that they had outwitted a living thing, imposed their will upon it' (p. 76). Symptomatically, the killings become ever more ferocious and orgiastic, culminating in a particularly vicious attack on a sow. Beside themselves with fear, the boys fling themselves at this female emblem of their own panic and vulnerability, determined to master and kill it once and for all. As the sexual undertones and disturbing orgasmic imagery of Golding's description signal, this is no mere killing, but also a rape, which facilitates the boys' initiation into the violent masculinity of big game hunters:

> the sow fell and the hunters hurled themselves at her . . . Roger ran round the heap, prodding with his spear whenever pigflesh appeared. Jack was on top of the sow, stabbing downward with his knife. Roger found a lodgment for his point and began to push till he was leaning with his whole weight. The spear moved forward inch by inch and the terrified squealing became a high-pitched scream. The sow collapsed under them and they were heavy and fulfilled upon her.

. . . Roger began to withdraw his spear and the boys noticed it for the first time. Robert stabilized the thing in a phrase which was received uproariously.

'Right up her ass!' (p. 149f.)

The boys engage in a relentless, ultimately self-annihilating battle against their own nature. In their attempt to assert themselves as men and avoid the stigma of being referred to as 'a lot of cry-babies and sissies' (p. 90), they determinedly violate and destroy their 'femininity'. Willingly, they metamorphose into what they are not, donning impassive, uniform masks of masculine strength intended to bring about an eclipse of the terror of individuality. Jack's response to his transformation into a savage by means of clay and charcoal is typical: 'He looked in astonishment, no longer at himself but at an awesome stranger . . . the mask was a thing on its own, behind which Jack hid, liberated from shame and self-consciousness' (p. 69). Notably, the mask of savagery is so compelling and indisputably masculine that, while wearing it, the boys feel free to tie their long hair back for comfort, an act previously perceived as girlish and hence entirely out of the question.

The boys' masculinity is a precarious construct, extremely paranoid and hypersensitive to the forever imminent threat of unmasking. Both Piggy and Ralph become guilty of disrupting the camouflage by reminding the other boys of the actual reality of their condition. Piggy accuses the hunters of 'acting like a crowd of kids' (p. 42); Ralph refers to them as 'boys armed with sticks' (p. 138). The need to silence these voices of emasculation becomes an imperative necessity. Piggy's authority is easily discredited as his outward appearance and intellectual disposition stand in stark contrast to the boys' ideal of masculinity. Piggy is also the only boy who has enjoyed a practically non-patriarchal upbringing. With both his parents dead, Piggy lives with his aunt whose authority he is never hesitant to invoke. '"Sucks to your auntie!"' and '"Shut up!"' are the other boys' unanimous standard responses to Piggy's female-authored rationality, whereas anecdotes of various fathers' heroic exploits never fail to find an eager audience. Piggy's deviation from the norm, his association with female (rather than male) authority, as well as his physical shortcomings, make him a paradigmatic candidate for ostracism. The boys quickly take to identifying themselves in opposition to him, whose deficient masculinity begins to function as a reference point for the suitability of their own conduct and appearance. Repeatedly, he is turned into 'the centre of social derision so that everyone felt cheerful and normal' (p. 164). The 'othering' of Piggy is finally complete when the pejorative epithet of his name is used to align him with the other victims of masculine self-assertion on the island. The answer to the question '"What would a beast eat?"' is '"Pig." – "We eat pig." – "Piggy"' (p. 91). The boys' initially playful transformation of Piggy into an outsider becomes so effective that even in death they find it impossible not to compare him to something less than human: 'Piggy's arms and legs twitched a bit, like a pig's after it has been killed' (p. 200). In contrast to Piggy's, the 'othering' of Ralph is a slightly more difficult task that is eventually accomplished by associating him inextricably with his companion and chief adviser. During the boys' last assembly meeting, Jack tells both Piggy and Ralph to 'shut up'. Soon afterwards, he suggests to his hunters that Ralph is 'like Piggy. He says things like Piggy. He isn't a proper chief' (p. 139).

The boys' refashioning of themselves and their environment is driven by the imperatives of a masculinity based on negative self-assertion. This kind of masculinity endlessly produces and consumes 'others' against which its superiority is defined. At the same time, it enforces a total annihilation of the self's own inherent complexity, prescribing, instead of individual self-fulfilment, the ritual enactment of a tautly scripted role. The process of becoming a man within the conceptual framework of this particular kind of masculinity necessitates a complete surrender of the individual self to totalitarianist, effectively self-oppressive rules and modes of behaviour, hence propagating not self-liberation but ritual self-oblivion. Recoiling in terror from the reality of being frightened little boys on a desert island beleaguered by a world at war, the boys seek refuge in the security of ritualistic role-play. Ironically, in order not to lose face, they resort to gender-specific masquerade. As Claire Rosenfield infers, the boys 'deteriorate into adults' (Rosenfield 1961: 100). They become men who categorically eschew a confrontation with their emotionality and intrinsic 'femininity' by covering it up with masks of authority and manly fearlessness.

As Peter Middleton argues, such an adamant refusal to apply 'the inward gaze' of self-inspection and self-examination is symptomatic of men's general inability to articulate and successfully negotiate their feelings 'for lack of a language for such reflection' (Middleton 1990: 3). Although the boys launch repeated attempts at discussing their communal quandary, their basic emotional inarticulacy remains conspicuous. Clearly, the boys' failure to communicate how they feel stands in immediate relation to their eventual decline into violence. Even feelings of joy and delight are translated into a playful enactment of combat, accompanied by a shouting of linguistically unintelligible neologisms of pure, physical excitement: 'Ralph danced out into the hot air of the beach and then returned as a fighter plane, with wings swept back, and machine-gunned Piggy. "Schee-aa-ow!" "Whizzoh!"' (p. 12).

According to Middleton, seemingly innocuous boyish behaviour like this hints at a grave masculine dilemma. As his detailed analysis of boys' comics shows, the fundamental emotional inarticulacy of superheroes is an indispensable constituent of their 'hard', infallible masculinity, at once the cause and effect of their apparent invulnerability. Heroes act; they do not engage in discussions about how they feel. Heroes are free, independent agents, unencumbered by a complicated emotional life, maintaining their superiority by means of a glamorously costumed outward appearance and a compelling style. In most cases, their heroism is facilitated by an explicit negation of their private persona. For example, unlike Clark Kent, Superman appears incognito, reduced to an exemplary icon of efficiency and action. The public role of heroic masculinity categorically excludes the individual man's private self. As Middleton states, all that can emerge from such a state of enforced impassivity is 'the meaningless cry, pre-linguistic and therefore impossible to have a dialogue with' (Middleton 1990: 27). Golding's boys are clearly influenced by representations of superheroic masculinity and show themselves prone to emulate its rigidly coded behaviour in situations of particular exhilaration or distress. They are inclined to mistake the fantasy of heroism for something real, learning and acting out its scripts until their individual identities become indistinguishable from the roles they play. Hence, the boys' tendency to express their feelings by dint of pre-linguistic neologisms can be read as a symptom of their incipient metamorphosis into men, that is, their gradual hardening and remote-controlled decline into emotional atrophy and self-oblivious role-play.

Apart from the 'littluns', who are as yet exempt from complying with imperative ideals of masculine behaviour and self-expression, the only three boys on the island that remain palpably troubled by their feelings throughout, and even dare admit to them, are Simon, Piggy and Ralph. However, their combined efforts to raise the issue, suggesting that 'the least part, the bit we can all talk about, is kind of deciding on the fear' (p. 89), are all stopped dead by Jack, who evermore persistently demands that they shut up. Instead of talk, which seems too feminine and 'cry-babyish' an option of going about the problem of fear, Jack offers his hunters an antidote concocted of silence, denial, stoical endurance and – most importantly – ever more self-assertive action. Notably, Jack's own ferocious masculinity is little more than a precarious pose. Earlier in the novel we find him struggling to explain to Ralph why hunting is so important to him. Stammering with embarrassment, he admits to his fear – and his fear of that fear – whose emasculating powers of subjection and victimisation he seeks to incorporate into his own being by casting himself in the role of a hunter:

> 'All the same – in the forest. I mean when you're hunting – not when you're getting fruit, of course, but when you're on your own –'
> He paused for a moment, not sure if Ralph would take him seriously . . .
> 'If you're hunting sometimes you catch yourself feeling as if –' He flushed suddenly.
> 'There's nothing in it of course. Just a feeling. But you can feel as if you're not hunting, but – being hunted; as if something's behind you all the time in the jungle.' . . .
> '. . . I know how they feel. See? That's all.' (pp. 57–8)

Fear is blanked out and compensated for by action. It becomes something unmentionable that continues to haunt the boys, ready to rematerialise from the petrified self beneath the mask at any unguarded moment. Eager to pass as manly, the boys comply with Jack's imperative 'to put up with' their fear instead of identifying, discussing and deciding on it (p. 90). Once again – as a brief reference to David Cohen's book on 'being a man' suggests – the boys implement a characteristically masculine code of behaviour:

> It isn't that our feelings are less intense than those of women but that certain feelings are shameful. Triumph and success are splendid. If you have cause for any other feelings – misery, fear, worry – it's best to hide them. Put on the mask. Assume the stiff upper lip. (Cohen 1990: 85)

The effort of acting masculine and forgetting about 'the depths of their tormented private lives' (p. 147) proves exceedingly strenuous. Hence, the hunters seem fortunate to find shelter in the natural fortress of Castle Rock on the outermost periphery of the island. Symptomatically, Jack orders this emotional stronghold and hideaway to be vigilantly guarded by the boys at all times to ensure that 'the others don't sneak in' (p. 177). It seems as if masculinity is never and nowhere safe from the threat of being penetrated, permeated, or in any other way either forced to shed its hard shell or induced to crumble from within.

The boys' grandiose establishment of a pure, fearless masculinity at Castle Rock, uncontaminated by feminine qualities, is continually at risk of a psychotic implosion. It can only succeed in sustaining itself if, first, its foundations are anchored in an infallible symbolic order and, second, a practical outlet for the boys' repressed emotionality can be found. It is erroneous to believe that the older boys have naturally grown out of the 'passionately emotional and corporate life' (p. 64) led by the 'littluns'.

Rather, they have been coerced to regard their fear and basic need for human warmth as shameful. In this respect, as Lewis's bitter reminiscences suggest, boyish life on Golding's desert island is no different from boyish life in an English public school. Both are marked by the same insidious group dynamics. Notably, Ian McEwan recalls his first reading of Golding's novel as an experience of self-recognition and total identification. 'I *knew* these boys,' he writes. 'I knew what they were capable of. I had seen us at it. As far as I was concerned, Golding's island was a thinly disguised boarding school'. Whereas McEwan adds rather naively that 'no one was to blame – it was how it was when we were together' (McEwan 1986: 158), Lewis blames 'the system' for undermining the boys' originally intact emotionality. According to Lewis, public-school pedagogy works systematically to isolate boys from one another, thereby reducing friendship, for example, 'to an endless calculation of cost and benefit' (Lewis 1991: 182). Naturally, so Lewis argues, once they find themselves on their own, without close friends or easy access to the loving embrace of their families, the boys develop an overwhelming desire to belong, to be part of something larger into which they can pour their pent-up emotionality:

> In school, the policing of experience and the competitive dynamic of a hierarchical system fill the emotional vacuum, inviting a boy's commitment to arbitrary constructions like team or house or school as a preparation for the world of work [and war!] that was to follow.
>
> (Lewis 1991: 180; my addition)

In Golding's novel, the boys' emotionality finds relief in a spurious tribal union, which barely conceals the fact that ultimately each boy remains on his own. There are no friendships on the island, only strictly purpose-bound, strategic alliances of convenience. Ralph's realisation that Piggy was his 'true, wise friend' (p. 223) rings hollow as a rather pathetic afterthought to a relationship not between equals, but between superior and inferior, teaser and taunted. The irresistible attraction of the tribe is facilitated by the boys' yearning for physical contact, for a sense of belonging as well as an opportunity to let themselves go. Significantly, the last two boys to join the tribe – and even then only reluctantly – are Sam and Eric, the twins, who between themselves share a physical bond unavailable to their peers. Sam and Eric do not need the tribe for comfort or emotional relief. They freely huddle and cuddle when distressed without ever being reprobated by the other boys who overlook their separate individualities and view them as one, as 'Samneric'.

As one of the central points of her 'twenty-first-century blueprint for boys' survival', which she regards as dependent on a societal unlearning of patriarchal masculinity, Rosalind Miles lists the following imperative. 'We must', she writes, 'help the boy to be genuinely strong and independent, teach him how to love and care for himself, so reducing his dependence on the female [and] on the gang as a substitute for the female' (Miles 1992: 300). Clearly, Golding's boys who, with the possible exception of Piggy, are exclusively of an English, middle-class, public-school background, would have greatly benefited from this recommendation. Due to their patriarchal conditioning they are all too willing to surrender their individual identities to a supra-individual common cause. Their fascination with the tribal is motivated by their desire to repossess themselves of the physical sense of belonging and security that they enjoyed before they were abruptly removed and ideologically alienated from their mothers and the feminine in general, that is, before they were forced to enter the paramilitary institutions of the patriarchal education system.

Strikingly, Golding's description of the boys' ritual dancing evokes a womb-like atmosphere. In the very act of celebrating their savagery and masculine self-sufficiency the boys conjure and reconstitute the presence of the female that they previously seemed so determined to exorcise. It appears as if they virtually regress to a semiotic, foetal state of absolute physical intimacy and ungendered primal being:

> The movement became regular while the chant lost its first superficial excitement and began to beat like a steady pulse . . . and the complementary circles went round and round as though repetition would achieve safety of itself. There was the throb and stamp of a single organism. (p. 167)

However, as it turns out, this is not a nurturant circle of organic becoming but a deathly anti-womb of destruction, driven by the boys' overpowering desire 'to squeeze and hurt' (p. 126). Rather than conjured to provide comfort and security, the female is perverted into a beastly maw, representative of the self-perpetuating dynamics of a relentless patriarchal totalitarianism. When the boys kill Simon, they act under the remote control of the Lord of the Flies who, like a diabolical radar beacon at the centre of the island, directs their circling, crunching and screaming movements. Simon falls down and loses consciousness 'inside the mouth' of the Lord's hypnotic, supra-individual being (p. 159) only to meet his death a chapter later in 'the mouth of the new circle' (p. 168). The boys and their imaginary projection of a supreme authority have become one. The moment of their mutual identification manifests itself in the senseless killing of truth. Simon had come to inform his peers of the true identity of the beast of which they were all so frightened. It is 'a dead man on a hill' (p. 168), a fallen superhero dangling limply from his parachute like a broken marionette, epitomising the inevitable detumescence of all the high-flying ideals and fantasies of masculinity.

It is crucial not to misinterpret the identity of the Lord of the Flies as a symbol of metaphysical evil forces or the inherent uncivilised depravity of human nature. The Lord of the Flies speaks 'in the voice of a schoolmaster' (p. 158) and is therefore representative of masculine authority, pedagogic discipline and patriarchal control. It does not stand for nature but for civilisation, and for patriarchal civilisation in particular, whose totalitarian presence depends for its erection and maintenance on a man-made perversion of nature. A nursing sow, symbolic of fertility and life, is hunted down and killed. Her severed head is then placed on a stick and left to rot into a symbol of masculine authority and patriarchal rule. The skull of the female becomes a chilling reminder of the parental, motherly care which used to infuse the boys' life and which has been superseded by the compulsory emotional atrophy of male adolescence. Golding's novel is not a generally applicable dystopian vision concerning the nature of humanity; rather, it constitutes a disturbing, gender-specific critique of English public-school pedagogy. All patriarchal societies thrive on a well-balanced mixture of wild savagery and lawful obedience in their male subjects' psychological make-up. Their often strictly anti-coeducational education systems purposely deprive boys of their skills of emotional self-expression by declaring everything vaguely 'feminine' – which in itself is a patriarchal term open to expedient redefinition – as shameful. This causes boys to become highly susceptible to patriarchally sanctioned, 'masculine' sentiments and causes, such as patriotism and war. Group identities replace individual identities, rendering men easily manipulable instruments within the various, hierarchically structured schemes and exploits of patriarchy.

Golding's use of boy characters as allegorical signifiers in a universally applicable fable is thwarted by the particular condition of boyhood, which is not so much a definitive state of generic being as a transitional process of becoming, catalysed and sustained by highly gender-specific, patriarchally manipulated needs and desires. Instead of depicting how humankind must inevitably descend into savagery when left in the absence of civilisational control, Golding gives an accurate description of boyhood's struggle to live up to the fantasy of adult masculinity. Problematically, an infallible, superheroic masculinity of grown-up men does not exist except in the boys' idealising imagination. And yet, although in Golding's novel there is no discernible difference between the worlds of boyhood and manhood, both of which are at war with themselves, the boys trust that there is and – needless to say – they find their own world lacking in comparison:

> 'Grown-ups know things,' said Piggy. 'They ain't afraid of the dark. They'd meet and have tea and discuss. Then things 'ud be all right –'
> 'They wouldn't set fire to the island. Or lose –'
> 'They'd build a ship –'
> The three boys stood in the darkness, striving unsuccessfully to convey the majesty of adult life.
> 'They wouldn't quarrel –'
> 'Or break my specs –'
> 'Or talk about a beast –'. (p. 103)

The fantasy of masculinity's superiority can only be maintained as long as boys remain strictly segregated from men, which in turn exacerbates the boyish desire to be granted admission to the masculine world of power and privilege. Middleton suggests that 'manhood is much more exclusive than womanhood' and that 'perhaps women welcome girls into their world in a way that men don't welcome boys' (Middleton 1990: 28). He continues to deplore that 'there is no place for boys who are less than men, and therefore no way to negotiate the transition into adult responses and their responsibilities' (Middleton 1990: 29). Similarly, Peter Lewis remembers that in the public-school environment 'there was no space in between being a boy and becoming a man for any distinctive style or assertion of identity' (Lewis 1991: 179). Within patriarchy, the initiation of boys into manhood is no gradual process; rather, boys are expected to take a jump as in a crucial test of courage.

Whereas girls and women are commonly believed to share the same gender, boys and men are not. As R.W. Connell points out, 'children of both sexes, being weak *vis-à-vis* adults, are . . . forced to inhabit the feminine position' (Connell 1995: 16). Hence, boys are regarded not only as quantitatively different from men – that is, as little, as yet incomplete males who will gradually and naturally mature – but moreover as qualitatively different, essentially feminine beings who must metamorphose into men. Boys have to break with their past in order to become men, signalling their essential change by acting differently, by showing that they are capable of fulfilling the ideals of masculinity. Yet, as they have normally had little contact with 'real' men, who shun and condescend to them, they act out masculinity as they imagine it, fashioning themselves in accordance with patriarchal fantasies and adopting fictional roles that are recognised as 'masculine' by their peers who, like them, are boys struggling to achieve manhood. As Middleton argues, the perpetuation of masculinity depends on boyhood's imitative invention of it. 'In return for admission to the picture palace of men's exploits', he writes, boys 'provide the credence which makes it possible'. Accordingly, 'manhood is a long-running fiction which men construct out of boyhood's worship generated by boyhood's exclusion' (Middleton 1990: 42). There are in fact no 'men' at all, only boys of different ages acting like 'men', each generation erecting their own respective Lord of War, Progress, Science, Capitalism, and so forth, whose awesome infallibility they strive to emulate, while its ultimate inhumanity invariably humiliates and destroys them.

As a normative construction, boyhood's fantasy of masculinity determines 'what men ought to be'. As R.W. Connell has shown, masculinity hence represents an impossible standard which 'hardly anyone meets', leaving the majority of men convinced they have failed (see Connell 1995: 70). Masculinity does not come naturally to men, but is an accomplishment dependent upon constant struggle. Patriarchy subjects men to its rules by ensuring that they never feel quite secure enough in their masculinity to assume a position of anarchic, independent power. Men's subordinate position is determined by the systemic projection of a masculine self-image that is at once normative and unrealisable. No real-life man can ever perfectly meet or embody the superheroic ideals of masculinity. Equally, the father who gives patriarchy its name is a purely symbolic construction. Like the permanent tumescence of the symbolic phallus, the phantasmatic image of an omnipotent, god-like father serves to keep men under systemic control by ideologically inscribing their feelings of inadequacy and impotence. Within patriarchy, manhood – like womanhood – is defined by lack and inferiority. No matter how 'masculine' men may succeed in becoming, the inevitable, much-dreaded realisation is that they cannot ever advance very far from being mere 'boys armed with sticks'.

As male violence and paranoia escalate in *Lord of the Flies*, one tends to become oblivious to the fact that Golding's protagonists are in fact boys, not men. All the greater then is the shock of recognition at the end of the novel when we are reminded that all of them – Ralph, Jack and Roger included – are in fact 'littluns'. Faced with the sudden appearance of a grown-up *miles ex machina*, the hunters spontaneously drop their masks of masculine prowess and determination. Their self-assertive agency wilts immediately to be replaced by an emotional display of feminine passivity and helplessness. A real man now occupies the superior position of masculinity that the boys struggled to usurp, an officer emblematic of the heroism the boys were so keen to emulate. However, like the boys before him, the soldier is only acting out a role, hiding his individual self behind a well-devised mask of 'white drill, epaulettes, a revolver, a row of gilt buttons down the front of the uniform' (p. 221). His fortuitous appearance saves Ralph and unmasks his persecutors, yet it does not resolve the novel's central problem. In fact, the soldier appears to epitomise the ordeal the boys have just been through, as he emerges from a world equally devastated by 'a jolly good show' (p. 223) of boyish 'fun and games' (p. 221).

Instead of effecting a genuine rescue of the boys from their gender-specific predicament, the officer only suspends it temporarily, delivering them back into the 'care' of the patriarchal order and its man-making imperatives that will eventually expect all of them to re-adopt the masculine role. Clearly, the officer himself has internalised all the imperative ideals of patriarchal masculinity: its mask-like uniformity, its paradoxical heroism-cum-servitude, its ethical ambiguity (this saviour carries a revolver!), and its peremptory unemotionality. The grown-up man's response to the boys' tearful display of despair and relief seems equally revealing: 'The officer, surrounded by these noises, was moved and a little embarrassed. He turned away to give them time to pull themselves together . . .' (p. 223). His masculine superiority expresses itself in a deliberate gesture of emotional detachment that serves to accentuate his own manliness in opposition to the boys' femininity. Moreover, his attitude of waiting for the boys to 'pull themselves together' is reminiscent of Jack's fateful earlier demand that the boys should learn how to 'put up with' their fear. The officer's appearance not only triggers the tears to which the boys succumb 'for the first time on the island' (p. 223); he also embodies the principle that is responsible for their tragic belatedness.

Patrick Reilly writes that *Lord of the Flies* was inspired by Golding's experiences as a soldier in World War II when 'the schoolroom of the world – masterless, bereft of authority – had been given over to the most monstrous mayhem. Murder had been committed on a massive scale by men, wicked children of a larger growth' (Reilly 1992: 7). What Reilly fails to address is that World War II – like most wars – was authorised, and its perpetrators and participants were not murderers (at least not in the legal sense of the word) but soldiers doing their heroic duty, and soldiers are respectable adult men, not children running amok. Significantly, even at the very end of Golding's novel there remains some ethical ambiguity as to the goodness or badness of male violence. On being informed that two boys have been killed, the officer asks if the children are all British, insinuating that if the boys had been fighting against German or Japanese 'enemies', their savagery might have been acceptable. After all there is a war going on!

Lord of the Flies seems a far more complex and complicated book than humanist critics like Reilly, discussing an entirely hypothetical *conditio humana*, appear to find conceivable. Its message is expressly gender-specific, testifying to the urgent accuracy of Middleton's statement that 'modern men have suffered greatly in a series of wars generated by largely masculine codes of behaviour whose close examination might be a useful step towards preventing their endless repetition' (Middleton 1990: 2–3).

5

·

The Height of Fashion

·

Anthony Burgess's A Clockwork Orange

Like Lord of the Flies, Anthony Burgess's *A Clockwork Orange* features a story of extreme boyhood violence against the background of an ethical problematisation of 'good' and 'evil'. Like Golding's setting of his novel on a remote desert island, Burgess's dystopian mode has encouraged humanist critics to read *A Clockwork Orange* both ahistorically and generically as a case study of man's free choice between vice and virtue. A gender-specific analysis of the novel's almost exclusively male cast, all of which are subject to severe patriarchal conditioning, has so far been neglected. Forty years after its original conception, the novel fails to shock or convince as an ominous allegorical prophecy concerning the future fate of human civilisation. However, it remains intriguing as the excessive and hyperbolic climax of a specifically male tradition in post-war British literature, namely the Angry Young Men movement of the 1950s and early 1960s.

Typical of the Angry Young Male hero, fifteen-year-old Alex, Burgess's central protagonist, displays a greater affinity with Jack, Golding's compelling antagonist, than Ralph, his mild-mannered hero. Both Jack and Alex employ domophobic action to assert their superiority against both real and imaginary others. Like Jack, Alex hides behind a mask, fashioning himself and his entourage of 'droogs' after the ideal of a highly stylised hypermasculinity. Symptomatically, 'nadsat' – Alex and his 'droogs' arcane sociolect – operates not only as a rebellious, anarchic counter-code but also as an elaborate adaptation of the neologistic diction favoured by comic-book superheroes. The more eloquent Alex's command of nadsat, the more successfully can he detach himself from the compromising emotionality of his boyish self. Nadsat forms a crucial, constitutive part of the droogs' manly masquerade, merging them into a uniform elitist group and thereby perfecting the artifice of their fearless and seemingly invulnerable warrior masculinity. Alex's extreme style consciousness signals that he lives his life in camouflage. In fact, he performs an almost grotesque drag act of masculinity, impersonating a phantasmatic superhero whose glamorous costume and exaggerated bodily contours he is eager to copy, yet of course hopelessly unable ever to match perfectly:

> The four of us were dressed in the height of fashion, which in those days was a pair of black very tight tights with the old jelly mould, as we called it, fitting on the crotch underneath the tights . . . Then we wore waisty jackets without lapels but with these very big built-up shoulders ('pletchoes' we called them) which were a kind of mockery of having real shoulders like that. (pp. 5–6)

The droogs' identity is a strenuous, adopted pose. Notably, the boys' incongruous outfit is not of their own making but fastidiously tailored after the fashion of the day which, in turn, reflects the hegemonic gender dictates of the totalitarian patriarchy in which they live. In Alex's world, masculine superiority manifests and expresses itself by dint of a hierarchically motivated dress code that accentuates a man's public rank and persona at the same time as it elides the uniqueness of his individual self. Instead of rebelling against such insidious ideological impositions, Alex internalises them, as his awe on meeting 'the Minister of the Interior or Inferior' demonstrates. According to Alex, 'you could viddy who was the real important veck right away, very tall and with blue glazzies and with real horrorshow platties on him, the most lovely suit, brothers, I had ever viddied, absolutely in the height of fashion' (p. 73). Although Alex takes great pains at presenting himself as a free, anarchic individualist, he remains highly susceptible to the impact of patriarchal imperatives whose most coercive implications appear entirely to elude him. Instead of striving to break out of totalitarianism's densely woven network of behavioural norms and rules, and create himself proprioceptively in opposition to the system he perceives as oppressive, Alex resembles Golding's Jack in that he readily dons the straitjacketing gender role of an essentially anti-individualistic, self-annihilating masculinity. As yet another boy keen to live up to the superheroic ideal, his desires and behaviour become predictable, rendering him extremely vulnerable to strategic manipulation as an instrument in the political plots and schemes of various patriarchal functionaries.

Whereas in *Lord of the Flies* the boys' assertion of their masculinity depends largely on the creation of 'feminine' others, *A Clockwork Orange* introduces actual female characters, if always only as expedient, super-numerary figures of contrast and never as protagonists in their own right. Primarily, however, it is the general civil inertia and domestic timidity of the majority of their contemporaries against which Alex and his droogs protest their own superiority as angry, violently non-conformist young males. The droogs' recklessly irresponsible pursuit of male adventure stands in stark contrast to the rest of society's placid, effeminate home-liness, an opposition strongly reminiscent of Jack's contempt as a hunter for Piggy and Ralph's ongoing concern with the building of shelters. In *A Clockwork Orange* domesticity comes to equal femininity, making it the non-negotiable opposite of the masculine domain of public action. Home – 'a gloomy sort of a name' (p. 19) – continually threatens to confine and terminate masculine fantasies of untrammelled freedom. Thus, the droogs' domophobic violence, culminating in the rape and death of a housewife and mother figure, must be regarded as an essen-tially ritualistic act designed to testify to the young men's masculine detachment and gender purity. Action and initiative become inexorable imperatives Alex and his droogs must obey lest they contract the emas-culating conformism and feminine passivity of ordinary familial domes-ticity. Whenever we find the droogs comfortably settled in their regular haunt, the Korova Milkbar, one of them turns to challenge his peers with the question of 'What's it going to be then, eh?' (pp. 5, 103, 140). Thus reminded of their shameful inclination to succumb to the easy pleasures of the domestic, the droogs must yet again venture beyond the *domus* to prove their adventurous spirit and masculine potency. Where they go, or what they do, is of little importance, as long as they 'keep walking . . . and viddy what turns up' (p. 8).

The droogs' ultraviolence, meted out with little apparent discrimina-tion as they roam the streets, is never gratuitous but serves to assert the boys' manliness which seems constantly at risk of domestic etiolation. Alex and his droogs are typical representatives of the in-vogue fantasy of young male rebellion against conformity, cherished in the 1950s by a whole generation of disenchanted men and most enduringly inscribed in mainstream culture by Hollywood movies celebrating the impetuous individualism of iconic vanguard figures like, for example, James Dean and Marlon Brando. Unlike the United States, however, post-war Britain was devoid of any such indelible national myths as the American Dream. Deprived of its erstwhile imperial opportunities for exotic self-expansion and self-aggrandisement, the nation was caught up in a gradual, if steady process of decline. The ideals of patriarchal masculinity seemed on the wane for lack of adequately heroic causes. Significantly, the central complaint of British literature's most renowned Angry Young Man, Jimmy Porter in John Osborne's play *Look Back in Anger,* is that 'there aren't any good, brave causes left' (Osborne 1993: 83). Jimmy's sentiment noisily reverberates in Alex's 'disappointment at things as they were those days. Nothing to fight against really. Everything as easy as kiss-my-sharries' (p. 14).

The violence perpetrated by Alex and his droogs is perhaps best explained as a desperate attempt at young, male self-assertion, escalating out of control due to the stagnancy and ideological immobility of the political system into which it unleashes itself. In the 1950s, British society found itself at a loss for viable means and strategies to accommodate the young male energies its own glamorisation of a certain kind of heroic masculinity had fostered. Conscriptive army service turned out to be a hopelessly inadequate substitute for the loss of real-life challenges like the war effort or the adventures opened up by the imperial enterprise. At the same time, attempts at domesticating the male by redefining the masculine role as that of a breadwinner, considerate partner in marriage, responsible father and DIY expert only resulted in the Angry Young Man backlash (see Segal 1990: 1–25), of which Alex and his droogs are symptomatic, if extremist representatives. Alex and his droogs appropriate the patriarchal ideal of heroism-cum-servitude, claiming the heroism for themselves while associating servitude of any kind with the emasculating sphere of feminine domesticity. In *A Clockwork Orange* militant heroism becomes its own anarchic cause and, freed of its employment in patriarchally sanctioned schemes, it soon reveals its fundamentally barbaric, droogish complexion. *A Clockwork Orange* holds the message that patriarchy is always at risk of producing masculinity as a violent, destructive force which – in case it cannot be appropriately contained – may turn against the system and attack it by dint of its own devices.

Like Jack in *Lord of the Flies,* Alex would no doubt make an excellent soldier if only his surplus energies could be reclaimed and applied to an authorised common cause. Significantly, one of the droogs (Dim) as well as the leader of another gang (Billyboy) reappear later in the novel as policemen, displaying the same old violent behaviour, only now it is authorised and perpetrated 'in the State's name' (p. 116). Subscribing to the proverbial wisdom that 'boys will be boys, as always was' (p. 116), Burgess presents adolescent male violence as inevitable. To him, the most crucial question seems to be if and how a system manages to tame and employ the raw aggressiveness of young men. After all, the difference between an anarchic terrorist and a good soldier or dutiful policeman, between what is commonly regarded as good or evil, is frequently determined by little more than the colour and design of their respective uniforms. Alan Sinfield has pertinently differentiated between 'violence which the state considers legitimate and that which it does not', concluding that 'violence is good . . . when it is in the service of the prevailing dispositions of power; when it disrupts them it is evil' (Sinfield 1992: 167–8). Accordingly, no matter how one may finally decide to gauge Alex's actions, one must not forget that his schooling has been determined by the same patriarchal system he subsequently turns to wreck. As Geoffrey Sharpless points out, Alex's disturbing behaviour and attitude in *A Clockwork Orange* seem often in conspicuous unison with the ideals of traditional English public-school education:

> Alex's brutal conditioning, his strange language and dress, his savage sexu-ality, his wickedness, cruelty, and sadism, his devious sensitivity to the ebb and flow of group power, were in fact essential to Arnold's Rugby School, and helped catapult it into international prominence as an unsurpassed institution of man-making. (Sharpless 1994: 12)

Far from expressive of his own free spirit, Alex's thuggish droogery and almost aesthetic commitment to ultraviolence are conditioned by his society's cultivation of a particular kind of masculinity that specialises in curbing the allegedly natural volatility of boys by imposing upon it a sportsmanly code of honour and fair play. Young male violence is stylised, even choreographed, in order to facilitate its systemic control and employment. According to Sharpless, 'we cannot only find the violence in the gentleman; we can find the gentleman in the violence' (Sharpless 1994: 19).

Even before Alex is subjected to the Reclamation Treatment of Ludovico's Technique, designed to make him a good person and valuable citizen, his behaviour is conditioned by the proprieties of conduct that structured and determined masculine gender performances in imperial Britain. Public-school pedagogy, which aims at rei(g)ning angry young male violence by codifying it, is so pervasive that it has left its mark even on working-class Alex, who lives in a towerblock and is on one occasion described as a 'wretched little slummy bedbug, breaking into *real* people's houses' (p. 51). Like Jack's in *Lord of the Flies*, Alex's savagery is far from wild or out of control; on the contrary, it follows the normative script of what finds societal approval as appropriate masculine behaviour and what does not. Keen to live up to the ideals of upper-class masculinity, Alex is a puppet on invisible strings long before he delivers himself into the hands of experimenting behavioural scientists. A substantial part of the delight and satisfaction Alex derives from lashing out against others comes from his expertise at implementing gentlemanly rules and techniques of combat. As Sharpless notes, Alex 'details with pleasure his own movements, and the violence softens into a gentleman's dance, with the expert's assessment of the opponent's weaknesses, and of proper footwork' (Sharpless 1994: 19).

In opposition to humanist interpretations of Alex's behaviour as 'psychopathic and perverse', as an exceptional 'type of mental derangement' (Parrinder 1981: 52), a gender-specific reading finds that Alex in fact epitomises a norm condoned and promoted by the patriarchal education system itself. The only difference between the droogs and 'ordinary boys' is to be found in the fact that the former's violent potential has so far remained unemployed in an authorised cause. Significantly, Alex's ultraviolence never pits itself against the dystopian regime itself, but invariably against physically weaker and culturally less refined others. For example, Alex makes a point of turning up his nose at his fellow droog Dim whose low-life, substandard manners and appearance he finds distasteful and despicable. The very presence of Dim, 'looking all dirtied over and too much von of sweat on him' (p. 24), threatens to spoil Alex's aspirations to pass as a sophisticated gentleman. Alex strongly believes in the hierarchical stratification of society and never hesitates to invoke or implement patriarchal imperatives. 'There has to be a leader', he states at one point. 'Discipline there has to be. Right?' (p. 26). Alex is no rebel, no exception to the rule, and definitely no anarchist; rather, 'Alex, in insisting on irony and rebellion, is merely recreating a conformist world in microcosm' (Sharpless 1994: 24). Alex must first and foremost be regarded as a deprived working-class youth reaching out for the power of the privileged upper-class male. Categorically excluded from the power benefits of hegemonic manliness, he overcompensates for his social inferiority by casting himself in the role of a superheroic leader, all the time copying, and thus perpetuating, the legitimate, 'educational' violence of his public-school oppressors.

The droogs' first victim in *A Clockwork Orange* is a frail, old schoolmaster on his way back from the library. By beating him up to teach him – as so many others who are to follow – 'a lesson' (p. 9), Alex testifies to his difficult love/hate relationship with the totalitarian system. He quashes schoolmasterliness only in order to establish his own equally schoolmasterly authority. As in *Lord of the Flies*, the supra-individual power principle with its network of compelling symbols proves invariably more resilient than any of its flesh-and-blood representatives. Patriarchal masculinity is a force that feeds on its practitioners who find themselves at constant risk of becoming casualties in masculinity's ceaseless and essentially arbitrary struggle for self-assertive dominance over whatever it chooses to perceive as its other(s). At the same time, the civilisational, communally beneficial aspects of patriarchy – embodied by the old schoolmaster in *A Clockwork Orange* or Piggy and Ralph in *Lord of the Flies* – seem subject to negotiations of systemic expediency and appear to be ultimately dispensable whenever masculinity, at once patriarchy's most essential and volatile constituent, finds itself under threat. While distinctions between victims and perpetrators, heroes and villains, law and tyranny, anarchy and civil obedience, good and evil, and so forth, are all open to redefinition, the phallus of patriarchal rule is guaranteed to retain its supreme, infallible authority forever. The rigid patriarchal clockwork invariably outlasts the individual orange, or *orang*, which in Malay signifies 'man', as Burgess must have learned when working as an education officer in the Colonial Service in Malaya and Borneo between 1954 and 1960.

Like Golding in *Lord of the Flies*, Burgess fails to unravel and effectively criticise the oppressive dynamics determining the dystopian condition he envisions in *A Clockwork Orange*. His didactic approach is in itself characteristic of a patriarchal humanism which unselfconsciously tends to universalise any historically or culturally specific problem. Only sporadically does Burgess allude to the social conditioning of Alex's identity; most of the time, he stresses his protagonist's indeterminacy as an exceptional and wildly anarchic individualist. Only in a couple of easily overread asides is there any mention of a power equivalent to Golding's Lord of the Flies as, for example, in a priest's article on 'Modern Youth' which Alex reads with great amusement over breakfast one morning. In Alex's paraphrase the priest is presented as:

> govoreeting as a man of Bog IT WAS THE DEVIL THAT WAS ABROAD and was like ferreting his way into like young innocent flesh, and it was the adult world that could take the responsibility for this with their wars and bombs and nonsense. (p. 35)

Similarly, only a fastidious reader is likely to interpret in gender-specific terms what the prison chaplain says to Alex about the ethical implications of the government's Reclamation Treatment: 'When a *man* cannot choose he ceases to be a *man*' (p. 67; my emphasis). Within the context of the present analysis, this statement evidently constitutes a major clue to the novel's central problem of Alex's struggle for masculine self-authentication.

Burgess's total indifference to the gender-specificity of Alex's condition shows itself perhaps most revealingly in his boy hero's ethical manifesto in which Alex outlines the reasons for his passionate commitment to the pleasures of droogery:

But, brothers, this biting of their toe-nails over what is the CAUSE of badness is what turns me into a fine laughing malchick. They don't go into the cause of GOODNESS, so why the other shop? If lewdies are good that's because they like it, and I wouldn't interfere with their pleasures, and so of the other shop. And I was patronizing the other shop. More, badness is of the self, the one, the you or me on our oddy knockies, and that self is made by old Bog or God and is his great pride and radosty. But the not-self cannot have the bad, meaning they of the government and the judges and the schools cannot allow the bad because they cannot allow the self. And is not our modern history, my brothers, the story of brave malenky selves fighting these big machines? I am serious with you, brothers, over this. But what I do I do because I like to do. (p. 34)

Addressing an exclusively male audience and clearly expecting sympathy and understanding, Alex refers to his ultraviolent badness as an inalienable constituent of his individuality. To deprive him of the freedom to act upon his bad impulses would not only represent a violation of his most basic human rights; ultimately, it would effect a total extirpation of the self. According to Alex's reasoning, patriarchal totalitarianism cannot tolerate his badness because it cannot tolerate the expression or manifestation of any kind of outstanding difference. As a result, Alex's badness becomes a morally good cause worth fighting for. His droogery, ultimately practised in defence of itself, becomes justified as a heroic means of resistance against systemic oppression.

The simplistic logic informing Alex's ethical argument can easily be dismantled. What is more interesting is that Alex chooses to portray his ultraviolent badness as natural, as innate to his self, although it clearly represents something socially acquired. Like Jack in *Lord of the Flies*, who hides behind a self-annihilating mask of savagery, Alex derives his heroic self-image from meticulously moulding himself after a certain masculine ideal. His gender masquerade is motivated by a deeply paranoid insecurity about his masculinity. In fact, Alex's violence and droogish self-fashioning seem designed to distract from his 'queerness' as a working-class boy who listens to Beethoven and is fond of displaying a sophisticated manner that borders on aristocratic snobbery. His conspicuous difference and striking lack of typically boyish, working-class interests make him potentially very vulnerable to ostracism and abuse by his peers. He strategically protects himself from being 'othered' and discursively feminised – as a boy not quite boyish enough – by taking the lead role of chief bully, a position which he defends with great ferocity and cunning. Rather than 'fighting these big machines', Alex appropriates the communal dynamics that ensure their continuing operation. What he describes as his self is little more than a by-product of skilful gender mimicry, a protective shell against ubiquitous threats of emasculation. Alex is a loose, if undoubtedly fitting, cog ready to be inserted into the patriarchal clockwork, a system that forces males to conceal the intrinsic complexity of their human disposition behind the imposing artifice of a self-oppressive, mask-like masculinity.

In his reading of *A Clockwork Orange* as a traditional *Bildungsroman*, Philip Ray insists that 'Alex's tale is still a story of liberation: he has escaped from not only the literal prison of Staja 84F but also from the figurative prisons of adolescent boyhood and "clockwork" humanity' (Ray 1981: 486). Ray is referring to the novel's final, twenty-first chapter which shows Alex's ascension from adolescent droogery to responsible manhood. However, even if one chooses to agree with Ray that Burgess included the last chapter 'in order to express the view that human growth is inevitable' (Ray 1981: 480), one cannot quite suppress a genuine wonderment at the great naivety and implausibility of Burgess's depiction of Alex's sudden maturation. Instead of signalling a triumphant liberation from the wicked impulses of irrational boyhood or the ideological clutches of totalitarianist coercion, Alex's growing up in fact adds the last finishing touch to a process of consistent patriarchal conditioning, a process so powerful and pervasive that even a self-professed individualist like Alex cannot escape it.

Burgess presents Alex's eventual surrender to oppressive gender norms in terms of a natural awakening to an adult sense of civil responsibility. As a result, the dynamics of 'human nature' and those of systemic conditioning become virtually indistinguishable, hinting at the deep complicitous embedment of Burgess's own thinking in the patriarchal ideology. Alex now yearns to become a good citizen and private family man. Suddenly, he seems ready to shrink himself into the decapitalised 'pee', 'dad' or 'papapa' of his own excessively docile father. Alex himself cannot explain what is happening to him. He is confused and overwhelmed by the suddenness of his mood change, which Burgess chooses to present as an obscure kind of nervous pre-marital tension all too obviously geared towards Alex's happy withdrawal into the grown-up world of nuclear-family bliss. Hormonally triggered rather than ideologically contrived, Alex's change remains rationally inexplicable, as numerous emotionally muddled passages throughout the last chapter illustrate:

> I didn't know what it was, but these last days I had become like mean. There had come into my gulliver a like desire to keep all my pretty polly to myself, to like hoard it all up for some reason. (p. 142)

> I couldn't explain how it had got there [into his wallet], but it was a photo-graph I had scissored out of the old gazetta and it was of a baby. (p. 143)

> There was something happening inside me, and I wondered if it was like some disease or if it was what they had done to me that time upsetting my gulliver and perhaps going to make me real bezoomny. (p. 144)

> Perhaps that was it, I kept thinking. Perhaps I was getting too old for the sort of jeezny I had been leading, brothers. I was eighteen now, just gone. Eighteen was not a young age. (p. 147)

> And all it was was that I was young. But now as I end this story, brothers, I am not young, not no longer, oh no. Alex like groweth up, oh yes. (p. 148)

Alex finally behaves in a fashion that totally refutes whatever subversive potential his droogery may have held. What the oppressive system requires of its citizens to maintain and perpetuate itself becomes Alex's most urgent and intimate personal desire. It is in the last chapter that Alex enters clockwork humanity for definite. Like a young Victorian heroine yielding her already considerably limited autonomy to the social institution of marriage, Alex consents to his own narrative death by conforming with 'human nature' and becoming like everyone else of his class and sex. Disconcertingly, Alex not only renounces his droogery and ultraviolence, which could be seen as a genuinely positive develop-ment. He abandons all resistance to a dystopia whose own systemic self-assertion by means of an omnipresent police force is becoming ever more droogish and authoritarian:

> I suppose really a lot of the old ultra-violence and crasting was dying out now, the rozzes being so brutal with who they caught, though it had become like a fight between naughty nadsats and the rozzes who could be more skorry with the nozh and the britva and the stick and even the gun. But what was the matter with me these days was that I didn't care much. (p. 144)

Burgess appears to suggest that the life of lower-class males falls into two discrete phases, invariably separated at the age of about eighteen by an abrupt, biologically pre-programmed change in attitude and behaviour. Also, according to Burgess, lower-class droogery, motivated by the need to overcompensate for social inferiority, represents a perfectly natural, self-perpetuating phenomenon, as indicated by Alex's ominous reflec-tions on his future son who:

> would not understand or would not want to understand at all and would do all the veshches I had done, yes perhaps even killing some poor starry forella surrounded with mewing kots and koshkas, and I would not be able to really stop him. And nor would he be able to stop his own son, brothers.

> And so it would itty on to like the end of the world, round and round and round . . . (p. 148)

Compounded by an air of general listlessness and disillusionment, prone to deteriorate into utter political inertia, the lower-class male's 'maturation' is triggered by a sudden urge to find 'some devotchka or other who would be a mother to this son' (p. 146). In short, ineffectual, uncoordinated rebellion against the system in imitation of its own heroic ideals is superseded by a voluntary retreat into politically innocuous domestic bliss. As a closer analysis reveals, both ways of life – droogery and civil adulthood – are the result of successful patriarchal conditioning. Only for a limited period of time and under strictly outlawed circumstances is lower-class masculinity allowed to revel in the glamour of heroic action that is normally reserved exclusively for upper-class males. Its ultimate subjection to the hegemonic order, in terms of both class and gender, is established by its allegedly natural, yet in fact ideologically facilitated withdrawal from the political scene into the easily supervised realm of the private.

As an ethical treatise on 'good' and 'evil', Burgess's novel is substantially flawed due to its total disregard for the wider systemic dynamics of class, gender and power. Alex is no free, unpredictable subject fighting for the survival of his spiritual self. The individuality he displays prior to his scientific conditioning is as scripted and acquired as the role he feels compelled to adopt at the end of the novel. Both are determined by political expediency. Had Burgess genuinely intended to portray the oppression of individual freedom by state power, he ought to have created his protagonist as an outsider for whom to follow the various scripts of patriarchal masculinity would have been an impossible act. What if, for example, Alex had been homosexual, forced to undergo not Ludovico's Technique to eliminate his droogery but Aversion Therapy to cure him of his sexual deviance? As Jonathan Dollimore comments with respect to the work of Joe Orton – an Angry Young Man of a totally different order, whose first play *The Ruffian on the Stair* was performed in 1963, just one year after the publication of *A Clockwork Orange* – 'sexual transgression and deviance could radically challenge an existing, repressive social order' (Dollimore 1983: 51) and in a way, one may add, that young male anger and even ultraviolence cannot. Anger and violence are no deviations from the norm and hence pose no insurmountable threat to the order of patriarchy. On the contrary, they represent constitutive, easily manipulable elements of the masculine standard, subject to systemic expediency and the vicissitudes of political fashion.

[handwritten margin note:] not really challenging anything

6

.

A Pretty Bad Case of Virginity

.

John Osborne's Look Back in Anger

JIMMY PORTER IN JOHN Osborne's *Look Back in Anger* epitomises a crisis in self-authentication endemic to post-war British culture in its entirety. The play is an index of the imminent postmodern decentring of the traditional masculine subject, accelerated by the collapse of the Empire and the incipience of a diversity of minoritarian liberation movements. *Look Back in Anger* presents us with a young anti-hero about to realise that man's centre-stage role in society has become precarious and questionable, destabilised by a general loss of certainty, faith and commitment, corrupted by a history of unjust, exploitative rule both at home and in the colonies, compromised by political apathy and opportunism, and contested by various subordinate identities beginning to voice and pursue their hitherto unacknowledged desire. In the 1950s, the majority of men were still conditioned to fashion themselves after masculine ideals devised under the aegis of patriarchal imperialism. As a result, Jimmy Porter's rebellious personality comprises a curious, ultimately untenable conflation of oppressive conformism with radical defiance. Also, as a university-educated intellectual of working-class origin, Jimmy straddles two diametrically opposed traditions in British society, one of elitist privilege, the other of social deprivation. Whereas society would no doubt welcome him with open arms, if only to testify to its own egalitarian principles, Jimmy is determined to resist systemic containment. At the same time, he remains essentially a man of the old order who, to affirm his masculine stature, feels compelled to identify with some kind of heroic cause that would help him detach himself from the spheres of the feminine and domestic.

However, the heroic tradition, as Jimmy knows it, has come to an end.

The great patriarchs have either reluctantly retired from their military careers in imperial service (like Colonel Redfern, Alison's father) or died an unmemorable death in the anticlimactic aftermath of the Spanish Civil War (like old Mr Porter, Jimmy's father). To pretend masculinity could still be won by means of adventure and the exploration of foreign lands is an anachronistic delusion, as Jimmy realises when his friend Hugh 'made up his mind he must go abroad – to China, or some God-forsaken place' (p. 43). With Hugh, Jimmy had briefly indulged in some mild, low-key droogery, mainly gate-crashing posh parties, using upper-class Alison 'as a sort of hostage from those sections of society they had declared war on' (p. 41). Unsurprisingly, their spontaneous act-up invasions of what purportedly are the strongholds of societal power result in little more than embarrassing moments of theatrical farce or slapstick comedy of no political import whatsoever. No matter what subversive strategies Jimmy decides on, they fail to empower him. Ritually predictable, his rebellious behaviour immediately petrifies into the artifice of a histrionic pose. Far from shocking or unheard-of, the counterdiscourse of the Angry Young Man is a fully integrated and securely framed product of the established order against which it exerts itself. Jimmy's dilemma remains unresolved because he cannot possibly conceive of reconstructing himself *ex nihilo*, that is, without recourse to the man-making ideals endorsed and promoted by the society in which he lives. He cannot envisage, let alone practise, a non-patriarchal, anti-imperialist mode of manly being that would genuinely challenge the system while, unprecedentedly, setting him free.

Since 'there aren't any good, brave causes left' (p. 83), all the grand conflictual tensions between Jimmy and the world at large release themselves in hurtful, often excruciatingly petty rhetorical tirades against Alison, his wife. Lynne Segal's comment on the extreme misogyny expressed in Angry Young Male writing in general aptly captures the atmosphere of *Look Back in Anger*. 'While male protagonists see themselves as opposing all authority', she writes, 'in reality the battle is with wives and mothers alone' (Segal 1990: 13). Indeed, Jimmy's hatred of the Establishment is most pronounced in his disparagement of Alison's mother: 'That old bitch should be dead!' (p. 51). For Colonel Redfern on the other hand, a representative of the old order if ever there was one, Jimmy harbours a kind of nostalgic sympathy rooted in secret admiration and respect. As Alison says to her father: 'Oh, [Jimmy] doesn't seem to mind you so much. In fact, I think he rather likes you' (p. 65). Osborne himself was never hesitant to declare which of his characters he thought responsible for Jimmy's predicament. In his 1993 introduction to the

Osborne

play, he blames Alison for cruelly refusing to understand her husband, quite as if the wife were herself totally unaffected by historical circumstance and – more importantly – in supreme control not only of Jimmy's fate but the whole of British world politics. It is Osborne's unselfconscious use of Conradian adjectives that gives him away as an inveterate misogynist while at the same time poignantly disclosing the play's suppressed concern with masculine hysteria and paranoia on being denied absolute authority. As a closer look at Osborne's authorial note brings to light, the basic motivation of Jimmy's recurrent rhetorical onslaughts on Alison seems little different from the imperial desire to break the intransigence of the Black African woman's alterity in Conrad's *Heart of Darkness*:

> I tried to explain that it was [Alison], not her husband, who was the most deadly bully. Her silence and her obdurate withdrawal were *impregnable*. The ironing board was not the plaything of her submission, but the bludgeon and shield which were *impenetrable* to all Jimmy's appeals to desperate oratory.
>
> (Osborne 1993: xii; my emphasis)

Look Back in Anger is only secondarily concerned with the etiolation of youthful zest within the claustrophobic confines of female-governed domesticity. The primary issue at stake is the hegemony of imperial English masculinity. Deploring a political climate in which 'nobody thinks, nobody cares', Jimmy expresses his desire for 'something strong, something simple, something English', adding that he 'can understand how [Alison's] Daddy must have felt when he came back from India, after all those years away' (p. 13). The grand imperial design is 'unsettled' (p. 42) and, irrespective of their class or generation, Englishmen are united in their nostalgic mourning of 'the England [Colonel Redfern] left in 1914' (p. 66). As Jimmy confesses, 'if you've got no world of your own, it's rather pleasant to regret the passing of someone else's' (p. 13). Jimmy's rhetoric is transfused with references to the Empire, alluding to Alison's domestic chores as 'the White Woman's Burden' (p. 7) while calling Cliff, the Porters' lodger and friend – notably a Welshman – 'a savage' in constant need of Jimmy's magnanimous supervision: 'What do you think you're going to do when I'm not around to look after you? Well, what are you going to do? Tell me?' (p. 12). Clearly not satisfied with sprawling in the central limelight, Jimmy expands his presence until he is in a position to occupy the whole stage at all times, imposing his psychological territorialism upon Alison and Cliff by means of endless oration, obnoxious pipe smoke and, while offstage, bouts of noisy trumpeting. Jimmy's hegemonic sense of self depends for its affirmation entirely on the responses he is able to elicit from others. Should his audience suddenly disperse instead of clustering attentively around him, and for once begin to concentrate on an exploration of their own interiority rather than eternally answering to the urgency of his allegedly superior needs, Jimmy's leadership would crumble and his claim to heroic status evaporate. As Osborne's stage directions indicate, Jimmy's frantic last-minute attempts at consolidating his position cannot pre-empt his imminent dematerialisation: 'He has lost [Alison and Cliff], and he knows it, but he won't leave it' (p. 10).

It is tempting to read the Angry Young Man's struggle for an ana-chronistic kind of masculine dominance, already lost to devolutionary processes of ever greater societal diversification, as symptomatic of the definitive break-up of the British Empire in the 1950s. Both patriarchal masculinity and European imperialism rely for their superiority on the unconditional subservience of a clearly defined margin of others. As colonies all over the globe took the end of World War II as a chance to opt for national independence, in *Look Back in Anger* we witness the first stirrings of organised self-assertion amongst women, gay men and – in Cliff's case – the minoritarian Anglo-Celtic subnations of Great Britain. Cliff eventually decides to move out and get married. Alison leaves her husband, if only temporarily. Her friend Helena is introduced as a woman with a 'sense of matriarchal authority [that] makes most men who meet her anxious, not only to please but to impress' (p. 36). Also, earlier in the play we hear Jimmy express jealous admiration for Alison's gay friend Webster and his 'Michelangelo Brigade' (p. 33) for having, unlike him, a cause worth fighting for. Naturally, all these subversive destabilisations of the old order must provoke some kind of backlash from Jimmy who, despite his self-professed role as a working-class rebel, appears to identify first and foremost as a heterosexual English male and hence as a standard representative of the patriarchal norm.

As David Cairns and Shaun Richards argue, Osborne's hero has internalised the discourse of imperialism with the result of 'producing a complex and paradoxical personal politics which denies the Establish-ment, and implicitly the Empire, at the very moment when the supposed retreat from that world reproduces it in all its most repressive features' (Cairns and Richards 1988: 202). Like Marlow in *Heart of Darkness*, Jimmy projects his own feelings of inadequacy onto the opposite sex, pompously accusing Alison of pusillanimity: 'That's my wife! That's *her* isn't it? Behold the Lady Pusillanimous' (p. 18). Even more significantly, in Jimmy's view Alison comes to constitute, 'as woman, one of the terrains on to which the discourse of metropolitan superiority vis-à-vis the colonial [is] transposed in decolonising and "post-colonial" Britain' (Cairns and Richards 1988: 194). Postcolonial woman is regarded as a monster whose predatory sexuality and maternal omnipotence threaten the male not only with infantilisation and disempowerment but total annihilative containment. '[Alison] has the passion of a python. She just devours me whole every time, as if I were some over-large rabbit', Jimmy informs Cliff. 'That's me. That bulge around her navel – if you're wondering what it is – it's me. Me, buried alive down there, and going mad, smothered in that peaceful looking coil' (pp. 34–5). In a passage that emotively merges the rhetorics of misogyny and racism, Jimmy identifies woman as the Ultimate Savage whose subjection to man's civilising mission becomes a compelling imperative:

> Have you ever noticed how noisy women are? . . . Have you? The way they kick the floor about, simply walking over it. Or have you watched them sitting at their dressing tables, dropping their weapons and banging down their bits of boxes and brushes and lipsticks? . . . I've watched [Alison] doing it night after night. When you see a woman in front of a bedroom mirror, you realize what a refined sort of a butcher she is. . . . Did you ever see some dirty old Arab, sticking his fingers into some mess of lamb fat and gristle? Well, she's just like that. Thank God they don't have many women surgeons! Those primitive hands would have your guts out in no time. Flip! Out it comes, like the powder out of its box. Flop! Back it goes, like the powder puff on the table. (pp. 20–1)

Despite its domestic setting, the trajectory of *Look Back in Anger* is informed by the classic imperial hero's twofold desire to make an honourable contribution to civilisational progress and to prove himself as a man by colonising the *terra incognita* of an imagined monstrous alterity. Perversely, Jimmy perceives his emotional dependence on Alison as a threat that acutely compromises his masculine autonomy. To break her 'other' self becomes his one and only obsessive desire: 'I want to see your face rubbed in the mud – that's all I can hope for. There's nothing else I want any longer' (p. 58). The play culminates in Alison's uncondi-tional surrender to her husband's superiority which ironically involves woman's initiation to man's corruption and utter futility. Neither Jimmy nor Alison can liberate themselves from the coercive ideological struc-tures of hegemonic gender formations; both must eventually succumb to the oppressive spirit of their age that is rigidly prohibitive of subversive self-fulfilment. Jimmy's question if he was 'really wrong to believe that there's a – a kind of – burning virility of mind and spirit that looks for something as powerful as itself' (p. 93) must be answered in the affirma-tive. Since it thrives on a subjugation of all its others, patriarchal virility will never tolerate an equal. In fact, virility is an attribute reserved exclusively for the system itself, representing a supra-individual quality that men (and women) can only ever align themselves with by proxy and on a precariously revocable basis. As Cairns and Richards suggest, in the 1950s deliberate impotence seemed the last dignified resort for all those who valued personal integrity more highly than social integration, but then, even the choice of becoming 'a lost cause' (p. 93) – as Osborne puts it – may be significantly marred by the delusion of individual autonomy and (anti)heroic assumptions of masculine superiority:

> The position of the alienated intellectual at the end of Empire was that in retreating from a world supposedly lacking in 'good brave causes' they – or their stage representative Jimmy Porter – reproduced the discourse of that to which they were nominally opposed, and in the powerful dramatic evocation of impotence made impotence not so much a condition to be rejected, as a sign of intellectual integrity in the face of a world which now, supposedly, lacked the ability to provide them with a cause.
>
> (Cairns and Richards 1988: 204)

Importantly, the Angry Young Man first entered the British national consciousness as the lead part in a stage production; only afterwards was his obtrusive prominence also detected in the less immediately affective terrain of contemporary post-war narrative. Like all theatre, *Look Back in Anger* signals that human life is based on imitation, the enactment of roles authorised, and possibly censored, by the societal order within which they display and arrange themselves. Although these given identities are open to varying degrees of individual improvisation, a refusal to accept any part at all is bound to result in invisibility and radical disenfranchisement. In a transitional age of general social mobility and potential ideological change, like that portrayed in Osborne's play, the desire of individuals for a new order of self-authentication and fulfilment clashes violently with their obligation to fashion themselves in compliance with what Judith Butler designates as the old order's 'regulatory fiction' (Butler 1990: 141). Hence, the always inevitable tensions between who one wants to be and who one ought to be assume tragic proportions. Jimmy's specific predicament is additionally compounded by the fact that he seems unable to re-imagine himself constructively, resolutely rejecting an order whose imperatives he has already perfectly internalised and thus perpetuates inadvertently. Finding the identity packages that are available to him either outdated, too prohibitive or politically irrelevant, he ends up with the unbecoming basic blueprint of a patriarchally conditioned manliness. Jimmy demands substance and authenticity without realising that these must be created out of the essential malleability of each generation's imitative repetition of its predecessor's role-playing traditions.

In *Look Back in Anger*, being and acting continually coalesce and interpermeate. For instance, Alison experiences Jimmy's emotional outbursts as 'carefully *rehearsed* attacks' (p. 19; my emphasis). Real lives present themselves as ritual routines of little distinctive authenticity. In the third act Helena, an actress, adopts Alison's part as 'wife of Jimmy' quite as if the role struck her as a peculiar professional challenge. As Robert Egan suggests, Jimmy's eventual dissatisfaction with Helena's mock-conjugal performance may be 'equivalent to his dissatisfaction with histrionic performance as an end in itself' (Egan 1989: 422). However, rather than revealing the fundamental inauthenticity of her own impersonation of 'the real thing', Helena's performance questions the ideological assumptions that underlie the nature of Alison's real-life existence. All social life is scripted, and no script is ever natural or authentic, although some scripts may be compulsory. Helena cannot resist standing in for Alison. Significantly, however, she is free to reject the part once the suffering becomes too much to bear. As her self-conscious role-play intimates, a certain kind of real-life pain is produced by an individual's social position rather than her psychological disposition. The conflict and suffering of *Look Back in Anger* are pre-programmed by Osborne's script which, despite momentous changes in the make-up of post-war society, chooses to cast men and women in the traditional poses of mutually injurious masculinity and femininity. Rather than expressive of natural female and male behaviour, Jimmy and Alison's volatile relationship reflects back on Osborne's unimaginatively conservative conception of gender. As Butler argues, 'the strategic aim of maintaining gender within its binary frame . . . cannot be attributed to a subject, but, rather, must be understood to found and consolidate the subject' (Butler 1990: 140). Jimmy and Alison are products rather than perpetrators of binarist oppositioning, which is why Jimmy fails to rethink his masculinity and Alison must return to her position of domestic inferiority. In fact, if somehow they managed to accomplish the impossible and act against their predictably gendered parts, Jimmy and Alison would transgress the virtual reality of Osborne's conservative script and thereby cease to exist altogether.

Despite its solid embedment in the specific historical climate of the 1950s, *Look Back in Anger* has remained a popular play that offers the theatrical imagination plenty of leeway for innovative re-interpretation. This seems mainly due to its heroic thrust being markedly impaired by a recurrence of interrogative, counterdiscursive voices. These voices are so obtrusive that it seems hardly conceivable Osborne did not intend to allow for an immediate deconstruction of the traditional masculine ideals he appears to be re-asserting. In many respects, *Look Back in Anger* resembles a kind of post-war rewrite of Shakespeare's most renowned tragedy, with Jimmy Porter representing 'a modern Hamlet' torn between irreconcilable old and new imperatives (see Banerjee 1993). Introducing numerous elements of cultural intransigence, destabilisation and resistance that are bound to proliferate in the audience's imagination, both plays subvert what at first appears as a definitive restoration of the old order. Most significantly, in Osborne's play, the fierce intensity of Alison's eventual subjection to her husband's rule finds relief in the couple's withdrawal into the private fantasy of 'Bears & Squirrels' – 'all love, and no brains' (p. 45) – with which the play concludes. The symbolic order of relentless hierarchical oppositioning, that motivates Alison and Jimmy's mutual infliction of suffering, is replaced by the unifying harmony of ludic togetherness beyond the reach of divisive class and gender formations. While seemingly signifying little more than pure escapism, 'Bears & Squirrels' gives voice to the exceedingly unbearable pressure exerted on Jimmy and Alison by the normative script of ordinary heterosexual role-play. As Alison explains to Helena:

> It was the only way of escaping from everything – a sort of unholy priest-hole of being animals to one another. We could become little furry creatures with little brains. Full of dumb, uncomplicated affection for each other. Playful, careless creatures in their own cosy zoo for two. A silly symphony for people who couldn't bear the pain of being human beings any longer. (p. 45)

Jimmy has internalised the remote-controlled existence of an actor desperate to impress as a consistent character. Confined to an author(is)ed theatrical script, he remains incapable of taking any meaningful action in the domain of real-life politics. With reference to an emended paraphrase of Robert Egan's interpretation of Jean-Paul Sartre's comments on the theatre, Jimmy could be described as someone 'who unrealizes his own being in the service of [a regulatory] fiction, allowing the substance of his self to be "devoured by the imaginary [ideal of traditional masculine power and integrity]"' (Egan 1989: 423; my additions). And yet, at least in seminal form, *Look Back in Anger* contains manifold suggestions as to which suppressed aspects of himself Jimmy would need to develop in order to re-invent himself as a New Man.

Throughout the play, one wonders if Jimmy could perhaps learn to embrace the demise of his hegemony and begin to appreciate the advantages of his own intrinsic self-and-otherness. After all, the disintegration of the traditional masculine subject does not signal the end of identity; rather, it bears the promise of a liberating re-assemblage of identity in continuous processes of communal re-identification. As indicated by Osborne's introduction of his central character as 'a disconcerting mixture of sincerity and cheerful malice, of tenderness and freebooting cruelty' (p. 5), Jimmy spends most of his time in adamant denial of his own psychological complexity. Also, it seems rather defeatist to suggest – as Helena does – that anybody is ever fatefully 'born out of his time' and thus given no chance to decide on 'where he is, or where he's going'. Helena's analysis of Jimmy as someone who will 'never do anything, and . . . never amount to anything' (p. 88) essentially serves to consolidate the myth of man as a pre-packaged victim of fate debarred from constructively (co-)authoring his life. Although the hitherto uncontested ideal of patriarchal masculinity is about to come under attack, this is ultimately no reason why the individual man ought to suffer. Jimmy could choose to leave the broken armour behind, breathe a sigh of relief and start to heal. He could reconstitute himself in solidarity with other newly released identities that are beginning to emerge from among the ranks of his own formerly captivated margin of others.

Commenting on general trends in post-war American men's writing with particular reference to the 'School of Virility' of Ernest Hemingway and Norman Mailer, Peter Schwenger identifies the rise of a new male self-consciousness that, rather than instigating a thorough critical overhaul of the old masculine tradition, perpetuates the glorification of an anachronistic show of traditional manliness. The old imperatives still appear to prevail. However, all they produce now is a well-rehearsed swagger marred by its own exaggerated perfection. Action, which used to come 'naturally' to a man, has become an apprehensive act of histrionic bravado:

> Action, which is so central to the traditional idea of manhood, becomes 'sicklied o'er with the pale cast of thought'; the he-man becomes Hamlet. He is perfectly capable of acting, it's true, but without the same spontaneity and confidence in his natural virility. As the moments of 'natural' virility elude a man over and over again, he begins to shore up his sense of manhood with theory, with language, with artifice. He begins, perhaps, to 'protest too much'. His manly actions have become a style. (Schwenger 1984: 155)

Clearly, Schwenger's analysis of the New American Macho is equally applicable to post-war Britain's Angry Young Man. Continuing to look back in anger and regret, English men of all generations, if for varying reasons, appear unable to accommodate and adjust to historical change. As Alison says to her father, 'you're hurt because everything is changed. Jimmy is hurt because everything is the same. And neither of you can face it. Something's gone wrong somewhere, hasn't it?' (p. 66).

Jimmy and Colonel Redfern are hurt by history, stunned by change, which has left them stranded on the margins of a new beginning. The future has started to thrive on something they fail to deliver. The heroic principle has become impractical, a cumbersome impediment rather than a potent tool of action. Patriarchal man, modelled after the phallic ideal of traditional manliness, is too one-sided and monologic to successfully contain the new pluralism of post-war society. Significantly, Osborne introduces the Colonel by pointing out that 'forty years of being a soldier sometimes conceals the essentially gentle, kindly man underneath' (p. 61). Once again we realise that masculinity asserts itself at the expense of a man's inherent emotional and psychological complexity. However, a simple retrieval of hitherto suppressed emotions bears its own hazards, as Cliff's enactment of a gentler, less imposing and detached mode of masculinity demonstrates. His role as 'a soothing, natural counterpoint to Jimmy' (p. 6) keeps him consistently in the background in a subordinate position of virtual invisibility. Instead of crystallising into a viable New Man alternative to Jimmy's impersonation of a phallic anachronism, Cliff's promising potential quickly exhausts itself in the ever-widening rift between the extreme polarities of traditional masculinity and femininity. He pertinently identifies himself as 'a no-man's land' (p. 58) between Jimmy and Alison and, as the marital conflict escalates, Osborne clearly loses all interest in him.

As Arthur Flannigan-Saint-Aubin's innovative exploration of the literary metaphors of masculinity suggests, Cliff's gradual disappearance from the scene of *Look Back in Anger* may in itself already signal a reassertion of the phallic principle. Flannigan-Saint-Aubin argues that 'masculinity as it expresses itself within patriarchy derives from a very selective and partial conception and experience of the male body [that] makes masculinity monolithic, seemingly without contradiction' (Flannigan-Saint-Aubin 1994: 241). Delineating 'another bio-logic' that would displace the penis/phallus and (re)inscribe the testicles, he proposes a radical reconception of the traditional male body image and its symbolism. While it is, perhaps, only natural for men to identify with the phallic, they are patriarchally conditioned to do so exclusively, at the expense of the testicular mode, which a man experiences when he is 'nurturing, incubating, containing, and protecting' (Flannigan-Saint-Aubin 1994: 250). To reach perfect bodily and mental completeness a man must remove 'the steel fig leaf' (Flannigan-Saint-Aubin 1994: 254) and discover himself as constituted by both the phallic and the testicular. Interestingly, the two different modes of manly being 'have been historically depicted as complementary in varying degrees in male "couples" in fiction and myth' (Flannigan-Saint-Aubin 1994: 252). Comprising a wide range of examples from Achilles and Patroclus to Superman and Clark Kent, Flannigan-Saint-Aubin's list could easily be continued by adding Victor Frankenstein and Henry Clerval, Golding's Ralph and Jack, as well as Osborne's Jimmy and Cliff.

Ideally, a man ought to reconcile the phallic and testicular modes within his own being. However, since in patriarchy the testicular is often ironically perceived as a set of emasculating qualities, the hero is mimetically disassociated from his *testi*fying companion, who authenticates his friend's masculine stature at the same time as he infiltrates it with a permanent risk of compromise and potential subversion. Accordingly, Cliff's subordinate, generally rather low-key presence in *Look Back in Anger*, as well as his eventual retreat into a life of his own, signal an acute imbalance in Jimmy's masculinity towards the excessively phallic. After recounting his father's death from war wounds, Jimmy tells his audience that he 'learnt at an early age what it was to be angry – angry and helpless' (p. 56). Of these two emotional responses anger features quite obviously more prominently in Jimmy's life than helplessness. In fact, his deliberate cultivation of anger serves to eclipse and distract from the helplessness underneath. While he finds an outlet for his anger in a pursuit of aggressive self-assertion, Jimmy fails to alleviate his helplessness by developing his testicular faculties of love and endurance. Describing 'anyone's who's never watched somebody die [as] suffering from a pretty bad case of virginity' (p. 55), he not only implicitly presents his loss as some kind of heroic achievement but also, more importantly, ignores that most of the emotional *terra incognita* of his own self has so far remained uncharted virgin territory. Of man's human complexity the traditionally masculine aspects have calcified into mere pretence and artifice, while its traditionally feminine aspects find their only expression in little more than 'a muffled cry' (p. 72).

The Angry Young Man's aggressive despair seems symptomatic of a fundamental panic befalling the traditional masculine subject on confrontation with its postmodern destabilisation. In his discussion of James Cameron's film *Terminator 2: Judgment Day* Thomas Byers designates this panic as *PoMophobia*, a syndromic condition that encompasses the whole 'set of deep and persistent fears on the part of a formerly dominant order that has begun to recognize that it is becoming residual' (Byers 1995: 6).

Jimmy Porter's temper tantrums foreshadow, or are in fact analogous to, the death throes of patriarchal imperialism. Since the 1950s, traditional masculinity – like Western subjectivity in general – has been in an existential crisis, provoked not so much by society's mere transition from an old to a new order as postmodernity's momentous threat 'to transform or even overthrow the whole *concept* of identity' (Byers 1995: 7). As Western civilisation faces the challenge to reconstruct itself virtually from scratch, man is undergoing a process of serious decentralisation. Significantly, the ending of *Look Back in Anger* presents us with both a restorative reassertion of the old symbolic inexorabilities and a visionary possibility of regressive escape into our child-like, perhaps even instinctual beginnings. No matter what Osborne himself may originally have intended, what his play conveys to a postmodern, gender-conscious audience or readership is 'the need to move away from the investment of belief in a coherent masculine identity that was always already imaginary (always pumped by ideological steroids)' (Byers 1995: 27). Naturally, rather than simply subscribing to the semiotic abandonment of playing at 'Bears & Squirrels', future generations of men and women will need to devise a more practical and effective alternative to patriarchy's symbolic order.

7

·

The Successful Zombie

·

John Braine's Room at the Top

WORKING-CLASS JOE LAMPTON is no droog (like Alex) or thwarted rebel-intellectual (like Jimmy Porter). Having worked hard to qualify as an accountant, Joe is a social climber intent on furthering his career by moving from 'Dead Dufton' (p. 16) to the only slightly less provincial town of Warley. Once there, he begins an affair with the unhappily married thirty-something Alice Aisgill before finally marrying Susan Brown, the teenage daughter of Warley's wealthiest entrepreneur and businessman.

Although Joe appears to share Alex's sartorial obsessions with clothes and – perhaps to a lesser degree – uniforms, the crucial difference is that Joe does not dress to shock but to blend in and succeed. As in *A Clockwork Orange*, a man's outward appearance signals class and status, and is strictly regulated by a tacit common consensus on what is appropriate and what is not. For instance, Joe never grows a moustache like Jack Wales, Susan's suitor, for 'it was an officer's adornment . . . if you wear one and haven't been commissioned people look upon you as if you were wearing a uniform or decorations you weren't entitled to' (p. 40). Joe is a coldly calculating opportunist who, mesmerised by the allure of upper-class luxuries and privileges, cultivates his anger against the Establishment to enter its clockwork and thus get 'to the Top, into a world that even from my first glimpses filled me with excitement' (p. 9). Carefully abiding by the normative rules of a system he purports to resent, his aim is not subversive infiltration but profitable manipulation. His project is to beat post-war society by means of its own devices.

Unlike other Angry Young Men, most notably perhaps Arthur Seaton in Alan Sillitoe's *Saturday Night and Sunday Morning*, Joe knows 'which side

[his] bread is buttered on' (p. 213), strategically embracing 'law and order against which [Arthur] had been fighting all his life in such a thoughtless and unorganized way that he could nothing but lose' (Sillitoe 1994: 180). Significantly, one of the first things Joe does on arriving at his new destination is join the local theatre group and become a 'Warley Thespian'. Eager to learn the script and play a part, he seems impervious to the various problems of self-authentication, dignity and personal autonomy that trouble his more rebellious contemporaries. Joe escapes the dilemma that must inevitably ensue from trying to be 'me and nobody else; and whatever people think I am or say I am, that's what I'm not, because they don't know a bloody thing about me' (Sillitoe 1994: 138). Instead, he fancies himself in the role of a reckless Hollywood newcomer, readily appropriating his sense of self in the assumption of a silver-screen persona: 'I was the devil of a fellow, I was the lover of a married woman, I was taking out the daughter of one of the richest men in Warley, there wasn't a damn thing I couldn't do' (p. 84).

Despite its initial appearance as a book that sings the praises of a young man's social ascent in direct consequence of his exemplary conformity, Braine's novel is perhaps the most intriguing and genuinely revolutionary work of the entire school of Angry Young Male writing. *Room at the Top* is a fictional autobiography told in retrospect by Joe Lampton himself, ten years after the events depicted, thus introducing the perspective of a self-conscious inward gaze hitherto unprecedented in men's writing. Young Joe's ostentatious heroism is badly marred by his older self's recurrent articulations of guilt and regret. Repeatedly, the older Joe gives voice to his acute disenchantment with his present position of power and authority which he consistently describes as a dead-end trap that puts him under enormous pressure to keep up the appearances appropriate to his elevated social status. His authorial comments are informed by the bitter realisation that he has metamorphosed into 'the Successful Zombie' (p. 123), the kind of functionary and official for whom he and his friend Charles had nothing but disapproval and scorn when they were young. As the older Joe admits, he has become not a ruler wielding absolute power from the top of the Establishment's hierarchical pyramid but an instrument, conditioned and straitjacketed (quite literally) by the prescriptive fashions of patriarchal masculinity:

> I've no desire to be ill-dressed; but I hate the knowledge that I daren't be ill-dressed if I want to. I bought the cheap rayon garment to please myself; I bought the expensive silk garment because always to wear clothes of that quality is an unwritten term of my contract. (p. 13)

For the sake of his career and general advancement in society Joe relinquishes his one chance at true love and happiness. He foregoes his only opportunity to experience, with Alice, a real-life version of the kind of ecstatic mutual self-fulfilment that Jimmy and Alison in *Look Back in Anger* try to establish for themselves in their escapist fantasy of playing at 'Bears & Squirrels'. Discarded by Joe as a compromising encumbrance and emotional burden, Alice, the independent woman who would not 'be possessed . . . dominated [or] owned by anyone' (p. 120) and with whom Joe could talk 'like a man' (p. 55), is killed in a horrific suicidal car accident. Despite his love for Alice, Joe resembles Jimmy Porter in that he cannot free himself of the insidious influence of patriarchy's misogynous archetype of woman as the witch-like enemy of man, intent on draining him of his virility to possess herself of his power. Symptomatically, in a perfectly innocuous encounter with Elspeth, Alice's best friend, Joe is overcome by a nightmarish 'sensation of black water closing over my head', followed by a totally irrational upsurge of fear of suddenly finding himself 'turned into an old man and see[ing] her laughing at me, a girl again, rosy and plump with my stolen youth' (p. 105). Like Jimmy, Joe excels at misogynous rhetoric, denigrating and disempowering women as 'stupid and unaccountable, ruled by the moon one and all, poor bitches'. And yet, apart from 'witch' and 'bitch', woman also features as a mother figure with 'a physical goodness about [her] as sacred as milk'. As Joe feels obliged to add, 'there's no such thing as a bad woman, because their soft complexities are what give us life' (p. 165).

Between these extreme, ultimately irreconcilable images of woman as both superior and inferior, deadly and nurturant, the crisis of the traditional masculine subject reveals itself, lashing out against whom he needs and desires most, reasserting himself at the very moment his assumption of an appearance of natural stability is discovered to be nothing but precarious, brittle artifice. Reminiscent of Marlow's mendacity in *Heart of Darkness*, neither Joe nor Jimmy ever tells his woman the truth. Like Kurtz, they maintain their sense of heroic autonomy by concealing their essential fragility 'in the magnificent folds of eloquence' (Conrad 1996: 85). This general masculine quandary has been succinctly analysed by Butler:

> The masculine subject only *appears* to originate meanings and thereby to signify. His seemingly self-grounded autonomy attempts to conceal the repression which is both its ground and the perpetual possibility of its own ungrounding. But that process of meaning-constitution requires that women reflect that masculine power and everywhere reassure that power of the

reality of its illusory autonomy. This task is confounded ... when the demand that women reflect the autonomous power of masculine subject/ signifier becomes essential to the construction of that autonomy and, thus, becomes the basis of a radical dependency that effectively undercuts the function it serves. But further, this dependency, although denied, is also *pursued* by the masculine subject, for the woman as reassuring sign *is* the displaced maternal body, the vain but persistent promise of the recovery of pre-individuated *jouissance*. The conflict of masculinity appears ... to be precisely the demand for a full recognition of autonomy that will also and nevertheless promise a return to those full pleasures prior to repression and individuation. (Butler 1990: 45)

Only once, on a short holiday with Alice away from Warley, does Joe leave his pre-scripted self behind and experience the sensuous reality of love as a reservoir of unlimited potentialities beyond the restrictive symbolic role-play of patriarchal heterosexuality. For a brief period of time, Alice and Joe escape the ideological deep freeze of post-war Britain that renders men and women abstracted variables in a regulatory design of oppositional polarity, 'friendly strangers with the appearance and functions of women [and men]' (p. 183; my addition) rather than com-plex sexual beings capable of genuine intimacy based on the articulation of their own distinctly individual desires. With Alice, Joe experiences himself as singular and authentic, as an individual in perfect bodily, mental and intellectual communion with another individual who stands for much more than mere complementary alterity. At an epiphanic moment redolent of D.H. Lawrence's conceptualisation of marital togetherness in *Women in Love*, Joe recognises that with Alice, he 'could enter into marriage, not just acquire a license for sexual intercourse' (p. 173). What the two of them experience as a couple is a unique ecstatic realisation of love unmoulded by society's ultimately divisive formulae of gender-specific role-play:

> I had discovered what love was like, I had discovered not, as before, its likeness to other people's but what made it different from other people's. When I looked at [Alice] I knew that here was all the love I'd ever get; I'd drawn my ration. It would have been better if she'd been ten years younger and had money of her own, just as life would be more agreeable if the rivers ran beer and the trees grew ham sandwiches. I was past being sensible.
>
> (p. 183)

However, on returning from their holiday together, Joe quickly realises that his love for Alice is incompatible with society's standards of propri-ety. Within patriarchy, marriage is primarily a contractual agreement securing the future administration of property by confining a man and a woman to certain, traditionally defined roles. It is not originally designed as an emotionally satisfying experience facilitating the mutual self-authentication and fulfilment of two autonomous selves. When Joe informs Alice that 'it's impossible for us to love each other in Warley, and I can't love anyone anywhere else', she responds that 'places don't matter' (p. 214). It is Joe's timid or, rather, systematically intimidated frame of mind, warped by a prioritisation of patriarchal values, that stands in their way. Ultimately, Joe's dismissal of Alice is equivalent to what R.D. Laing describes in *The Divided Self* as 'the abdication of ecstasy, the betrayal of our true potentialities, [the sad fact] that many of us are only too successful in acquiring a false self to adopt the false realities (Laing 1965: 12; quoted in Dollimore 1983: 79). The system exerts normalising, conformative pressure on both Joe and Alice. Yet, whereas it moulds the ambitious young male into shape by draining him of his intrinsic self-and-otherness, it ostracises the abandoned female and crushes her to death. Only in retrospect does Joe see through society's apparent harmony to the inexorable clockwork underneath, describing the outlines of 'a huge machine that . . . had been designed and man-ufactured for one purpose, to kill Alice' (p. 220).

Warley is a perfectly self-contained, securely framed patriarchal world in which women are deprived of all independent human agency. Their commodification as mere vehicles in men's business transactions, per-sonal feuds and general social warfare is total. Woman is man's purely decorative asset. Charles and Joe work out 'a grading scheme for women, having noticed that the more money a man had the better looking was his wife' (p. 36). Within the context of the Angry Young Man's ambitions, women feature about as prominently as cars. Alan Sillitoe's hero dreams of making a lot of money and 'settl[ing] down somewhere with fifteen women and fifteen cars' (Sillitoe 1994: 36) while Joe sets out to claim 'an Aston-Martin , . . a three-guinea linen shirt [and] a girl with a Riviera suntan' (p. 29). As the heiress to a considerable fortune, nineteen-year-old Susan Brown – 'not trained for anything. They always said there was no need' (p. 157) – becomes in Joe's eyes an irresistible icon of her father's success as well as 'a justification of the capitalist system . . . a human being perfect of its kind, a phoenix amongst barnyard fowls' (p. 128). Her individuality – or humanity, for that matter – does not signify. Susan has been produced to be consumed, an expensive stimu-lant appealing to all that is left of the new Warley man's sensuality:

I was undecided as to which to taste first; the plain dark chocolate of going out with a pretty girl, the Turkish Delight of vanity, the sweet smooth milk of

93

love, the flavour of power, of being one up on Jack Wales, perhaps the most attractive of all, strong as rum. (p. 70)

Reduced to the status of a fine delicacy, with no active identity of her own, Susan cannot but collude in her own oppression. To her, Joe seems a saviour, even – or especially – when he rapes her. He is a Christ-like figure about to initiate her to life(-in-death), a process which, as for Alison in *Look Back in Anger*, necessitates her total surrender and obliterates whatever residues there are left of her own original self:

> 'I love you, Joe. I love you so much that I'd let you walk over me if you wanted, I'd let you tear me to bits and I wouldn't mind . . . I want you to hurt me here. Oh God, you're so beautiful. You've lovely eyes, like Christ's –'. (p. 157)

It seems as if, not unlike Frankenstein's female monster, post-war woman still poses a threat to man's autonomy. To escape her otherwise inevitable annihilation, she has little choice but to welcome her ideological dismemberment and subsequent reconstitution in man's superior image.

Independent Alice, of course, disrupts the carefully woven web of man's authority and control. Hers is a presence apt to unravel the hoary certainties of Warley's patriarchal agenda that brainwashes women like Mrs Thompson, Joe's landlady, into thinking that 'men's friendships are much deeper than women's . . . not so possessive, they never stand in each other's way' (p. 18). For example, by asking uncomfortable questions about the war, Alice interrogates the very foundations of post-war British masculinity which appears so safely anchored in a seamless network of ubiquitous male bonding: 'All these men, so well-mannered and mild and agreeable – but what's behind it all? Violence and death. They've seen things which you think would drive anyone mad. And yet there's no trace' (p. 103). She is the only one not to have forgotten about men's recent employment in a worldwide scheme of unspeakable horror and seems genuinely perplexed at the peace, silence and communal perfection that surround her. Alice is wary of the men's calm resumption of civility, their apparently unscathed recovery from the savage brutality of total war. It seems as if she suspects post-war man's gentleness to harbour an uncanny *doppelgänger* with blood on his hands, ready to venture out and kill again at a moment's notice. What about Charles, for instance, who claims to have 'killed forty Japs at least, not to mention that Wog I ran over in Calcutta' (p. 192)? Alice runs a probing finger along what Joe refers to as 'a sort of Plimsoll line of decency which marks the difference between manhood and swinishness [or monstrosity]' (p. 214; my addition). As a result, she becomes a severe security risk.

Notably, her gruesome death, ultimately brought about by systemic pressure, ruptures the smooth surfaces of Warley life only momentarily, being quickly covered up by a general consensus that 'it was all for the best' (p. 235). In the pre-feminist era of the late 1940s, which constitutes the setting of *Room at the Top*, the status of an intellectually independent and sexually liberated woman of Alice's calibre can only be recognised as that of a worthless, entirely dispensable 'old whore' (p. 211).

At the time of his first encounter with Alice, Joe's transmogrification into his own *doppelgänger*, 'the Successful Zombie', has only just begun. Gradually, the system renders him one of its own by depriving him of his ability to feel and express emotions and thereby moulding him into a robot-like prototype of masculine perfection. He becomes 'Joe Lampton Export Model Mark IA, warranted free of dust, flaws, cracks, or pity' (p. 220). Cruelty, fraudulence and ruthlessness prevail over love, tenderness and trust. As if he were Dr Jekyll fleeing from Mr Hyde, or Victor Frankenstein haunted by his Monster, Joe eventually starts referring to himself in the third person, terrified that at any moment 'Joe Lampton would take possession of me again' (p. 220). Braine's hero has suffered an irreparable psychic split, isolating him not only from other people but also alienating him, most incisively, from himself. 'I hate Joe Lampton', he declares at one point, 'but he looked and sounded very sure of himself sitting at my desk in my skin; he'd come to stay, this was no flying visit' (p. 219). What originally started as a challenging experiment in masculine self-fashioning, fuelled by anger and ambition, has turned into a remote-controlled process of relentless patriarchal conditioning, satisfied with nothing less than the individual's total systematic commodification. Joe's older self speaks of 'a transparent barrier between myself and strong emotion. I feel what is correct for me to feel; I go through the necessary motions. But I cannot delude myself that I care' (p. 123). Remembering, only vaguely, the ecstatic joy he was capable of experiencing with Alice, he concludes that he 'could have been a different man . . . a real person' (p. 124). As it is, Joe finds himself in bondage to the laws of patriarchal capitalism which render him, quite literally, an ideal 'model' of successful masculinity:

> I'm like a brand-new Cadillac in a poor industrial area, insulated by steel and glass and air-conditioning from the people outside, from the rain and the cold and the shivering ailing bodies. I don't wish to be like the people outside, I don't even wish that I had some weakness, some foolishness to immobilize me amongst the envious coolie faces, to let in the rain and the smell of defeat. But I sometimes wish that I wished it. (p. 124)

Braine's novel concludes with a detailed portrayal of Joe's delirious response to Alice's suicide, featuring a kind of *psychomachia*, or conflict of the soul, between man's complex stock of human emotionality and, grafted upon it, his depersonalised role as a promising scion of patriarchal masculinity. The ending of *Room at the Top* resembles that of *Frankenstein* in that both novels concentrate on a man's vain attempt to deny his own artifice and cancel the hegemony of a robotic ideal that has started to consume him like a cancerous growth. Joe is overwhelmed by an upsurge of painful self-consciousness from which he is, unsuccessfully, seeking relief in self-oblivious inebriation. Looking at himself in horror, he realises that by becoming who he always wanted to be, he has unleashed a monster intent on killing his loved ones as well as destroying the emotional authenticity of his self. As the older Joe's self-declarations indicate, this monster eventually grasps hold of the man and possesses him totally, rendering him an empty shell, a mere façade without substance. Like Kurtz's in *Heart of Darkness*, the subjectivity of the Angry Young Man is drained of its life-giving zest and rendered a 'hollow sham' (Conrad 1996: 85), not by woman, as his misogynous rhetoric suggests, but by his own easily manipulable, tragic compliance.

Exceptionally, Braine's novel highlights the Angry Young Man's gender-specific, rather than purely class-related dilemma by steeping the narrative in authorial self-consciousness. Joe's autobiography is motivated by his need to be blamed for what he has done, the desire not to evade but embrace responsibility. *Room at the Top* presents itself as Joe's attempt at becoming intelligible to himself as an individual who has his own story to tell. Joe is desperate to elude his systemic (al)location as an exemplary representative of his kind whose identity has always been securely emplotted within a patriarchal framework that allows for no excursive ventures into the potentially self-liberating domain of the postscripted. *Room at the Top* is also presented as the product of a man's refusal to collude any longer with patriarchy's imposition of silence on an outlawed woman's narrative death. It takes Joe ten long years to re-open the case and disrupt the sense of closure that the community of Warley enforced on the account of events that led to Alice's suicide. Apparently unafraid of implicating himself and revealing his own complicity, Joe's autobiography reflects on the gender trouble caused by society's positive endorsement of even the cruellest instances of masculine failure. Joe's breakaway gesture and expression of unease at the end of the novel are conspicuously indicative of a change in man's self-representation. This man's sense of authenticity is patently at odds with the untarnished image society – all the more insidious for being represented by a female – urges him to cultivate of himself:

> Eva drew my head on to her breast. 'Poor darling, you mustn't take on so. You don't see it now, but it was all for the best. She'd have ruined your whole life. Nobody blames you, love. Nobody blames you.'
>   I pulled myself away from her abruptly. 'Oh my God,' I said, 'that's the trouble.' (p. 235)

Room at the Top is not a typical example of Angry Young Male writing, sanctioning 'complex forms of mystification and exploitation which facilitate rather than challenge patriarchal power' (Dollimore 1983: 69). On the contrary, the hitherto unacknowledged literary, historical and socio-political importance of Braine's novel resides in its explicit refusal to condone patriarchal structures whose detrimental, even deadly impact on both men and women it seeks to expose and condemn, rather than merely drawing them, as Jonathan Dollimore puts it, 'into unintended visibility' (Dollimore 1983: 70). For a male author writing in the pre-feminist 1950s, Braine displays an astonishingly acute understanding of patriarchy's relentless commodification of women as well as its manipu-lative deformation of men into perpetrators of systematic oppression. Significantly, after Alice's death, Joe suffers 'an attack of the truth', realising that 'there were no more dreams and no mercy left in the world, nothing but a storm of violence' (p. 221). His sensitivity heightens to such an unprecedented degree of self-consciousness that the drab interior décor of an otherwise non-descript pub suddenly comes to strike him as a fitting image of the remote-controlled pathos of all of man's ambitions within the normative order of patriarchal organisation:

> I ordered a rum and a half of bitter, and stood at the bar staring at the pictures which were hung round the walls and on the staircase leading to the Ladies'; they were all battle scenes, rather pleasant coloured prints with energetic marionettes waving swords with red paint on the tips, firing muskets which each discharged one round puff of white smoke, planting their standards on little cone-shaped hills above the perfectly flat battlefield, advancing relentlessly in perfect parade-ground formation and, occasionally, dying very stiffly with their left hand clutching their bosoms and their right hand beckoning their comrades on to victory. (p. 221)

As Schwenger points out, 'becoming self-conscious of their sex, male writers are now labouring under a disadvantage that was formerly women's alone' (Schwenger 1984: 10). In their introduction to a collec-tion of essays on men's writing and gender criticism, Laura Claridge and Elizabeth Langland take Schwenger's diagnosis a step further by expressing an interest in the manifold difficulties men must inevitably encounter on developing a gender-specific sense of self and experimenting with modes of writing that go against the grain of their patriarchal conditioning. Their questions concern what it is like 'to be a symbol of a power group, yet to find oneself self-alienated as the result of belonging to, or being constructed by, such a group', as well as what it means 'not to belong to that which it is assumed one belongs to' (Claridge and Langland 1990: 8). *Room at the Top* constitutes a seminal text in that it heralds the beginning of male-authored anti-patriarchal writing in Britain, in which men expose and, if possible, seek to distance themselves from the oppressive implications of the gender they traditionally inhabit. As the rare instance of Braine's novel suggests, the rise of a gender-specific self-consciousness in post-war British men's writing may not be solely attributable to the influence of feminist thought, although the latter has no doubt considerably assisted in facilitating its articulation and refinement over the last fifty years. The self-image cultivated by young men in the 1950s seems in itself so deeply fraught with impossible tensions and contradictions that it must ineluctably begin to destabilise and ultimately subvert the traditional success of its own maintenance and perpetuation.

According to Claridge and Langland's investigation of the possible development of a new kind of male-authored literature, the most urgent question remains what exactly male writers 'who feel fettered by the patriarchal literary tradition [can] do to escape a language implicitly – and often explicitly – defined as their own' (Claridge and Langland 1990: 11). It seems as if a new men's literature can only emerge from a self-conscious reiteration of the old traditions because, as Butler wisely points out, 'all signification takes place within the orbit of the compulsion to repeat; "agency", then, is to be located within the possibility of a variation of that repetition' (Butler 1990: 145). Braine's novel gives a brilliant example of this kind of subversive repetition. It recounts the conventional tale of the Angry/Ambitious Young Man from an introspective, revisionary viewpoint, thus breaking up the highly stylised codes of omission and denial that constitute the genre's classic symptoms of masculinist articulation.

Part III

Man's Progeny:

Towards an *écriture masculine*

THE FOLLOWING READINGS OF four male-authored texts – accompanied by a reading of Angela Carter's *The Passion of New Eve* – investigate the emancipatory impact feminist thought has had on the emergence of a plurality of post-patriarchal masculinities in contemporary British men's writing. The feminist demolition of traditional ideals of femininity has triggered a gradual disintegration of all patriarchal gender formations. As Michael Kimmel asserts, 'the "New Woman" redefined femininity . . . and this redefinition [has also] called into question the definition of masculinity, given that the two are relational constructs' (Kimmel 1987: 14). In consequence, some male authors have become highly self-conscious of the gender-specificity of their writing and have started to search for constructive solutions to men's double-bind dilemma of being at once both chief perpetrators and self-professed victims of patriarchal oppression.

Iain Banks, Alasdair Gray and Ian McEwan effectively contest the traditional perception 'that men and women are "opposite sexes" . . . [which] creates the expectation that one is either a man or a woman and that these two categories are essentially disparate' (Gutterman 1994: 221). Like Angela Carter, they envision a *gynandric* complexity of the human subject, a multi-gendered self-and-otherness which would significantly surpass Virginia Woolf's famous imperative in *A Room of One's Own* that 'one must be woman-manly or man-womanly' (Woolf 1993: 94). Unlike Woolf's ideal of androgynous self-formation, gynandricity does not merely stand for a personal trait or individual quality but is moreover expressive of a continuous communal appropriation and re-invention of gender. Thus, as a theoretical concept, it resembles Homi Bhabha's envisioning of cultural hybridity in *The Location of Culture* which, by prioritising new forms of intercultural communication that would accentuate 'the "inter" – the cutting edge of translation and negotiation, the *in-between* space', seeks to enable both individuals and whole communities eventually to 'elude the positions of polarity and emerge as the others of [their] selves' (Bhabha 1994: 38–9).

The concept of gynandricity seeks to incorporate the utopian potential of Bhabha's hybridity, not in order to create a new gender category but to disclose a 'third space' of mutual encounter within which men and women would be free continually to renegotiate their own – as well as one another's – differences. By thus transforming both men and women into Kristevan subjects-in-the-making, a gynandric gender dynamics would radically subvert the patriarchal inscription of polarity between a hegemonic masculine self and its margin of feminine or 'effeminate' others. Gender would cease to be a fixed, tautly scripted assignment of either empowering or disempowering symbolic allocation. Instead, it would come to express itself in a vast repertoire of invariably momentary configurations produced by a never-ending communal dialogue between differently embodied, yet equally enfranchised voices. It is this gynandric dynamics of a continuous (re-)engendering that Hélène Cixous has invoked in her designation of writing as a fundamentally deconstructive, 'bisexual' activity. However, gynandricity crucially reaches beyond Cixous's theorising in that it aims to involve both *écriture féminine* and *écriture masculine* together in:

> a process of different subjects knowing one another and beginning one another anew only from the living boundaries of the other: a multiple and inexhaustible course with millions of encounters and transformations of the same into the other and into the in-between. (Cixous 1976: 883)

The term *écriture masculine* is derived from Cixous's programmatic imperative that 'woman must write woman. And man, man . . . it's up to him to say where his masculinity and femininity are at' (Cixous 1976: 877). Rather than intending to re-inscribe a categorical separation of men's writing from women's writing, it is employed to describe the anti-phallogocentric and non-patriarchal disposition that characterises (pro)-feminist men's writing, while at the same time clearly indexing this new disposition's indebtedness to feminist thought. As a male 'writing from the body', the concept of *écriture masculine* also responds to Harry Brod's proposition that, whereas 'women's studies has seen much of its task as "enculturating" women . . . men's studies would aim at "embodying" men, as its share of the task of overcoming the Western mind/body dualism that has often operated to the detriment of women' (Brod 1987a: 273–4). No doubt, even in the hands of its most well-intentioned practitioners, *écriture masculine* is not always successful. As far as Banks, Gray and McEwan are concerned, they seem cautious enough not to fall prey to the masculinist fallacy of appropriating and thus upstaging women's femininity instead of exploring and negotiating their own. In contrast, Irvine Welsh's attempt at criticising patriarchal power relations is ultimately sabotaged by a latent horror of feminine alterity, leading the author to conclude his novel not on a note of reconciliation but with a nightmarish vision of man and woman's mutual castration.

8
·
Dams Burst
·
Iain Banks's The Wasp Factory

ANY WORK OF LITERATURE written by an author born or bred in Scotland will inevitably be vetted for traces of a distinctive, typical Scottishness to see if it merits incorporation into the canon of Scottish national literature. The Scottish literary establishment still tends to concern itself primarily with the question of national identification at the expense of other, perhaps more fundamentally identity-bearing issues that have started to emerge in contemporary Scottish writing, such as gender, sexuality and non-white/non-Scottish ethnicity. Even the problem of class, which – since James Kelman – has become a hallmark of Scottish literature, does not seem realised in its full complexity within the framework of a nationalist agenda inclined to regard a person's middle- or upper-class status as categorically indicative of their English-ness or, at least, compromisingly anglicised disposition. It seems as if in Scotland critical writing has so far failed to catch up with the exponen-tially increasing diversification of its creative counterpart. Contemporary Scottish literature, authored by both women and men, riddles the tradi-tionalist conception of national identity as definitive self-containment, bombarding the myth of closure with a self-conscious proliferation of ambivalence and heterogeneity. Iain Banks's first novel, *The Wasp Factory*, is part of this new tradition in Scottish writing, protesting that Scotland's imminent secession from England must not result in the creation of yet another insular monolith but give birth to a vibrant communal con-glomerate, aware of its own constitutive self-and-otherness and appre-ciative of the nation's affiliative dependency on a wide spectrum of fully emancipated others.

The neo-Gothic design of Banks's novel, its macabre celebration of violence, horror and death, is not an end in itself but aims to unmask the fraudulence of the old order and, ultimately, to demolish the Law of the Father by probing the subliminal turmoil that both upholds and potentially subverts it. In *The Wasp Factory*, patriarchal masculinity, traditionally the bedrock of all communal and individual identification, undergoes an elaborate process of ironic unwrapping. Banks employs gender parody to reveal the imitative artifice of normative standards that compel individuals to fashion themselves in compliance with an imperative ideal that does not originate in biological nature but is in itself a derivative of social conditioning. The chief objective of Banks's narrative is a deconstruction of traditional gender formations that present themselves as manifestations of a congenital inevitability. In unison with Butler's theorising of gender as a performative 'imitation without an origin', which can only perpetuate itself by hazardously disclosing its own immateriality, *The Wasp Factory* eventually releases its central characters, Frank and Eric, into 'a fluidity of identities that suggests an openness to resignification and recontextualization . . . depriv[ing] hegemonic culture and its critics of the claim to naturalized or essentialist gender identities' (Butler 1990: 138).

Banks's novel reverberates with allusions to a wide variety of classic literary masculinities – from *Frankenstein, Heart of Darkness* and *The Turn of the Screw* to *Lord of the Flies* and *A Clockwork Orange* – all of which dismantle themselves in light of Banks's central coup of presenting his readers with a typical boy's tale whose hero is *really* a girl. At the novel's climax Frank realises that he has lived his whole life in drag: 'I'm not Francis Leslie Cauldhame. I'm Frances Lesley Cauldhame. That's what it boils down to' (p. 181). Far from natural or authentic, his assumption of masculinity turns out to have been a monstrous impersonation synthesised by his Frankensteinian father, 'a doctor of chemistry, or perhaps biochemistry – I'm not sure' (p. 14). Expertly parodying psychoanalytic theories about the child's inevitable submission to patriarchal law and its symbolic order of phallocentric gender differentiation, Banks shows how Frank's sense of self is warped, virtually beyond repair, by his father's arbitrary fabrication of a castration complex. At the age of three, so his father's story goes, Frank was maimed by the family's pet dog, an incident of spurious authenticity that leaves the child traumatised by penis envy. The now male-identified girl begins to deny and discriminate against her own femaleness, which embarrasses her as an 'unfortunate disability' (p. 17). The boy she becomes, on the other hand, appears as a manufactured, entirely fictitious creation, obsessively overcompensating for an imaginary, patriarchally inflicted lack of natural manliness by pursuing an extremist ideal of violent masculine perfection. However, despite his apparent endorsement of a constructionist theorising of gender, Banks refuses ultimately to commit himself to any one definitive explanation of Frank's behaviour in terms of either nature or nurture. Frank's ultraviolence may be motivated by his detrimental internalisation of traditional gender norms. Alternatively, it may be triggered by the male hormones Frank unwittingly imbibes with the food his father prepares for him.

Predictably, the parodic multi-layeredness of Banks's novel – all of whose central protagonist's efforts at manly self-assertion are ironically undermined by their own intrinsic deviancy as a girl's appropriation of allegedly natural masculine behaviour – has never once been interpreted in terms of gender. Rather, reviewers and critics alike have shown themselves eager to integrate *The Wasp Factory* into the Scottish literary tradition, emphasising its generic resemblances with other canonical texts instead of meeting the challenge of its profoundly subversive, deconstructive potential. In a typical manoeuvre to manage the novel's bizarre oddity, Thom Nairn quickly resuscitates the stereotyping myth of the Caledonian antisyzygy, first introduced by Gregory Smith in 1919 to describe the recurrent dichotomy of the realist and fantastic modes in Scottish fiction and ever since applied as a term of critical convenience that explains the occurrence of practically any kind of contradiction, incongruence or irreconcilability in Scottish literary representation. Insensitive to the possible gender-specificity of the *doppelgänger* motif, Nairn perpetuates the given paradigm of traditional Scottish criticism which – seemingly impervious to strategies of appropriation, parody or subversion – concentrates exclusively on pointing up traces of historical continuity and national self-constancy. 'Potential schisms in the individual (schisms piled on schisms of all kinds) are constantly present in Banks's fiction', Nairn writes, 'making it comparable to R.L. Stevenson's *Dr Jekyll and Mr Hyde* and James Hogg's *Confessions of a Justified Sinner* . . . or Alasdair Gray's *Lanark*' (Nairn 1993: 129).

Interestingly, Adrienne Scullion suggests that this inferiorist, pathologistic imaging of Scotland as 'a culture of madness, or at least mental and emotional instability' may in fact be motivated by attempts to both obscure and contain 'society's fear of the *unheimlich* aspects of the feminine' (Scullion 1995: 201). Perhaps it is even more plausible to argue that the conspicuous popularity of the *doppelgänger* motif in both creative and critical Scottish writing, and men's writing especially, discloses the Scottish male's fear not only of a feminine other but also – more significantly – his own intrinsic self-and-otherness, or 'effeminacy'. Within the imperial framework of English–Scottish relations, the Scottish male is already feminised as a disempowered native (br)other. His condition is one of subordinate marginalisation which, while sensitising him to the plights of the systematically oppressed, makes it all the more important for him to disassociate himself from the female in order not to compromise his masculinity even further. The result is a psychic split expressing itself in precarious and highly conflictual assertions of the integrity of a self continuously embattled and destabilised by its own irrepressible alterity.

Scottish masculinity occupies no fixed position of indisputable social hegemony but is caught up in continuous oscillation between the diametrically opposed sites of (post)colonial marginality on the one hand and patriarchal dominance on the other. This simultaneous inferiority and superiority make an uneasy blend, highlighting Scottish men's complicity with a system of oppression while, at the same time, necessitating their commitment to counterdiscursive resistance. This quandary appears to find an apt analogy in the odd brotherhood of Eric and Frank in *The Wasp Factory*, which features both a girl obsessively preoccupied with asserting what she believes to be her congenital masculinity and a boy whose feminine disposition disintegrates under patriarchal pressure. Parallel to the representations of other phallic/testicular male couples in men's writing already discussed in this study (Victor Frankenstein and Henry Clerval in *Frankenstein*; Jack and Ralph in *Lord of the Flies*; Jimmy and Cliff in *Look Back in Anger*), Eric and Frank crucially complement each other's realisations of masculinity. Only superficially does Banks perpetrate a confrontation of two different discourses: one of heroic normality, the other of psychopathic madness. Despite Frank's resolute assertion that '[Eric] is mad and I am sane' (p. 118), reinforced by his position of authority as the novel's first-person narrator, the brothers appear in fact to be equally disturbed. Moreover, as Frank himself acknowledges, their insanity directly reflects the systematic perversity that is encouraged, even necessitated, by the societal order in which they live:

> The madder people. A lot of them seem to be leaders of countries or religions or armies. The real loonies.
> . . . Or maybe they're the only sane ones. After all, they're the ones with all the power and riches. They're the ones who get everybody else to do what they want them to do, like die for them and work for them and get them into power and protect them and pay taxes and buy them toys, and they're the ones who'll survive another big war, in their bunkers and tunnels. (p. 112)

In his analysis of the deconstructive potential of Freudian thought, Jonathan Culler infers 'that "sanity" is only a particular determination of neurosis, a neurosis that accords with certain social demands' (Culler 1983: 160). Accordingly, Frank is able to think of his own madness as sanity because, unlike Eric's, it appears to have patriarchal sanction. Although it results in the deaths of two cousins and his younger brother, Frank's ultraviolent behaviour ultimately poses no threat to the societal order but, like the ill-fated group dynamics that control Golding's boys in *Lord of the Flies*, seems to remain – almost – within the socially acceptable boundaries of what boys naturally tend to get up to. Despite the fact that Frank does undoubtedly go too far, his actions are never deviant or subversive but follow the normative guidelines of masculine propriety. Actually, considering the unremitting circulation of idealised images of a violent, domineering masculinity within contemporary society, it seems quite astonishing that Frank's behaviour strikes us as exceptional at all. Albeit extreme, Frank's masculine self-fashioning is by no means a monstrous aberration but the result of a meticulous self-formation in accordance with hegemonic ideals:

> I believe that I decided if I could never become a man, I – the unmanned – would out-man those around me, and so I became the killer, a small image of the ruthless soldier-hero almost all I've ever seen or read seems to pay strict homage to. (p. 183)

While busily blowing up rabbit warrens and declaring war on the entire animal kingdom, Frank does not hesitate to express dismissive exasperation at Eric's compulsive immolation of dogs: 'This burning dogs stuff is just nonsense' (p. 109). One wonders if in contrast to his brother's destructive excesses, Eric's violence is considered unacceptable because it targets man's best friend and unleashes itself amidst society, in the public sphere, rather than Frank's peninsular seclusion. Alternatively, it may be the case that there are both more complex and sinister reasons for Eric's rendition as a mad misfit and social outcast.

Before he went mad, on witnessing a horrific incident in a hospital during his time as a medical student in the city, Eric was Frank's picture-book hero, 'doing what he had to do, just like the brave soldier who died for the cause, or for me'. Like other truly great men before him, Eric seemed consumed by 'that outward urge . . . and it took him away from me, to the outside world with all its fabulous opportunities and awful dangers' (p. 138). Frank worships his brother who strikes him as a perfect embodiment of all the heroic ideals of patriarchal masculinity. It is against Eric's example of an immaculate adult manliness that Frank, the boy, defines his own position of lack and femininity. His identification is a negative one, conditioned by his 'injury' or (con)genital wound, which in accordance to the prevalent laws of gender differentiation confines him for ever to the sphere of the domestic. At the same time, Eric's imaginary progress in the world at large instigates Frank's own microcosmic cultivation of a compensatory, exaggerative masculinity. 'I had a vicarious feeling of manly satisfaction in the brilliant performance of Eric on the outside', Frank declares, 'as, for my own part, I slowly made myself unchallenged lord of the island and the lands about it' (p. 139).

However, as in *Lord of the Flies*, the boy's idealisation of adult masculinity's perfect heroism reveals itself as a naive make-believe projection, as Eric's masculine integrity is shown to have always been but a half-hearted performance that eventually breaks under patriarchal pressure. The older brother's nervous disintegration is equivalent to a total collapse of the phallic ideal. In Frank's view, Eric fails because he allows himself to be permeated by the feminine. His madness is an immediate corollary of his emasculating susceptibility to emotion, pain and trauma:

> Whatever it was that disintegrated in Eric then, it was a weakness, a fundamental flaw that a real man should not have had. Women, I know from watching hundreds – maybe thousands – of films and television programmes, cannot withstand really major things happening to them; they get raped, or their loved one dies, and they go to pieces, go crazy and commit suicide, or just pine away until they die. Of course, I realise that not all of them will react that way, but obviously it's the rule, and the ones who don't obey it are in the minority. (pp. 147–8)

Emotionality is considered unnatural in a man, a weakness and mad affliction, whereas violence is not. Unaware of his own fraudulently engendered subjectivity, Frank blames Eric's breakdown on his father's interference with nature, 'that nonsense in Eric's early years, letting him dress as he wanted and giving him the choice of dresses and trousers' (p. 148). Frank refuses to accept Eric's sensitivity and nurturant, testicular rather than phallic, qualities as a natural given. As a reader, one begins to long for Eric's own first-person account of his upbringing and socialisation. One would expect such a narrative to comprise numerous memories of coldly straitjacketing moments when Eric must have been terrified at his own outstanding deviance from the masculine norm. 'Once he picked me up and gave me a kiss on the lips which really made me frightened' (p. 143), Frank remembers. The reader is left to imagine Eric's alarm at his younger brother's horror and revulsion in response to this perfectly innocuous gesture of fraternal affection. Under pressure, Eric makes an attempt at living up to the stereotype, but even as a medical student he appears drawn to the nurturant and caring (traditionally feminine) rather than scientific (traditionally masculine) aspects of the profession. Significantly, his final emotional collapse does not result in hysteria, or *testeria* (a harmful inversion of the testicular), but in a mad, excessive emulation of phallic heroism. Like Frank's (or Alex's in *A Clockwork Orange*), Eric's ultraviolence is motivated by an overwhelming sense of his own inadequacy, failure and incompetence as a 'real' man. Accordingly, it is not the feminine that softens him, as Frank suggests, but the masculine that makes him harden beyond the humanly bearable, to the point of cracking up.

Eric's violence is ultimately designated as madness and thus deprived of all societal authorisation because it discloses – in public, for all to see – the deformative potential inherent in the masculine ideal itself. Man's insanity is encouraged and fostered, up to a certain non-negotiable limit, by the system itself:

> The conflagration in his head was just too strong for anybody sane to cope with. It had a lunatic strength of total commitment about it which only the profoundly mad are continually capable of *and the most ferocious soldiers and most aggressive sportsmen* able to emulate for a while. (p. 127; my emphasis)

In *The Wasp Factory*, Banks appropriates the motif of the *doppelgänger* to demonstrate that masculinity is informed by a systemic confusion of the normative with the normal/natural. No matter if they are labelled 'mad' or 'sane', boys feel compelled to exert their energies in a continuous effort to maintain an attitude of self-contained mastery, if necessary by means of violence. Consequently, within patriarchy masculinity develops, more often than not, into a neurosis of compulsive self-assertion.

Whereas according to psychoanalytic discourse 'woman is not the creature with a vagina but the creature without a penis, who is essentially defined by that lack' (Culler 1983: 167), man's physical nature enslaves him to the law of 'the fictitious phallus and its *hard-(w)on* masculinity, that precarious and ephemeral power that has to put itself constantly on the line to prove itself and to merit its status' (Flannigan-Saint-Aubin 1994: 254). In irreconcilable contrast to masculinity's projection of a forever augmenting phallic plenitude, the immediate reality of a man's bodily experience is marked by the flaccid penis, not a state of permanent tumescence but the trauma of impotence. Of course, Frank's dilemma in *The Wasp Factory* is even more problematic. Incapable of ever mustering an erection, he becomes a mere impersonator of masculinity, the irreparably emasculated shadow of heroic man: 'I saw myself, Frank L. Cauldhame, and I saw myself as I might have been: a tall slim man, strong and determined and making his way in the world, assured and purposeful' (p. 48). In order to compensate for his failure to embody the ideal, he must inscribe the phallic principle in whatever he does, assertively expanding his self by assimilating the world in acts of virtually autistic identification. Pretending to be as autonomous and neatly enclosed as 'a state; a country or, at the very least, a city' (p. 62), Frank abandons 'the real world' (p. 24) to re-imagine it as a narcissistic reflection of who he would like to be. Deeply insecure in himself, the island on which he lives becomes his self-aggrandising fantasy, forever reconstituting itself 'to boost [his] ego' (p. 63). Only at his god-like command, after he has imposed his supposedly indelible mark on them, do certain parts of the island emerge out of their primordial formlessness and take experiential shape as 'Black Destroyer Hill' (p. 36), 'the Snake Park' (p. 41) and 'the Skull Grounds' (p. 107), mirroring the lethal trajectory of Frank's extremist masculine self-fashioning.

However, as Frank gradually comes to realise, the territorialist boundaries of traditional masculinity are permeable and ultimately revocable. The artifice of patriarchal law must eventually yield to nature's insurmountable alterity, which disperses the phantasmatic integrity of the man-made subject by continuing to proliferate unpredictable change. Unsurprisingly, Frank identifies nature with femaleness and fluidity, both of which threaten to upset and decentre the carefully established order of his insular world:

> My greatest enemies are Women and the Sea. These things I hate. Women because they are weak and stupid and live in the shadow of man and are nothing compared to them, and the Sea because it has always frustrated me, destroying what I have built, washing away what I have left, wiping clean the marks I have made. And I'm not all that sure the Wind is blameless, either.
>
> (p. 43)

Intriguingly, Banks renders the eventual collapse of Frank's masculinity, as well as that of the patriarchal order in its entirety, not as a ruinous defeat but as some kind of liberating rebirth or regeneration. In *The Wasp Factory*, true authenticity is found in the release and acknowledgement of a hitherto repressed otherness, in madness, chaos and familial confusion. The cherished, ferociously guarded self is revealed to have always been a fraudulent imposition, not the result of free self-fulfilment but of remote-controlled self-(de)formation. Determined to pre-empt yet another successful insurrection of the female – similar to that initiated by Frank's overly autonomous mother, which leaves him limping for the rest of his life – Frank's father manipulates his daughter into identifying herself against her congenital sex. Like all patriarchal discourse, his tale of Frank's accidental castration is designed to disable woman, to keep her in check by inculcating in her an awesome respect and envy of the penis. Frank's father assures himself of his own superior able-bodiedness, badly damaged by his wife's rebellious onslaught on his authority, by projecting his fear of impotence and fallibility onto his daughter. Clearly, patriarchy can only perpetuate its structural hegemony if it manages to establish a general worship of the infallible phallus, thereby controlling all alterity, in any shape or form, in both its female and male subjects, within and outwith the boundaries of the self. In this context, Frank's statement on the science of dam-building can be read as a pertinent comment on the manipulative practices and strategies of systemic containment:

> But I have a far more sophisticated, even metaphysical, approach to dam-building now. I realise that you can never really win against the water; it will always triumph in the end, seeping and soaking and building up and under-mining and overflowing. All you can really do is construct something that will divert it or block its way for a while; persuade it to do something it doesn't really want to do. (p. 25)

The child's originally chaotic, intransigent nature is moulded into shape by the Law of the Father and its imposition of a rigid societal frame of *Bildung*. Frank's father is shown to wield absolute power over his daughter's understanding of the world, once having her believe 'that the earth was a Möbius strip, not a sphere' (p. 12). Language becomes a tool of arbitrary indoctrination and insidious make-believe. 'For *years*', Frank confesses, 'I believed Pathos was one of the Three Musketeers, Fellatio a character in *Hamlet*, Vitreous a town in China, and that the Irish peasants had to tread the peat to make Guinness' (p. 14). Frank is introduced to a universe dominated by his father's 'grand scheme' of fraudulent meaning-making and informed by his father's obsession with 'silly Imperial measurements' (p. 12), which the child is required to absorb by rote. As Frank remembers well, to rebel against the obtrusive omnipresence of the father's symbolic order is to court punishment and exclusion:

> Ever since I can remember there have been little stickers of white paper all over the house with neat black-biro writing on them. Attached to the legs of chairs, the edges of rugs, the bottom of jugs, the aerials of radios, the doors of drawers, the headboards of beds, the screens of televisions, the handles of pots and pans, they give the appropriate measurement for the part of the object they're stuck to. There are even ones in pencil stuck to the leaves of plants. When I was a child I once went round the house tearing all the stickers off; I was belted and sent to my room for two days. (p. 11)

As a teenager Frank believes he has totally emancipated himself from his father's 'little bits of bogus power [that] enable him to think he is in control of what he sees as the correct father–son relationship' (p. 16). Yet, not only is he still living the lie of a paternally engineered gender identity, his supposedly alternative existence replicates in minutest detail the symbolic order he aims to replace. In striking correspondence to the boys on Golding's desert island, Frank's desire to protest his autonomy ironically effects a re-erection of the phallic self of patriarchal authority. The Wasp Factory is identical with the Lord of the Flies; both constitute centralised reference points of (remote) control, order and legitimacy. Like his father, Frank re-maps the world in which he lives, intent on construing symmetrical patterns of regulatory signification from life's elusive contingencies: 'From the smaller to the greater, the patterns always hold true, and the Factory has taught me to watch out for them and respect them' (p. 37).

However, as it turns out, these patterns are not natural givens but man-made imperatives. In everything he does, Frank is guided by the Factory's oracular prophecies providing him with truths that are ultimately of his own making. His 'personal mythology, with the Factory behind it' (p. 128), is not any less fraudulent and oppressive than his father's scheme of interpreting, and hence manufacturing, the world virtually at random. Frank projects and identifies with the artifice of an imagined authority that does not erase but substitute his father's hold over him. Once caught up within the order of the symbolic, the subject finds it impossible to retrieve the indeterminacy and proprioceptive freedom that characterise the lives of young children 'before the insidious and evil influence of society and their parents have properly got to them' (p. 87). In *The Wasp Factory*, any conceptualisation of an original, authentic identity is spoilt by the patriarchal law of binarist oppositioning, which promotes a cultivation of the self at the expense of its other(s), splitting the individual himself into desirable manliness on the one hand and despicable femininity on the other. As Frank realises, otherness is invariably a deliberate creation, a particular *breed* of being, designed to facilitate the self's hegemony. With respect to domestic animals and – more controversially – women, Frank suggests that they really represent 'not their own stupidity, but our power, our avarice and egotism' (p. 145). The world of *The Wasp Factory* is riven by traditional masculinity's desire to present itself as pure, self-contained and uncontaminated by (its own inherent) alterity. What is needed to put it back together again, to cure it of its deadly schisms, is not synthetic closure but an eruption of regenerative chaos.

Frank's dilemma not only illustrates how within patriarchy the female is manipulated into experiencing her own bodiliness as an 'unfortunate disability' (p. 17), as 'too fat . . . chubby . . . strong and fit, but still too plump' (p. 20). It also indicates how even the most dedicated and compliant enactment of the phallic ideal fails to result in a satisfactory incorporation of the heroic masculine body that remains forever out of reach as a purely symbolic, impossibly idealised and exclusive icon of perfection. Frank's desperate emulation of the masculine ideal is rooted in his desire 'to look dark and menacing; the way I ought to look, the way I should look, the way I might have looked if I hadn't had my little accident'. Significantly, he adds that 'looking at myself, you'd never guess I'd killed three people. It isn't fair' (p. 20). Against the patriarchal standard of bodily perfection, both males and females must perceive themselves as physically inadequate, as either hopelessly incapacitated by the fact of castration or haunted by the fear of it. Ironically, as Flannigan-Saint-Aubin notes, despite 'the privileged position that the complex occupies in psychoanalytic theory, neither Freud nor his disciples have ever commented on the paradox that castration literally means the removal of the testicles' (p. 248). Not only does the cultural predominance of phallic symbolism obscure the integrity of femaleness, it also eclipses the originary gynandricity of the male body. Phallocentric thought effects a selective disembodiment of man, stressing the hard and erect over the malleably soft and vulnerable. It champions an ideal of self-centred, monologic and divisive autonomy over principles of communal dialogue and togetherness. In patriarchy's pursuit of the phallic ideal, testicular as well as traditionally feminine qualities – such as love, nurturance, peace and harmony – inevitably fall by the wayside, obstructing men's access to a wholesome fulfilment of their congenital complexity.

It seems symptomatic of man's patriarchal conditioning that, when Frank protests his bodily intactness by referring to his 'uncastrated genes' (p. 118), he does not assert his human indeterminacy or innately gynandric disposition. On the contrary, he is keen to affirm his indisputable natural manliness which, ironically, can only develop into proper masculinity once the boy has internalised the phallic ideal and, with it, every real man's unremitting fear of castration. Taking his father's word 'for anything that had happened' (p. 173), Frank succumbs to patriarchal imperatives and becomes a one-dimensional functionary of 'the harder sex', eager to incorporate 'what men are really *for*. . . We strike out, push through, thrust and take' (p. 118). Gender, as we know it, inflicts a sentence of definitive, unequivocal closure on an individual's processes of self-identification or, as Tina Chanter puts it, 'before you know it you are a girl or a boy, and acting like one' (Chanter 1997: 52). However, as Frank is to discover eventually, there is more to human identity than either masculinity or femininity.

On being confronted with the reality of having lived a lie, Frank resorts to proprioception to maintain a sense of self-constancy. 'I *am* still me', she claims, 'I *am* the same person, with the same memories and the same deeds done' (p. 182). Proprioception, originally a physiological term defined in contradistinction to perception, designates the means by which the individual receives and interprets self-authenticating information from within herself. Reared on false premises, Frank can only retrieve her proprioceptive faculties once her inferiority complex – imposed by her father, yet internalised and perpetuated by herself – has been lifted off her. As patriarchal *Bildung* aims at a standardisation of society in terms of gender, it strategically interferes with the self-formation of society's others: women, sexual minorities and, most overtly perhaps, children. Since patriarchy encourages self-alienating mimicry and conformism, prone to result in monstrous deformations rather than an authentic fulfilment of individual difference, subjects displaying visible aberrations from the standard norm are particularly susceptible to proprioceptive impairment which causes them to fall ill with *Bildung*-induced misperceptions of themselves. Only once her father's symbolic order has been revealed to represent neither nature nor the truth but a fraudulent scheme of arbitrary engineering, does Frank stop perceiving herself as disabled and physically inadequate. Her quest for self-identification is bound to resume. However, this time she will search for authenticity not within the enclosures of patriarchal gender formations but in an acknowledgement of her own proprioceptive indeterminacy, as her final conclusion indicates:

> Inside this greater machine, things are not quite so cut and dried (or cut and pickled) as they have appeared in my experience. Each of us, in our own personal Factory, may believe we have stumbled down one corridor, and that our fate is sealed and certain (dream or nightmare, humdrum or bizarre, good or bad), but a word, a glance, a slip – anything can change that, alter it entirely, and our marble hall becomes a gutter, or our rat-maze a golden path. Our destination is the same in the end, but our journey – part chosen, part determined – is different for us all, and changes even as we live and grow. (pp. 183–4)

In correspondence with Butler and Chanter's theorising of gender, Banks is careful to avoid 'the extremes of complete determinism or absolute freedom' (Chanter 1997: 52) by suggesting that although our identities are inevitably engendered against a certain cultural background, there is always plenty of leeway for self-determinative change. Banks urges traditional man to open up to what he has learned categorically to exclude from his psychological make-up. What is abject to the patriarchal system may not necessarily be abject to the individual male. On the contrary, as in Frank's case, what man is conditioned to regard with (self-)loathing may begin to initiate processes of genuine self-authentication. The ending of *The Wasp Factory* hints at a remedial reassemblage of human subjectivity. Injurious distinctions between femininity and masculinity, madness and sanity, have collapsed into a vision of restorative unity beyond the systemic inscription of woman's congenital lack in opposition to man's phallic plenitude. Banks defeats the patriarchal image of woman as man's enemy, as either 'an object of horror and revulsion, living proof of the possibility of castration, or else . . . an altogether superior and autonomous being, complete in herself with nothing to lose or gain' (Culler 1983: 169). Banks's newly born female is introduced not as a monster or domineering mother figure but as her brother's sister. Promisingly, Eric and Frank's final embrace signals a liberating reconstitution of gender relations beyond patriarchal pressure in an ambience of equality and mutual affection.

Banks's interrogation of patriarchal gender norms is grounded in a general problematisation of tensions between standard and difference, centre and margin, the established order and its subversive regeneration from within. Thus, albeit only analogically, *The Wasp Factory* also clearly addresses the issue of Scottish postmodernity, that is, contemporary Scotland's communal struggle for national (re)identification. Significantly, Frank must eventually abandon his project of heroic self-fashioning. The hitherto unchallenged lord of the island becomes a Kristevan *sujet en procès*, eager to resume his quest for self-authentication but now required to do so from a position of feminine marginality rather than phallocentric independence: 'I don't know what I'm going to do. I can't stay here, and I'm frightened of everywhere else. But I suppose I'll have to go' (p. 182). Stripped of its spurious self-consistency and fraudulent traditionalism, the new Scotland is left to re-inscribe itself in a dialogic exploration of its own as well – as its others' – alterity. Banks's vision of subversive change is not apocalyptic but epiphanic, deconstructive rather than purely annihilative. 'Poor Eric came home to see his brother', the novel concludes, 'only to find (Zap! Pow! Dams burst! Bombs go off! Wasps fry: *ttssss!*) he's got a sister' (p. 184). The apparent cataclysm is parenthetically contained within the notion of a revelational homecoming. Although the old order has undergone an explosive decentralisation, it is not radically destroyed but transformed into a welcoming refuge for the uprooted and temporarily insane.

In their confusion, Frank and Eric set fire to the picture-book icons of the Scottish pastoral (rabbits, dogs, sheep). Miraculously, however, despite the fact that it sits on a basement full of cordite, hoarded by the boys' grandfather, the family estate of the Cauldhames emerges unscathed from this panoramic conflagration. The old Scotland is not totally erased by the angry insurrection of 'an evil demon we have lurking, a symbol for all our family misdeeds' (p. 53). Rather, like the traditional gender formations that have sustained it so far, it finds itself at the beginning of a period of regenerative change.

9

.

The Exquisite Negative of His Sex

.

Angela Carter's The Passion of New Eve

IN HER COMMITMENT TO a radically subversive analysis of the strategies and practices of patriarchal power Angela Carter never fails to distinguish between individual men as potential friends and lovers on the one hand and the normative societal standard of generic man on the other. In Carter's work, men are comprehended not only as the oppositional factor in an oppressive equation but also as ultimately indispensable allies in the creation of a new order.

Carter employs feminist strategies of interrogation to demolish the apparatus of patriarchal conditioning that harms and deforms all of us, segregating us categorically into women and men before, and often instead of, allowing us to grow into a solidary community informed by close-knit, mutually empowering and supportive relationships between the sexes. Protesting that it is our common humanity that is at stake rather than the maintenance of a supposedly natural balance or interplay between the polarised essences of the male and female, Carter's work sets itself off against the general majority of feminist debates in the 1970s by aiming not at a simple reversal or redistribution of power but at a deconstruction of all individual and societal moments of hierarchical oppositioning. According to Carter, a truly revolutionary feminist movement must not categorically dismiss and denigrate men to realise its objectives. Mere biological maleness does not necessarily signal a wholehearted, complicitous endorsement of patriarchal oppression. There are in fact men who not only appreciate the example of women's invention of powerful new femininities (that incorporate traditionally masculine attributes) but also feel compelled to work on an equally liberating invention of fully emancipated masculinities (that would incorporate

117

traditionally feminine attributes). As a decisively anti-patriarchal movement, feminism bears the potential of re-introducing women and men to
each other as victims of the same processes of symbolic castration,
processes that induce women to internalise their 'nature' while engaging
men in a life-long battle against theirs.

Hinging on the creation and subsequent quest for self-fulfilment of a
wo/man, *The Passion of New Eve* represents perhaps Carter's most dedicated endeavour to reconcile man and woman in their struggle against
the patriarchal system that enslaves women at the same time as it
systematically brutalises men. However, with most of her work commonly rubricated as 'women's writing', Carter's concern with the problematic position of men in patriarchy often remains unacknowledged.
The overwhelming majority of Carter's critics focus on the representation of femininity and femaleness in her work, quite as if a sympathetic
discussion of men and masculinity would seriously compromise or call
into question their feminist commitment. *The Passion of New Eve* clearly
intends to do much more than merely reveal the symbols of femininity
'as reflections of male desire', or show women's subjectivity 'to be de-
formed by the social power of patriarchal stereotypes of femininity'
(Schmidt 1989: 73). The novel is first and foremost about the recruitment and conversion of a 'typical' man to the counterdiscursive principles and tenets of women's liberation. It concentrates on one man's
drastically experiential initiation to the sufferings of women as perpetrated by the patriarchally conditioned male he himself used to be. In
Lenora Ledwon's words, Carter poses the question, 'if femininity is a
masquerade, is masculinity equally a masquerade? And is there any way
to control this economy of masquerade through play, so that one can be
whomever (or whatever) one desires?' (Ledwon 1993: 27). Carter's ironic
exposure of the dynamics of gender stereotyping and the performativity
of sexual identities constitutes but a necessary backdrop to what lies at
the heart of her investigation. And that is a rigorous exploration of the
wasteland between the iron-curtained enclaves of traditional masculinity
and femininity, the binarist carve-up of the body of human potential into
male and female or, as Paul Magrs puts it, 'the bits in between performances' (Magrs 1997: 195).

From the beginning, the dystopian New World setting of *The Passion of
New Eve* alerts us to the quality of Carter's novel as an enquiry into the
desirability of utopia as a fixed condition rather than a historical impulse
motored by continuous change and progressive development. While
America regards itself as the perfect new beginning that has once and
for all overcome 'those vile repositories of the past, sewers of history, that

poison the lives of European cities' (p. 16), its greatest achievements of utopian self-fashioning have already begun to deteriorate into tragic hallmarks of inevitable decline. Permanence is anathema to utopia whose irresistible vigour is mainly derived from the elementarity of flux which, in turn, is the bane of order and symbolic consistency. Seeking to immortalise itself in a pose of filial superiority, America has not replaced but simply exceeded its progenitor's phallocentric narcissism up to the point of suffering some kind of climactic stroke. The phallic principle of absolute perfection is about to give in to the strain of ideological exhaustion. By the time of Evelyn's arrival in America, New York is already falling apart, releasing 'the entropic order of disorder' (p. 15) on whose suppression it was founded. As in Iain Banks's *The Wasp Factory*, the constructs of cultural engineering and masculinist self-fashioning must eventually yield to the increasing pressure of what they were originally designed to exclude, dam in, and hide from view.

Far from representing a genuine new beginning, America is the product of colonisation, its history fuelled by countless instances of systematic Cartesian splitting, which manifests itself perhaps most incisively in the triumph of masculinist architectonics over the unruly wilderness of indigenous space. Carter draws a meaningful parallel between the city of New York 'built on a grid . . . planned . . . in strict accord with the dictates of a doctrine of reason' (p. 16), and Leilah, Evelyn's African-American mistress. Both native land and female body are portrayed as systematically dissected and incarcerated by the inscriptive aesthetics of an arresting male gaze:

> [Leilah] rolled the mesh stocking down one black, matte thigh, upon which the coarse mesh had left indentations as tragic as if the flesh had been pressed against barbed wire in an attempt at an escape from a prison camp in which she had always lived, would always attempt to flee, would always fail. (p. 24)

Against the truism that one man's utopia always inevitably constitutes another wo/man's dystopia, Carter goes a step further to show how the symbolic order of patriarchal phallocentrism also exerts a profoundly detrimental impact on the masculine subject himself. Mary Daly's argument that 'sexist society maintains its grasp over the psyche by keeping it divided against itself. Through stereotyping it harnesses the power of human becoming' (Daly 1973: 128), is revealed to be applicable to both women and men. The masculinity of Evelyn and his kind has been cut to definitive measures to suit an allegedly perfect environment which they are authorised to administrate, yet never to govern. Men's privileged position is won and maintained at the high cost of internal repression. It is vitally imperative for their ongoing success that they 'must not breathe a word of [their] desires in the pure, evangelical fusion of form and function, even if the black rats of these desires gnaw away at [them] constantly, all the time eroding' (p. 16). At least half of men's humanity is subjected to self-oppressive processes of abjection that converge and harden into a permanent state of acute paranoia. 'The bright, rich smell of shit [that] added a final discord to the cacophony of the city's multiple odours' (p. 17), for example, is thus a direct result of patriarchal masculinity's cultivation of a pose of impossible purity. Ultimately, the pressure on men always to project an attitude of impervious control provokes a powerful return of the repressed, unleashing desires as 'fat as piglets and vicious as hyenas' (p. 17) that trigger the system's eventual collapse into total semiotic dissolution. Ironically, this 'catastrophe of the city' (p. 15) heralds not a moment of apocalypse but a moment of rebirth. The insurrection of 'Blacks, Mexis, Reds, Militant Lesbians, Rampant Gays, etc etc etc.' (p. 16) is inspirited by a desire for utopian regeneration. The disintegration of normative man becomes a necessary prerequisite for the liberation of all wo/men.

Carter dismantles the masculine viewpoint without ever eliminating it altogether. Hence, Evelyn's female-authored transformation into Eve can also be seen as an attempt to rehabilitate masculinity as an integral component in Carter's eventual reassemblage of humankind's utopian potential. Since *The Passion of New Eve* invests so much time and effort in the inspection and overhaul of patriarchal man, Evelyn's initial encounter with Leilah ought perhaps not to be read primarily as a serious feminist probing of the destructive dynamics of heterosexual desire, but as a deliberate parody ringing with relentless, yet essentially curative Medusan laughter. At the time of writing, woman already knows man inside out: his response to feminine seduction, his proclivity for annihilative subterfuge as well as his inevitable panic in the face of paternal responsibility. As it dawns on Eve towards the end of the novel, Evelyn is strategically set up. 'Had [Leilah] all the time been engaged on guerilla warfare for her mother?', Eve wonders. 'Had that gorgeous piece of flesh and acquiescence been all the time a show, an imitation, an illusion?' (p. 172). To teach him a lesson and bring him quite literally back to his senses, woman corners man at his weakest, when he has already begun to disintegrate together with the world he designed or, rather, the world that designed him.

Patriarchal masculinity seems so predictable in its dependency on woman as its discursive opposite that Evelyn is easily manipulated to behave in perfect accordance with Mother's plan. What strikes him as an authentic gesture of escape from the threat of domestic entrapment is in reality little more than a pre-programmed corollary of his domophobic conditioning. Notably, 'lusting after the prototypical all-American quest, the solipsistic male journey into the desert to find himself' (Ledwon 1993: 33), Evelyn marginalises himself, a circumstance which not only considerably destandardises his position of authority but also motivates the first tentative, if still rudimentary, stirrings of a growing self-consciousness and sense of emotional interiority:

> At first, I was exhilarated. I thought I left behind a fatal sickness that had been bred of the city; yet the darkness and confusion were as much my own as that of the city and I took the sickness with me since I was myself infected, or had brought it from the Old World to the New World with me, was myself a carrier of the germ of a universal pandemic of despair. But I wanted to blame my disease upon somebody and so I chose Leilah, for she was the nearest thing to myself I had ever met. (p. 37)

In the desert, 'the abode of enforced sterility, the dehydrated sea of infertility, the post-menopausal part of the earth' (p. 40), Evelyn finds masculinity at its purest, expressing itself in a symbolic landscape of negation and lack, which ultimately discloses that man deprived of woman equals nothingness and annihilation. Confounding self-determination with self-termination, man's quest, his dead-end search for 'the exquisite negative of [his own rather than her] sex' (p. 27), ends here. Ironically, only woman's intervention can at this point still save man from the certainty of an untimely narrative death. Carter appears to suggest that history depends for its continuation on a radical iconoclastic interrogation of the phallus. Evelyn's quest is refuelled at a site of violent feminist protest and resistance, 'a stone cock with testicles, all complete, in a state of massive tumescence. But the cock was broken off clean in the middle' (p. 47). His emasculation and transsexualisation revive him so that he becomes a productive subject-in-the-making, newly conscious of gender's unremitting dystopian subjugation of the flesh.

Evelyn is captured by the women of Beulah, the inhabitants of a matriarchal civilisation underneath the desert, whose subversive location indicates its programmatic intention to undermine the self-annihilative ideals of patriarchal man. However, the reader's expectation of being introduced to a system grounded in maternal fecundity and cyclical regeneration is quickly frustrated on confrontation with an earth mother who, in both appearance and attitude, differs only insignificantly from the salvationist ideologues and totalitarian dictators of male-authored dystopias. While each of her devout subjects has internalised the pose of a 'satisfied Calvinist who knows he has achieved grace' (p. 79), Mother herself is likened to idolisations of Karl Marx, her face bearing 'the stern, democratic beauty of a figure on a pediment in the provincial square of a people's republic' (p. 59). Carter's unfavourable description of the politics of Beulah constitutes an engaging critique of a certain kind of militant feminism that, instead of radically deconstructing oppositional hierarchies to engender a new, alternative order, only reverses the oppressive dynamics of systemic victimisation. Now it is men suffering under matriarchy rather than women suffering under patriarchy. As Ledwon writes, 'Mother merely replaces one set of false universals (phallocentricity) with another set (gynocentricity)' (Ledwon 1993: 37), the only major difference consisting perhaps in Beulah's inexorable sense of mission.

Mother's regime is not satisfied with man's mere submission to matriarchal law and his interpellation into a position of subordination and passivity. Rather, by re-designing Evelyn's physical nature after a normative (masculinist!) blueprint of ideal femaleness, she seeks to extirpate once and for all whatever congenital essence of maleness his self may still be susceptible to. Mother's realm turns out to represent an unnatural, inhuman, woman-made world in which cosmetic surgery in the name of feminine perfection is replaced by a belief in the fundamental political correctness of the female body. And yet, despite the apparent sacredness of the female principle, Beulah's women are all marked by arcane practices of ritual maiming (single-breastedness) or surgical enhancement (multi-duggedness). Significantly, Carter refers to Mother as 'the hand-carved figurehead of her own self-constructed theology' (p. 58), recurrently emphasising her syntheticity: 'She was her own mythological artefact; she had reconstructed her flesh painfully, with knives and with needles, into a transcendental form as an emblem, as an example' (p. 60). Ultimately, 'in Beulah, myth is a made thing, not a found thing' (p. 56). The symbolic orders of matriarchy and patriarchy seem equally unsatisfactory; both result in the circumscription of our humanity. Or, to express it in Carter's own words in *The Sadeian Woman*, 'mother goddesses are just as silly a notion as father gods' (Carter 1979: 5).

Beulah is no oasis or utopian herland but a site of negation originating in woman's discontent with man's image of her as 'the antithesis in the dialectic of creation' (p. 67). Mother's body politic is primarily aimed at confounding and repelling the inscriptive faculties of the male gaze, seeking emancipation from patriarchal control in a fantastic exorcism of man-made forms and symbols of femininity. However, Mother's 'painful metamorphosis of the entire body' (p. 49) is profoundly fallacious. While no doubt successfully disrupting man's habitual approval of the suitably feminised female body, her excessive self-fashioning still clearly orients itself against his response to it. Rather than authenticating itself by its own standards, Mother's new womanhood depends for its validation entirely upon man's shock and bewilderment on confronting it. Far from originary and self-motivated, Beulah represents a residual derivative of man's history of destruction, with Mother's brave new world unfolding and identifying itself in the mirror of his previous monstrosities. 'Perhaps this desert, since the nuclear tests they had performed here . . . spawned mutations of being', Carter suggests, 'hitherto unguessable modes of humanity, in which life parodied myth, or became it' (p. 77).

Ultimately, the feminism of Beulah strikes Carter as such a disappointing and unsuccessful attempt at emancipation because it denies and fails to address its roots in man's history of deliberate or compulsive self-(de)formation. There is no resistance that can operate entirely *ex nihilo*. In the light of Tina Chanter's reflections, even Mother's spectacular pose as 'the Great Parricide . . . the Castratix of the Phallocentric Universe' (p. 67) must be regarded as an angry backlash to centuries of oppression and hence, ultimately, as a patriarchally determined construct:

> even if individuals react to stereotypical injunctions by refusing them, there is still a sense in which those injunctions govern individual reactions, albeit negatively or indirectly. If a woman prefers wearing black leather to pink flowery dresses, this choice is far from incidentally related to the ideal of femininity that culture holds up for her. (Chanter 1997: 47)

Beulah fails to deconstruct the essentialist conception of gender as an individual's inalterable destiny. As long as Mother continues to rival patriarchal man's mythical feat of autonomous self-authentication, her oppositional radicalism will never mature into a truly alternative world view. Instead, it comes to resemble yet another tedious manifestation of sexual unequivocality that merely reconfigures and supplants, rather than resolutely eradicates, previous constellations of power. The self is still subjected to a traumatic allocation of identity exclusively determined by gender. Notably, Mother's masterstroke of congenital 'psycho-surgery' is inspired by the idea that 'a change in the appearance will restructure the essence' (p. 68). Accordingly, Beulah's main objective, which consists in the creation of 'the Messiah of the Antithesis' (p. 67), constitutes an act of female self-assertion as problematic in its conscriptive totalitarianism and hierarchical orchestration as Victor Frankenstein's ill-omened project of man-making. Like Frankenstein, or Frank's father in *The Wasp Factory*, Mother assumes the pose of 'a great scientist who makes extra-ordinary experiments and [Evelyn] was destined to become the subject of one of them' (p. 49).

In anticipation of Butler's critique of fundamentalist feminism, Carter exposes the artifice of Mother's new woman by indicating how the feminist ideology of Beulah 'presumes, fixes, and constrains the very "subjects" that it hopes to represent and liberate' (Butler 1990: 148). As Ledwon asserts, the most commendable achievement of *The Passion of New Eve* consists in its indefatigable attack on:

> the assumption that identity can be whole and complete, whether it be femininity incarnate (Tristessa), maternity incarnate (Mother), masculinity incarnate (Zero), or hermaphroditism incarnate (Mother's project to create a completely self-sufficient being in Eve). We desire the self made perfect, but the self escapes our attempts at perfection. (Ledwon 1993: 38)

Since it does not automatically result in a seamless aggregation of self and body, Evelyn's 'change in ontological status' (p. 71) challenges the very concept of sexual identity as consistent, definitive self-containment. 'I have not yet become a woman', New Eve declares, 'although I possess a woman's shape' (p. 83). Problematising the role of both artifice and nature in the construction of gender identities, Eve's incomplete trans-formation also questions the notion of sexual originality. Biological sex is exposed as a symbolic (al)location, at the same time arresting and irresistible, a kind of self-imprisonment to which the individual must involuntarily subscribe and conform. As Eve realises, he 'must climb inside the skin of the girl willy-nilly, whether [he] liked it or not, and learn, somehow, to live there' (p. 80).

While the motivation, success and legitimacy of Mother's attempt at creating the perfect female remain questionable, Evelyn's castration and subsequent reconstruction as a woman have a curious effect on his understanding of himself as a man. For the first time ever he experiences himself as a gendered, one-dimensionally sexed being. Forced into the marginal position of woman, masculinity becomes visible to him, not as a referential standard but as a manifestation of difference. At the same time, the sense of lack that is traditionally associated with femaleness is identified not as inherent in woman alone but as endemic to the whole system of patriarchal heterosexuality within which both men and women find themselves permanently embarked upon quests for their other, allegedly complementary halves, who at once attract and tragically repel them. Significantly, situated between the male and female, Eve is not left with nothing but with a chaotic overabundance of possible orientations, suggesting that only in between or outside of the traditional polarities of gender has wo/man got a chance to retrieve and fulfil her innate gynandricity. Thus, after her eventual escape from Beulah, Eve's story departs from the trajectory of traditional male quests that seek conclusive fulfilment in the self's triumphant penetration or self-expansive assimilation of its other(s). From a domophobic escape narrative *The Passion of the New Eve* changes into a 'journey back to the source . . .' (p. 53) and becomes illustrative of a gradual process of evolutionary regression towards a new beginning, a utopian moment at which the self prepares for its rebirth as its own other. As Ledwon argues, Eve's passions are all 'driven by the passion for identity, for the self'. Yet, as the self cannot ever be found, made, or even known, 'the best you can do is embrace the self by embracing the Other' (Ledwon 1993: 41).

The Passion of New Eve comprises a sequence of picaresque adventures devised ultimately to empower the traditional subject to emancipate itself from the symbolic impositions of systemic control. However, before Eve is free to address her proprioceptive indeterminacy and transport herself into a future beyond the grasp of oppressive gender formations, she must confront and submit to the whole gamut of injurious myths and allegories of the flesh. No sooner has she escaped from her assignment as the key character in Beulah's salvationist plot of feminist liberation than she falls into the hands of Zero, an archetypal embodiment of patriarchal tyranny. Interestingly, Zero is portrayed as consumed by his own excessively self-centred imaging of himself as the alpha and omega of human achievement and perfection, the be-all and end-all of historical experience. His monomaniacal cultivation of the phallocentric ideal has exerted an entirely detrimental influence on his bodily self, leaving him one-eyed, one-legged, sterile and permanently ill-tempered, crippled and crazed by power. As Carter suggests, man's total identification with patriarchy renders him a paranoid robot-like caricature of human nature, emotionally disabled and intellectually autistic. With respect to Zero, the inherent fraudulence of the system translates into a compulsive and self-delusive appropriation of the world within as well as outside of his desert kingdom. Not only is he intent on regulating his wives' 'understanding of him and also [their] understanding of themselves in relation to him' (p. 97), he also 'no longer needed news of the world, since he manufactured it himself to his own devices' (p. 101).

Zero's autocratic rule is undermined by Eve's increasingly ambiguous, multi-gendered self-consciousness. Most importantly, Eve cannot help identifying with Zero as a ghostly apparition from her own past as a

125

man. 'I felt myself to be, not myself but he', s/he declares, 'and the experience of this crucial lack of self, which always brought with it a shock of introspection, forced me to know myself as a former violator at the moment of my own violation' (pp. 101–2). On the other hand, Eve can barely resist giving in to the masochistic, self-annihilating pleasure of feminine passivity, to 'all the lure of that narcissic loss of being, when the face leaks into the looking-glass like water into sand' (p. 103). Due to her position in between the sexes, Eve is able to recognise the man she used to be, as well as the woman she now finds herself compelled to impersonate, as an artificial creation necessitated by patriarchy's divisive misapprehension of human nature. As Eve realises in her encounter with Zero, under patriarchy men and women are prone to lose their autonomy as unique individual beings to a systemically inscribed antagonism of mutually destructive or neutralising desire. Under patriarchal pressure, man violates woman to assert his masculinity, while woman is dehumanised to such a degree that she becomes prone to welcoming her subjugation as evidence of her feminine authenticity.

Patriarchal heterosexuality seems patterned by expedient necessities according to which men and women are modelled to suit each other rather than themselves. Without his wives, Zero 'would have been nothing' (p. 100), Carter points out, 'his myth depended on their conviction . . . Their obedience ruled him' (p. 99). Moreover, convinced that 'women were fashioned of a different soul substance from men, a more primitive, animal stuff' (p. 87), Zero becomes at least as limited and predictable in his self-expression as his harem of wives. As Carter shows in *The Sadeian Woman*, once men and women have internalised their absolute hierarchical oppositioning in accordance with the anonymous, supra-individual categories of sex and gender,

> they cease to be themselves, with their separate lives and desires; they cease to be the lovers who have met to assuage desire in a reciprocal act of tenderness, and they engage at once in a spurious charade of maleness and femaleness.
> . . . The man and woman, in their particularity, their being, are absent from these representations of themselves as male and female. (Carter 1979: 8)

From the beginning, *The Passion of New Eve* is motivated by the search for a new America in which, should they so wish, men and women would be free to re-imagine themselves outside of, and/or in radical opposition to, normative gender standards. The novel contests the disingenuous logic of Evelyn's initial reasoning that 'our external symbols must always express the life within us with absolute precision; how could they do otherwise, since that life has generated them?' (p. 6). It is Evelyn's use of the possessive pronoun here, clearly intended to suggest a universal consensus, that betrays the androcentric bias of his approach. The symbols he refers to are the symbols of patriarchal man, inscribing his needs, desires and ideals while expecting everybody else, and woman especially, to subscribe to them. Inspired by the profound changes in Western society's emotional and intellectual make-up in the late 1960s and 1970s, Carter's novel protests that man's symbols have long been outlived by history and operate no longer – if ever they did – as well-intentioned moral guiding principles but as means of deliberate dystopian oppression. Keen to uphold the notion of utopia as an evolutionary impulse, Carter refrains from endorsing the establishment of any new, ostensibly counterdiscursive order. Instead, she proposes to suspend all symbolic certainty, 'for a while, until the times have created a fresh iconography' (p. 174). Applied to the women's liberation movement, this means that it must not precipitately settle for a female-authored alternative to patriarchy, thus creating a new centre with new margins, but remain in flux. Unlike patriarchal discourse in reverse, feminist counterdiscourses ought not to alienate woman from herself by alienating her from man. Both men and women deserve to be released into a socio-political climate that would allow them to relate to themselves and each other without ideological bias or conformative pressure.

As Carter concludes, 'the vengeance of the sex is love' (p. 191). Love, of which we catch a brief glimpse in Eve's encounter with Tristessa, may be able to overcome the divisive compartmentalisation of men and women's common human potential. However, in order to exert a viable and enduring influence, such love would need to find a firm foothold in human time, in history. Eve's union with Tristessa, establishing a bond between male-to-female transsexual and female impersonator, seems of necessity short-lived as it occurs 'outside history' between 'beings without a history mysteriously twinned by [their] synthetic life' (p. 125). Still, due to Eve's alleged pregnancy with Tristessa's child, their mutually liberating encounter beyond 'the false universals of myth' (p. 136) appears to anticipate the imminent incarnation of a new kind of human being, a messianic Tiresias or pansexual hermaphrodite impervious to the totalitarian violence of symbolic allocation. Paradoxical as it may seem at first, Tristessa's death is integral to the successful gestation of a new order of signification. Unlike Eve, who is made of flesh and blood, Tristessa is 'an anti-being that existed only by means of a massive effort of will and a huge suppression of fact' (p. 129). Eve's masquerade is 'more than skin deep', her femaleness 'a mask that now I never would be able to remove, no matter how hard I tried' (p. 132). In contrast, the identity of the transvestite, based on disguise and disembodiment, possesses little permanence, nor candour, perpetrating a deliberate dissubstantiation of the *realissimum* of the flesh.

Tristessa is little more than a specular mirage, a man-made illusion motivated by man's desire for 'the only woman he could have loved' (p. 129). As Carter emphasises, 'Tristessa had no function in this world except as an idea of himself; no ontological status, only an iconographic one' (p. 129). Far from representing Eve's counterpart or perfect partner, Tristessa constitutes in fact a glamorous reflection of Zero's monomania, his cinematic impersonation of the feminine exacting the same perpetuation of traditional gender roles as the latter's punitive battering of his wives. In fact, the very circumstance that Tristessa, like Zero (or Evelyn, for that matter), has sought refuge in the arid depths of the desert should suffice to alert us to 'the awfully ineradicable quality of his maleness' (p. 173). Far from defiant or subversive, Tristessa's masquerade as 'the perfect man's woman' (p. 128) is solidly embedded in the binarist structures that inform traditional sex and gender formations. Hence, his death becomes a necessary prerequisite for Eve's freedom to conceive (of) a genuinely new future, 'a new child, a new America, a new type of text . . . standing as a challenge to systems of entrapment' (Ledwon 1993: 39). To Eve, the old oppositional boundaries can mean but little as they freely intersect and blur on the experimental body of her liminal existence. Maleness and femaleness, masculinity and femininity, overlap here, even exert an influence, but they never manifest themselves as absolute epistemic certainties or symbolic structuring principles of human nature:

> Masculine and feminine are correlatives which involve one another. I am sure of that – the quality and its negation are locked in necessity. But what the nature of masculine and the nature of feminine might be, whether they involve male and female, if they have anything to do with Tristessa's so long neglected apparatus or my own factory fresh incision and engine-turned breasts, that I do not know. Though I have been both man and woman, still I do not know the answer to these questions. Still they bewilder me. (pp. 149–50)

Unlike Iain Banks's *The Wasp Factory*, Angela Carter's *The Passion of New Eve* aims not at a devolutionary empowerment of the subject to re-engender herself on her own terms, but at a radical departure from all knowledgeable sites of socio-historical interpellation, be they super-imposed or speciously self-authenticated. The novel seems driven by

Carter's desire to see humankind arrive at a state of pristine gynandricity, purged of gender and hence unencumbered by ideological inscription. Eve's narrative is geared towards a deliberately inconclusive point of embarkation at which wo/man-made artifice prepares to reconsign its destiny to the potential vicissitudes of its own indeterminate nature as 'Eve and Adam *both*' (p. 165; my emphasis). The reader witnesses a wo/man's struggle out of symbolic violence towards a moment of utopian initiative that holds the promise of salvaging the conception of a new kind of human being from the charted enclosures of given sex and gender formations.

Significantly, Carter's novel represents only the prologue to a story that remains to be told, a story that lies as yet hidden beyond the horizon of human conceivability. The apocalyptic demise of history does not simply make way for a celebration of her story, the story of New Eve. Rather, without envisaging a clear-cut destination for her protagonist or projecting a new world order, Carter lifts the pressure of emplotment to see Eve off in a setting that could be both an ending and a beginning, a site of arrival and a point of departure. As Ledwon explains, the peculiar narrative zest of *The Passion of New Eve* consists in its resolute unwrapping of systemic authority which results in a proliferation of hitherto unprecedented emancipatory potential. 'The New Eve's immersion in a series of symbolic systems and her sufferings under those systems leads not so much to any kind of "success" as we know it', Ledwon writes, 'as to a radical and ironic questioning of all systems' (Ledwon 1993: 30). In this respect, Carter's novel could perhaps also be read as a utopian configuration of the hope expressed by Butler:

> If identities were no longer fixed as the premises of a political syllogism, and politics no longer understood as a set of practices derived from the alleged interests that belong to a set of ready-made subjects, a new configuration of politics would surely emerge from the ruins of the old. (Butler 1990: 149)

However, what may eventually spring from the vertiginous mixture of Evelyn's uncastrated genes, Eve's anatomical reassignment, and Tristessa's performative artifice is left to the reader's imagination. As the pregnant body of orphaned Eve is about to escape the dystopia of narrative closure, the union of transsexual mother and cross-dressing father is perhaps still as likely to produce a monster as a messiah.

10

·

This Stiff State Does Not Suit Man

·

Alasdair Gray's 1982 Janine

M IDDLE-AGED SCOTSMAN JOCK MacLeish, the first-person narrator of
Alasdair Gray's *1982 Janine*, resembles Evelyn, Carter's protagonist, in that both are presented to us as 'typical' men. 'I could be
hundreds of men just now' (p. 11), Jock explains at the beginning of
the novel. Gray's narrative, like Carter's, is concerned with one man's
gradual departure from the behavioural traits of the masculine norm,
focusing on his problematic rediscovery of the bodily as well as psychic
complexity of himself as a human rather than one-dimensionally gendered being. Jock, characterised by one critic as 'a thoroughgoing Jekyll
and Hyde' (Boyd 1991: 109), must somehow learn to suspend and
distance himself from the manifold processes of psychic splitting that
continue to divorce him from the sensual, nurturant and passionate
aspects of his self. Only if Jock manages to retrieve and wholeheartedly
embrace his repressed alterity does he stand a chance to emancipate
himself from patriarchal man's monologic self-confinement.

Being a man has seriously affected Jock's emotional maturation and
brought his life to a virtual standstill. The ensuing tedium and insufferable
monomania find symptomatic relief in a compulsive reiteration of self-
aggrandising masturbatory fantasies of mastery and control. Unprecedented in its self-conscious, scrupulous honesty, *1982 Janine* represents a
male author's exposure of traditional masculinity as little more than
delirious, automatised self-abuse. Patriarchal man is portrayed as permanently engaged in a pathetic wrangle with his own inadequacies and
insecurities, eliciting a quandary that, in itself, would perhaps be hardly
worth our attention. However, man's paranoid fear of impotence and
inferiority tends to find a dangerous outlet in wrecking the lives of women

and other men; it poses in fact – so Gray asserts – an existential threat to the survival of all of us as a species.

Gray is clearly in favour of a radical deconstruction of hegemonic gender formations as envisaged and pursued by contemporary feminisms and, despite all his blatant shortcomings as a man severely disabled by the masculine role, Jock seems principally ready to reconstruct himself. Unlike Evelyn in *The Passion of New Eve,* Jock experiences masculinity not as a continuous triumphant celebration of the self's prowess, independence and superiority but as a neurotic affliction effecting violence, guilt and psychic self-mutilation. Jock's masculinity hurts, even more so because a deep-seated horror of emasculation – compounded by a lack of viable alternatives of manly being that would not find their foothold in vicious circles of sado-masochistic power relations – debars him from ever productively re-imagining himself. He seeks out his ex-girlfriend Sontag's feminist counsel but chronically fails to even try to act upon her advice. Moreover, although he protests that he is 'not a bad man . . . but a good man' (p. 57) and quite obviously finds it hard to identify with the image of man as an oppressor and natural born rapist, more than half of his narrative consists of a graphic description of exploitative fantasies of torturing and systematically humiliating a select group of women, whose most prominent member is the eponymous Janine. Desensitised and intellectually debilitated by excessive drinking, Jock continues to suppress his discontent with the vacuity of his life in self-indulgent projections of extremely misogynous violence for which, when sober, he seems incapable of forgiving himself. Ironically, his adamant refusal to recognise himself as 'a representative of general male swinishness' (Boyd 1991: 113) causes him to become just that. Dodging the inward gaze of responsible self-interrogation, Jock fails to awaken to himself by identifying, and resisting, his condition as a typically masculine, patriarchally determined dilemma.

As William Harrison points out, 'Jock's long alcoholic decline corresponds with his employment by and integration into the military-industrial complex' (Harrison 1995: 164). Far from being a free, independent agent Jock, a supervisor for security installations, represents an exploitative system based on a rigidly organised hierarchy of power that renders the individual male at once a perpetrator and victim of systemic oppression. According to David Stenhouse, Jock 'has absorbed the political structures which characterise his working life to such an extent that even his name (McLeash) represents constraint and control' (Stenhouse 1996: 115). It is perhaps equally significant to take note of his family name's constitutive patronymic prefix ('son of') as an index of Jock's at once

privileged and subordinate position within the symbolic order of patriarchal relations. In *1982 Janine* Gray sets out to explore the predicament
of an unremarkable, average male who, like Kurtz in *Heart of Darkness*,
seems irreparably damaged by his loss of youthful idealism, yet who,
unlike his renowned predecessor, never musters the courage to run out of
systemic control and achieve (anti-)heroic greatness for himself. Jock's
exceedingly claustrophobic entrapment could not possibly be any more
pronounced had he been straitjacketed and left to lose his mind in the
solitary-confinement unit of a high-security prison. In fact, one gets the
impression that to Gray such an image would seem quite an appropriate illustration of Jock's lamentable condition as an unreconstructed,
pre-feminist man.

Still, despite the hopeless state he finds himself in, Jock balks at
confronting and constructively devising possible strategies of resistance
to his dilemma. Paralysed by the imperative, non-negotiable demands of
his public persona, Gray's protagonist comes to ventriloquise the monologue of the phallus that in solipsistic bliss continues to discourse solely
with and upon itself. Conspicuously, Jock's masturbatory fantasies never
seem to answer, let alone satisfy, a deep-seated physical or emotional
need. Rather, by preventing Jock's voyeuristic gaze from ever closely
zooming in on himself, they constitute the corollary of an ideologically
motivated automatism designed not only to divert but to erase the
articulation of individual desire. The underlying logic is simple: while
permanently frustrated arousal and a traumatic fear of ultimate impotence shackle and enslave the individual, orgasm – and orgasm experienced in a loving embrace especially – would effect at least a temporary
release. Also, since it is imperative to keep the monumentality of the
phallus uncompromised by the subversive weaknesses of the individual
flesh, a man's body is considered perfect only as long as it is hard and
erect. This means that the emotionality of a man like Jock must remain
inarticulate lest it radiate its emasculating influence and irremediably
destabilise the masculine standard. When finally Jock's interiority threatens to surface, suicide appears to be the only valid response. It seems as
if only a radical disembodiment and complete elimination of feeling can
ultimately safeguard the traditional, phallic iconography of man.

Jock has been brought up systematically to unlearn behaviour that
used to come naturally to him as a boy. As a reward for this feat of
remarkable self-discipline he claims to be entitled to cultivate fantasies of
whatever he desires, no matter if these are contemptuous of or demean-
ing to other people and women especially. 'Since the age of thirteen I
have not shed a single tear', Jock declares. 'Surely, inside the privacy of

this body and the secrecy of this skull I have earned the right to enjoy any woman I want in any way I can?' (p. 57). Little does he realise at this point that his abuse of imaginary women is in fact symptomatic of his own violently repressed condition. Significantly, the manly, solitary independence of Jock, and other men of his kind, only gives rise to feelings of profound loneliness and angst. As Sontag points out to Jock, 'you have no friends, only colleagues and an occasional one-night stand with women as lonely as you are' (p. 52). As it turns out, this loneliness is not a random but perfectly functional result of man's systemic conditioning. The individual man's isolation constitutes the bedrock of patriarchy. His ensuing paranoia and desperate need to belong make him extremely susceptible to the allure of manifold processes of integrative systemic advancement that appear to hold the key to an exclusive, almost ersatz-heroic sphere of homosocial bonding. Only much later when, as in Jock's case, one's loyalty and total identification with systemic power are revealed to have never been more than an expedient means to an expedient end, do disenchantment and a deep sense of acute meaninglessness set in:

> I am not a man, I am an instrument.
>
> I am the instrument of a firm which installs instruments to protect the instruments of firms which produce meat cloth machines and whisky, instruments to feed, dress, move and stupefy us. But the National [Securities Ltd] installs most of its instruments around nuclear reactors – instruments powering the instruments which light, heat and entertain us – and banks – instruments to protect and increase the profits of the instrument owners – and military depots where the weapons are kept which protect the nation's instruments and profits from the protective instruments of the Russian instrument-makers. Mirrors reflecting mirrors are the whole show? No. Instruments serving instruments are the whole show. (p. 105)

At the same time as we get the impression that it would perhaps take just one man to break the circle, Gray alerts us to the fact that the patriarchal processing of young boys into instruments of power has become institutionalised to such a degree that their emotional atrophy almost appears to be the result of a natural, inevitable development. As Jock reflects on his (de)formative experiences with Mad Hislop, his teacher, 'the more I think of my childhood the queerer it seems although it was perfectly ordinary' (p. 54). 'To produce that steady glare of hatred which proved he had made the thing he called a man' (p. 85), Hislop never tires of maltreating the boys in his class whom he addresses as 'nothing but a bunch of big lassies' (p. 54). However, Hislop himself is only a remote-controlled instrument of patriarchal oppression, badly scarred by his past as a soldier and prisoner-of-war and totally dependent for emotional sustenance on his paralysed, bedridden wife. When she dies, his mask of dutiful authority momentarily falls off him, revealing not 'a monster' but a 'small, lonely and haggard, very ordinary and dismal' man (p. 84).

While Gray remains reluctant to exonerate the individual man from the burden of taking responsibility for his life, his critique is clearly interested in highlighting the roots of masculine self-deformation in the perversity of society's political unconscious, from which absolutely no one can claim to be exempt. 'Women don't despise themselves for weeping, why do they admire men who won't or can't?', Jock laments. 'Why are so many of them attracted by bullies and killers? Why are so many MEN attracted by bullies and killers? Shit. Shit. Shit. Shit. Shit. Shit. Shit' (p. 85). In this context, Gray's most poignant indictment of the system's straitjacketing, deadly grip on individual life – and its organised pressure on men to live up to a dehumanising ideal especially – can be found in his description of the suffering of young soldiers in World Wars I and II:

> Behind them was an organisation which shot them as deserters if they turned round and walked away, and behind that organisation stood their mothers/ fathers/sisters/girlfriends/the newspapers/British Industry/Capital/ Labour/The Church/The Law/The Government/The King/The Empire saying: 'Go forward lad! It's your duty! Only you can save us from being raped and plundered by those German boys in the trench before you.'
>
> (p. 128)

Clearly, gender is not simply a natural given informing the social and sexual intercourse of men and women; it is a political tool of ideological indoctrination by which every single one of us is allocated a certain inescapable role within the patriarchal order of things. As long as we obey this bio-logic of sex, we will continue to act not as independent men and women in pursuit of a fulfilment of their individual desires, but as remote-controlled, expediently (de)formed variables in an equation of supra-individual interests of power.

The personal is always of necessity political. As Jock declares at one point, 'I would like to ignore politics but POLITICS WILL NOT LET ME ALONE. Everything I know, everything I am has been permitted or buggered up by some sort of political entanglement' (pp. 231–2). Sex is never secondary to our lives but constitutes the matrix in which our selves originate. Rather than making us human, it holds the capacity of dehumanising us, rendering us automatons or mere structuring principles in the service of a totalitarianist regime of 'nature'. As Angela

Carter suggests, reduced to its most basic, pornographic axiomatic, sex deprives men and women of their humanity, a circumstance perhaps best illustrated by 'the ambivalence of the word "to fuck", in its twinned meanings of sexual intercourse and despoliation: "a fuck-up", "to fuck something up", "he's fucked"' (Carter 1979: 27). In their pornographic totality, the non-egalitarian dynamics of 'fucking' make an ideal blueprint of the politics of patriarchal capitalism whose main representatives and agents – depersonalised, paranoid and motivated solely by the ethos of masculine domination – are men. Against this background, Gray's deployment of sexual imagery in his pithy summary of World Wars I and II may seem not just apt but positively inspired. 'In 1914 and 1939', he writes, 'the big industrial nations, having fucked the rest of the planet (in the vulgar sense of the word) started wanking all over each other. None of them enjoyed it but they could not stop' (p. 151).

Since its first publication, *1982 Janine* has repeatedly been accused of comprising gratuitously detailed descriptions of the exploitation of women as objects of male sexual gratification. It is quite astonishing how, despite Gray's reputation as an incorrigibly mischievous postmodernist, his second novel could so triumphantly succeed in provoking reviewers and critics alike to divulge their own inveterate prudery and disingenuous conservatism. As David Stenhouse asserts, 'to characterise a novel which deals with pornography and fantasy as a piece of pornography itself is an example of critical and cultural illiteracy' (Stenhouse 1996: 113). True, *1982 Janine* does contain degradingly stereotyped representations of women (Janine, Superb, Helga, Big Momma), yet its ultimate objective is clearly neither the author's nor the reader's titillation or quick and easy gratification. Jock's projection of a never-ending sequence of sexual conquests invariably concludes with a deeply frustrated sense of defeat, painfully exacerbated by his realisation that no matter how many women he manages to consume, he will always remain 'absolutely alone' (p. 55). His horror of post-orgasmic tristesse becomes so intense that he acquires the skill of delaying ejaculation virtually *ad infinitum*. Giving in to the eventual inevitability of orgasm is a sign of weakness and loss of control, a hazardous moment of emasculation. Jock's 'illusion of ABSOLUTE MASTERY which real life has never never never allowed [him] in any way whatsoever' (p. 43) lasts only as long as his penis stays erect. Its inevitable detumescence testifies to its fallibility which, in turn, becomes emblematic of Jock's own shamefully inadequate attempts at emulating the phallic ideal.

Jock has manoeuvred himself into an inescapable Foucauldian trap. The part of his life that he considers the least circumscribed and repressed is also the site on which he surrenders most willingly to remote control and self-alienation. Seeking relief from societal pressure Jock withdraws into a prison-house of strictly anti-therapeutic, phantasmatic narratives of power that serve to recharge, rather than relax or question, his instrumentality. What seems to him a talking cure reveals itself as a talking curse instead. His mind is inundated by blue movies not of his own imaginative inscription but reeled off by the internalised propaganda machines of systemic surveillance. The unfolding of individual, potentially subversive desire is obstructed by a never-ending supply of pornographic stereotypes of lust and gratification borrowed from the ideological archives of society's political unconscious. Not very surprisingly, Jock is extremely slow at unravelling the axiomatic contradictions that inform his psychological make-up and cause it to be permanently at odds with itself. 'I am attracted by most of the women I meet, I fear and despise most of the men', he notes, 'yet I am excited by fantasies of worlds where men have total control' (p. 68). Only gradually does he come to realise that his faculties of reflection have become seriously impaired by systematic reflexes learned rather than inborn. What he regards as manifestations of individual desire turn out to be patriarchally sanctioned phantasmagoria of megalomaniacal, masculine compulsion.

Against this background it becomes evident that Gray's novel is far removed from pornography of the salacious, sleazy top-shelf variety. Rather, it represents a genuine enquiry not only into the reasons for Jock's addiction to misogynous representations of sexual intercourse, but also the general tendency within society to mystify sex as a politically innocuous leisure activity that ought to remain private and therefore exempt from artistic or intellectual probing, which is often categorically rejected as gratuitous, prurient and intrusive. Apart from shedding light on the injurious impact of traditional gender formations on individual men and women, Gray's portrayal of a 'typical' man also seeks to disclose, fathom and suggest remedies for the trauma of sexism. Institutionalised sexism not only obstructs a mutually fulfilling coming together of the sexes but moreover threatens to sabotage even the most well-intentioned attempts at establishing peaceful understanding, rather than conflictual strife and binarist oppositioning, as the political principle of worldwide communal interaction. Like Carter, Gray appears convinced that 'sexual relations between men and women always render explicit the nature of social relations in the society in which they take place and, if described explicitly, will form a critique of those relations' (Carter 1979: 20). In this respect, Gray epitomises the moral pornographer Carter characterises in *The Sadeian Woman*:

A moral pornographer might use pornography as a critique of current relations between the sexes. His business would be the total demystification of the flesh and the subsequent revelation, through the infinite modulations of the sexual act, of the real relations between man and his kind. Such a pornographer would not be the enemy of women, perhaps because he might begin to penetrate to the heart of the contempt for women that distorts our culture even as he entered the realms of the obscenity as he describes it.

(pp. 19–20)

1982 Janine is concerned with the increasingly introspective dynamics that lead Jock to identify the cherished masturbatory 'I' of his voyeuristic fantasies as a miniature replica of the ubiquitous supra-individual eye of sexist stereotyping, pornographic remote control and ideological surveillance. Only once he has apprehended his supposedly private self as a mirror image of phallic masculinity's totalitarian monomania can he instigate the long, arduous processes of reconstructive disassociation and reassemblage that are geared towards making him 'a new man [or] not exactly the same man, anyway' (p. 340). Only then can he face up to himself as a human being twisted out of shape by the interpellative imperatives of his sex and admit to himself, without losing all hope of a viable future, that 'I am a bad man, I am what is wrong with the world, I am a tyrant, I am a weakling, I never gave them what they wanted, I grabbed all I could get' (p. 67).

It seems significant to remark that in this context Gray exploits and shrewdly deconstructs Scottish literature's penchant for a representation of divided personalities in the manner of Dr Jekyll and Mr Hyde. Notably, in Jock's case, it is the public persona that invades and corrupts the self. What Jock cherishes as illicit fantasies are in actual fact insidious measures of ideological conditioning and normative self-(de)formation. In contrast, the emergence of unpredictable, subversive Mr Hyde, an embodiment of the repressed, would have to be regarded as the assertive manifestation of a self as yet uncontaminated by societal programming, that is, as a vigorous, utopian herald of the return and fulfilment of individual desire. Intriguingly, in its celebration of the individual person's subversive potential, *1982 Janine* could also be read as an inspired rewrite of George Orwell's renowned dystopia, which one would in this context be tempted to re-title as '1984 Julia'. In both novels, the masculine self is portrayed as intolerably straitjacketed by totalitarianist constraints, eventually confronting itself in a claustrophobic, sado-masochistic encounter as potentially both an abject victim and complicitous perpetrator of despotic power. More significantly perhaps, in both novels the initiation of subversive desire emanates from the female. In *Nineteen Eighty-Four*, it is

Julia, Winston's lover – memorably characterised as 'only a rebel from the waist downwards' (Orwell 1989: 163) – whom Orwell portrays as the embodiment of desire. In *1982 Janine*, it is the eponymous heroine who, at the very end of the novel, unexpectedly affronts her tormentors instead of continuing to collude in her pornographic misrepresentation as a voyeuristic spectacle of sexist oppression: '"Act calm," thinks Janine. "Pretend this is just an ordinary audition." And then she thinks, "Hell no! Surprise them. Shock them. Show them more than they ever expected to see"' (p. 341).

1982 Janine falls in two halves divided by Chapter 11 as a crucial, pivotal turning point. Unable to bear the stale repetitiveness of his existence any longer, Jock takes an overdose of sleeping pills and temporarily slips into a delirious, semi-conscious state from which he re-emerges as a purged and newly born man, resolved now 'to tell truthfully how he reached this pointless place in order to say Goodbye to it and go elsewhere' (p. 191). The latter part of the novel takes the form of an autobiographical confession investigating 'the story [of] *how I went wrong* . . . called From the Cage to the Trap' (p. 191). Gray emulates the techniques and devices of what has become widely known as *écriture féminine* to indicate that Jock is now ready to extricate himself from the monologue of the phallus that dominates traditional modes of masculine self-representation. As Hélène Cixous explains, it would be fallacious to understand *écriture féminine* in strictly gender-specific terms as feminine or even female writing. In fact, she stresses that the concept aims 'at getting rid of words like "feminine" and "masculine" . . . which designate that which cannot be classified inside of a signifier except by force and violence' (Conley 1984: 129). It may thus be more beneficial to translate *écriture féminine* in less gender-specific terms as non-patriarchal or anti-logocentric writing. According to Cixous, however, still absolutely crucial for this mode of subversive self-expression would be the palpable textual manifestation of 'a decipherable libidinal femininity' (Conley 1984: 129).

Pertinently, in Chapter 11 Jock is saved from certain death by the intervention of a force explicitly designated as female, opening up a striking parallel to Evelyn's female-authored rescue from total narrative exhaustion in *The Passion of New Eve*. Reminiscent of Cixous's concept of a 'libidinal femininity', this force is depicted as whisking our man off the beaten dead-end track of his self-destructive masculinity and taking him through to a new, hitherto unheard-of destination:

The car, veering and twisting between the treetrunks, followed no track but went smoothly by going very fast. It skimmed through bracken-clumps and crossed ditches and hedges without the slightest jolt. I felt recklessly happy, recklessly sure of the driver's skill. *She* was driving dangerously but well, I knew I would laugh aloud and still love her if the car crashed. (p. 191; my emphasis)

Suggesting that what happens to Jock both before and during his break-down constitutes quite a typical masculine predicament, Madeleine Gagnon writes that within patriarchy 'man confronts himself constantly. He pits himself against and stumbles over his erected self' (Gagnon 1981: 180). However, although it represents possibly as much a gesture of ultimate manly self-assertion as a genuine effort at escape, in Gray's novel Jock's suicide attempt entails purely positive repercussions. Not only does it eventuate the first step in his gradual emancipation from the masculine standard; it also offers him an alternative mode of self-expression – that of *écriture féminine* – in whose exuberant, curative chaos he is at once to lose and fruitfully regain his senses.

According to Ann Rosalind Jones, *écriture féminine* designates a 'semiotic style . . . likely to involve repetitive, spasmodic separations from the dominating discourse' (Jones 1986: 363). This style ignores grammatical constraints, preferring a rhythmic, poetic, gestural mode to a logical sequence of referential objectivity. Control, power and truth as the standards of symbolic expression give way to a polyphonic chorus of voices courting a semantic climax, or *jouissance*, that manifests itself in orgasmic, deliberately out-of-control, verbal diffusion. At the beginning of Chapter 11, Gray's appropriation of *écriture féminine* is still quite tentative. Gray deploys the rather conventional image of rider and horse, for instance, to hint at the solid embedment of Jock's thinking in the Cartesian *cogito* of hierarchical oppositioning. Thus, typically, Jock does not refrain from deeply misogynous condescension in his reference to Denny, the first (and perhaps only true) love of his life, as a 'sturdy wee compliant pony, a lovely ride' (p. 175). He even describes his own suicide in terms of a hierarchical relationship between the mind and body: 'Jolly Jimmy Body has been slipped a Mickey Finn by his aristocratic jockey Melancholy Montague Mind and before sunrise both will drop out of the human race damn' (p. 174). However, from the very beginning of the chapter a different mode of representation is preparing to unleash itself. Word formations like 'easy-oasy' and 'okey-dokey' (p. 174), for example, appear to be inserted in the narrative solely for their euphonic delect-ability rather than any purposeful design of stringent meaning-making.

The rigid martial monotony of Jock's narrative voice is undermined and eventually superseded by the beating of his heart. Surprised, he notes that 'the pains are rhythmical, *dradadumba dradadumba*, a change from our old friend dradadum' (p. 177). Finally, Jock's received mode of self-representation explodes into a welter of pure heteroglot nonsense that threatens to proliferate beyond his control. This sudden upsurge of unbound significatory energies Jock can only dam in by abruptly return-ing to the definitive differences and equations that together constitute symbolic language:

> Queer feelings queer words are abroad in me, words like Chimborazo Cotopaxi Kilimanjaro Kanchenjunga Fujiyama Nagasaki Mount Vesuvius Lake Lugano Portobello Ballachulish Corrievrechan Ecclefechan Armaged-don Marsellaise Guillotine Leningrad Stalingrad Ragnorok Skaggerak Sur le pont d'Avignon Agincourt Bannockburn Cavalry Calvary Calgary Wounded Knee Easterhouse Drumchapel Maryhill West Kilbride Castlemilk Mother-well Hunterston terminal megawatt kilowatt dungaree overall kilowatt equals one-point-three-four horsepower I'm back to dradadum. (p. 177)

Jock's traditional masculine subjectivity – monologic, coherent, self-contained – eventually comes under close scrutiny in a section entitled 'The Ministry of Voices' where his self splinters into the three discrete Freudian components of superego, ego and id – represented by three typographically distinct columns – that are shown to vie for space and predominance over the next eight pages. Although initially the voice of the male ego launches into a vociferous attempt at re-inscribing its autonomy and independence, there is no doubt that its status and general influence are undergoing quickly accelerating, unstoppable processes of decline. Traditional structuring principles like syntax and punctuation that served to buttress the male ego's cultivation of self-aggrandising fantasies give in to the free, continuous flow of an originary stream of consciousness. In vain does Jock urge its audience to 'ignore the couple signalling from the wings everyone wants into the act but I am boss here I am the director' (p. 178). The male ego's hitherto uncontested hegemony has begun to disintegrate irreparably. It is forced to realise that it is, and has in fact always been, 'queer as a coot' (p. 180), tautly hemmed in by the behavioural straitjackets of a soul-destroying, maddening norm:

> hate sex hate my sex I can
> play no game in this tight
> suit doesn't fit cant move
> I shit stick stiffen stink
> I hate to sit in *this stiff*
> *state does not suit man*
> woman brutebird turdword
> name echoes fact act same
> verb as noun I shit my shit

> I ache my ache I dream my
> dream I scream my scream
> is an echo echo echolalia
> lovely echolalia name of
> brain diseeeeeeeeeeeeeeeeease
> (p. 182; my emphasis)

The most interesting element in 'The Ministry of Voices' is certainly the figure of God whom Jock erroneously believes to be identical with the superego of patriarchal rule. God assures Jock that he is 'no king judge director inspector supervisor landlord general manager or any kind of master no expert computer planner lawyer accountant clergyman policeman teacher doctor father who is cruel to be kind' (pp. 179–80). Rather, he incorporates 'light air daily bread common human warmth ordinary ground that drinks every stain takes back all who fall renews all who have not poisoned their seed' (pp. 180–1). God is no 'extraterrestrial Big Daddy who would one day screw up the earth like bumpaper and flush it down the stank' but 'the small glimmer of farseeing, intelligent kindliness which, properly strengthened and shared, will light us to a better outcome' (p. 314). In short, so Gray insists, the basic (meta)physical principle of life is communal in nature rather than self-centred and hence more in tune with what is traditionally construed as feminine. It appears that in order to legitimate their strictly hierarchical organisation of power, patriarchal societies have re-inscribed the face of God in their own image as that of a violent, monomaniacal bully, although in actual fact – according to Jock's flippant remark later in the chapter – he appears to be 'more like Groucho Marx or a critical housewife than the Universal Framemaker' (p. 194).

God's masculinity is a patriarchal projection; his true essence is revealed as gynandric: 'i [*sic*] split myself in two in making you' (p. 184). Perhaps God's omnipresent benignity is best signified by his refusal ever to capitalise (on) his supreme subjectivity. God unequivocally disassociates himself from his monumental image as the ultimate patriarch. Moreover, he reassures Jock that there is nothing biologically wrong with him. Not maleness but relentless conditioning within the order of patriarchal capitalism has reduced him to the deplorable state he currently finds himself in: 'listen not bad nature i [*sic*] am nature but the dull habits of a bad job make you nothing nobody a tool blunted by deliberate stupidity' (p. 184). Jock comes to realise that 'it is ignorance of my own nature which has made me an easy tool in the hands of others' (p. 195), hinting at the emergence of a kind of masculine self-consciousness missed so sorely ever since Walton in *Frankenstein* stated that 'there is something at work in my soul, which I do not understand' (Shelley 1992: 30).

Wedged in between the voices of God and its own body, Jock's ego approaches a cathartic crisis point. The urgency of its cry for help is accentuated by dint of a gradually contracting typographic design reminiscent of the religious hour-glass poetry of George Herbert and Dylan Thomas. As the discrete boundaries of the transcendent and physical begin to encroach upon it, the traditional phallogocentric certainties of the masculine subject falter and collapse. Intriguingly, it is Jock's body that saves him from suicide by taking control and revolting against his masculine verbosity. Having borne more than it can stomach, the body releases itself from the ego's death-bound strategies of self-assertion quite simply by throwing up. Coinciding with both the body's self-cleansing and God's final words of hope and comfort, Jock's monologue finally concludes on a consensual note of perfect unison, its final orgasmic 'o yea yeaaa yeaaaaaa . . .' (p. 185) curiously reverberating with Molly Bloom's affirmation of feminine subjectivity at the end of James Joyce's *Ulysses*. The dialogic excesses of 'The Ministry of Voices' are complemented by a period of restorative sleep, represented by three blank pages, after which Jock's narrative reconstitutes itself into a new order markedly inspired by its previous immersion in the regenerative chaos of *écriture féminine*.

While still precariously at risk of relapsing into his old habit of conjuring up positions of phantasmatic power for himself, in the latter half of *1982 Janine* Jock is seriously trying to pursue and act upon his newly gained insights into both his patriarchal conditioning and his often volitional complicity in the manifold exploits of systemic oppression. Most significant in this context seems his realisation that both the private and public lives of men and women are determined by the politics of pornographic discourse. Including himself, albeit as yet quite reluctantly, Jock describes technological men as 'lunatics who fuck and neglect everything in reach which has given them strength and confidence' (p. 313). For the first time also, Jock self-consciously probes the premises of his narration. Unlike Marlow in *Heart of Darkness*, for example, he acknowledges the blatant misogyny of his gaze, identifying it as a projective reflex that has its roots in an unspeakable horror of the reality of his own inferiority, inadequacy and failure. His seemingly incorrigible predilection for the pornographic is made to undergo a rigorous self-analysis. Contemplating the nature of his masturbatory fantasies, which invariably feature woman as a sexist stereotype 'corrupted into enjoying her bondage and trapping others into it', Jock comes to comprehend 'that this was the story of my own life' and that he has so far conveniently concealed this truth from himself 'by insisting on the *femaleness* of the main character' (p. 193).

Towards the end of the novel, Jock increasingly identifies with the potentially subversive position of feminine marginality. Intent upon re-entering and exerting an influence on the course of his story, he resolves to emancipate himself and eventually resigns from his job:

> For more than twenty-five years . . . I was a character in a script written by National Security. That script governed my main movements, and thereby my emotions . . . I made myself completely predictable so that the firm could predict me. I stopped growing, stopped changing. I helped the firm grow, instead of me. (p. 333)

When Jock finally bursts into tears, the narrative of *1982 Janine* once again gives way to a mode of representation that seeks to reconcile the physical with the verbal in an immediate merger of experience and expression. It is here, at the very end of the novel, that Gray puts into practice the principles of *écriture féminine* most effectively, consigning the articulation of Jock's emotionality to a pure writing from the body. His tears materialise as printed words on the page. Moreover, in yet another decisively anti-logocentric move, Jock refrains from encapsulating what is happening to him in unequivocal, definitive terms. 'What is this queer slight bright fluttering sensation as if a thing weighted down for a long time was released and starting, a little, to stir?', he ponders and immediately inter-jects, 'Don't name it. Let it grow' (p. 340). He seems afraid of this new development inside of him being captured and thereby halted or crushed.

Importantly, according to Kaja Silverman's investigation in *Masculine Subjectivity at the Margins*, 'to re-encounter femininity from within a male body is . . . to live it no longer as disenfranchisement and subordination, but rather as phallic divestiture, as a way of saying "no" to power' (Silverman 1992: 389). In this light, the ending of Gray's novel clearly features Jock as a newly born man, an unpredictable *sujet en procès*, determined in future to resist the joint impact of patriarchal condition-ing and unwholesome masculine conformity. Also, rather than being yet again conjured as an object of exploitative desire, Janine's femininity is now invoked as an irresistible emancipatory principle of counter-discursive guidance and inspiration:

> I will stand on the platform an hour from now, briefcase in hand, a neater figure than most but not remarkable. I will have the poise of an acrobat about to step on to a high wire, of an actor about to take the stage in a wholly new play. Nobody will guess what I am going to do. I do not know it myself. But I will not do nothing. No, I will not do nothing. Oh Janine, my silly soul, come to me now. I will be gentle. I will be kind. (p. 341)

Compared to *The Passion of New Eve*, Gray's envisioning of a radical re-invention of masculinity seems to constitute more of a political, real-life challenge in that it does not project change into a utopian, ahistorical future outside of the very real – if no doubt mythically informed – restrictive parameters of present sex and gender formations. Jock is bound to continue living in this world. He can jump neither out of his own skin nor out of culture. Thus, he cannot avoid negotiating discursive practices of signification as he finds them, not as he would ideally like them to be. In this respect, Gray appears to be in agreement with Judith Butler's understanding of gender subversion as a slow, hazardous and highly complicated enterprise entirely dependent for its success on the strength of every single individual's commitment and determination. 'The task is not whether to repeat [discursive practices]', Butler writes, 'but how to repeat or, indeed, to repeat and, through a radical prolif- eration of gender, *to dislocate* the very gender norms that enable the repetition in itself' (Butler 1990: 148). Jock seems ideally equipped for this task because, while he has changed, this may not be immediately obvious to others who may still be inclined to mistake him for the man he used to be. As David Gutterman suggests,

> whereas women and gay men often are forced to seek to dismantle the categories of gender and sexuality from culturally ordained positions of the "other", profeminist men can work to dismantle the system from posi- tions of power by challenging the very standards that afford them normative status in the culture. (Gutterman 1994: 229)

As far as Jock is concerned, there seem virtually no limits to the ways in which he could, if he so wished, infiltrate the strongholds of patriarchal authority and, once inside, subvert them from within.

However, the greatest counterdiscursive achievement of *1982 Janine* appears to reside in Jock's departure from what Mark Justad designates as 'the "phallusization" of the male body' (Justad 1996: 363) – a departure that constitutes a crucial first step towards a conceptualisation of new, post-patriarchal masculinities. As Justad outlines, 'in the West the body and those "others" associated with the *mater*-ial, have effectively been assigned to the realm of the female and feminine' (Justad 1996: 362). In *1982 Janine*, Gray commendably resists this axiomatic by reso- lutely and constructively re-embodying masculine narration. His self- conscious implementation of the techniques and devices of *écriture féminine* leads him not only to 'begin to address the privileges historically asso- ciated with the disembodied, masculine, male' (Justad 1996: 363) but also to disclose the enormous human detriment to which these privileges used to be – and are still being – won, maintained and passed on.

11

·

The Dark Continent of Masculinity

·

Irvine Welsh's Marabou Stork Nightmares

I N *MARABOU STORK NIGHTMARES* Irvine Welsh graphically portrays the impact patriarchal imperatives, norms and ideals exert on the psychological disposition of an underprivileged working-class youth, Roy Strang from Muirhouse, a council estate on the outskirts of Edinburgh. Excluded from the privileges of power that in patriarchy serve to consolidate masculine superiority, Welsh's structurally emasculated anti-hero finds himself under enormous pressure to assert himself as a man. To Roy, physical violence often seems the only instrument by which he can command the respect he deems himself entitled to as a man. It seems as if the more precarious and insecure a youth's masculine status, the likelier it becomes that he should overcompensate and resort not only to violence but, like Alex in *A Clockwork Orange*, to 'ultraviolence'. The world Roy lives in is ravaged by a continuous battle for superiority and power. Men do not fight for a fulfilment of their ideals; rather, fighting becomes its own cause, determining a man's social rank as either a winner or a loser. And whoever emerges as a winner today, may find himself defeated and utterly crushed tomorrow.

Power, which 'always goes on and on until it finds its limits' (p. 219), becomes the main driving force in Roy's life, infiltrating and corrupting all his other interests, principles and desires. As in Alasdair Gray's *1982 Janine*, if no doubt more bluntly, *Marabou Stork Nightmares* introduces us to a society thrashed and riven by the institutionalised politics of 'fucking'. Far from gratuitous, Welsh's use of strong, sexually explicit language pertains to his critique of hegemonic power relations that divide people, irrespective of their biological sex, into active 'men' and passive 'women', victors and victims, the powerful and the chronically disempowered. Rape and sexual(ised) violence constitute integrative, functional elements of patri-archal discourse and practice, best evidenced by the fact that the language of the law consistently echoes the attitude of the rapist: 'Put yourself in my hands and we'll give her damn good shafting, [the lawyer] said smugly, his smile crumbling around the edge of his mouth in realisation of a poor choice of metaphor' (p. 207). In this context, it also appears symptomatic that Roy should refer to his disadvantaged background in terms of rape and pillage as 'that fucked-up place which made me the fucked-up mess I was' (pp. 16–17). Within patriarchy, social deprivation connotes much more than the general stigmata of poverty, inferiority and failure. To men specifically, it signifies a state of emascu-lation, of violation and shameful impotence.

Since he can remember, Roy has been 'surrounded by latent and manifest violence' (p. 134), caught up in a vicious circle of abuse in which he 'batter[s] smaller/weaker kids [and in return gets] battered by bigger/stronger kids' (p. 21). Later, instead of initiating him to experi-ences of intimacy and togetherness, sex opens up yet another battle-ground on which the fighting/fucking continues. And yet, it seems facile to describe Roy, as Alan Freeman has done, as someone who suffers 'in an insensitive environment, where the patriarch is chief tormentor' (Freeman 1996: 137). In *Marabou Stork Nightmares* no one, not even John Strang, Roy's father, ever manages to consolidate his power and remain absolutely on top. Every victimiser is shown to have started life as a victim. Accusing Welsh of preferring sketchy, comic-book caricatures to plausible, fleshed-out characters, Freeman asks impatiently what 'we learn of John Strang's inner life, other than that he's a mad bastard' (Freeman 1996: 139). In fact we learn quite a lot. Rather than revealing the flawed and superficial nature of Welsh's characterisation, John's striking lack of interiority testifies to its skill and poignancy. Welsh's fiendish patriarch represents a case study in emotional atrophy, introdu-cing us to a man psychologically crippled by both personal experience and social conditioning. In a casual aside we are informed that John's 'old man had been put away for interfering with young boys' (p. 144), raising the question if it was sexual abuse by his father that turned John into a psychopath and Uncle Gordon, his brother, into the rapist of little Roy.

Forever translating violation into violence, abuse spawns abuse. One's own breakdown is successfully deferred by breaking others. Traumatised by Uncle Gordon's unforgivable breach of trust, Roy copes by victimis-ing an even younger boy at school who, contemptuously described as 'Dressed-By-His-Ma-Cunt' (p. 109), later in the novel briefly reappears as a muscle-bound thug. The young boy's innocence has grown a hard shell of experience constituting a love-proof apparatus exclusively aimed at pre-emptive defence. Across this non-negotiable, paranoically fortified boundary a man is led to view his own innermost desires as alien, smuggled-in devices designed to undermine and explode his hard-won masculine integrity from within. As a result, the irresistible other who, even if only potentially, triggers these desires is at once coveted and loathed, perceived as both a saviour and an unmanageable security risk. Hence, as regards Roy's rape of Kirsty at the dark centre of the novel, the cruelty and relentlessness of his assault are in fact indicative of his impossible longing to give himself up to his feelings for her, to court and love her. The embattled confines of the masculine psyche function as both a prison and a fortress. While promising to release Roy from his deep-rooted suffering and shame, love also threatens to emasculate him by disrupting his guise of self-contained security and power. In consequence, woman becomes the arch-enemy of man. To keep up masculine appearances and avoid a conflagration of the feminine inside of himself, Roy cannot but compulsively re-inscribe the (f)law of the father.

Welsh's novel seems written in direct response to one of its epigraphs which cites John Major on juvenile delinquency after the killing of little James Bulger by two ten-year-old boys in 1993: 'We must condemn a little more, and understand a little less'. Welsh clearly repudiates 'evil' as a satisfactory explanation for the seemingly self-perpetuating dynamics of angry young male violence. According to Welsh, evil is bred not born. In South Africa, freed of the stigma of class and newly privileged by the colour of his skin, eleven-year-old Roy 'could see possibilities' (p. 77), envisaging an academic career for himself as a zoologist. He obtains good grades at school and is commended by his teachers as highly promising university material. But 'the old man's piss-up blew that away' (p. 77) and the Strangs are deported back to the deprivation and hopelessness of dead-end Muirhouse. Importantly, Welsh never speculates that 'evil' and violence may be natural, inborn traits of the human male. In this respect his stance differs markedly from Blake Morrison's in *As If*, which gives a journalist's intimately personal account of the trial of Robert Thompson and Jon Venables, the child killers of James Bulger. Morrison writes that:

Boys beat boys up. Law of nature.
This was the climate I'd grown up in, where aggressors were the hero of every story. They weren't the headcases; the headcases were their victims,

requiring thirty or more stitches. Thirty years on, Robert and Jon grew up in the same culture. Northern, is it, this need for boys to show themselves hard? Not Northern, not British, not Western, perhaps not even human: fundamental to young males of most species. The social order, properly run, can help control their aggression. Non-violent role models might in time create a different kind of male. But instinct isn't easily quashed . . . (1997: 153)

According to Welsh, violence is not endemic to the male sex but to nature as a whole. Hence, what ultimately mars the cogency of Welsh's fathoming of the masculine psyche, and detracts from his enquiry into the origins of 'evil', is his fatalistic stance to the allegedly biological foundations of social injustice and inequality. Instead of initiating an open debate on the issues at stake, Welsh's employment of starkly reductive nature imagery forecloses the argument before it has properly begun. The problem is that Welsh seems all too ready to authorise and endorse John Strang's designation of 'the law ay the wild' (p. 74) as the most fundamental principle of human action and decision-making. As a result, the rape victim becomes a mere casualty of nature, her violated body resembling 'the unrecognisable corpse of an animal' half-eaten by vultures (p. 173). What would perhaps strike a more discerning and intellectually refined observer as a dystopian, man-made, and hence re-adjustable system is here presented as a primeval, natural, and thus ultimately inalterable truth.

Not only Thatcherite politics but human behaviour in general operates in Welsh's novel against the allegorical background of a group of ugly marabou storks slaughtering beautiful, Bambi-eyed flamingos. 'The world we live in is not run by cuddly, strong bears, graceful, sleek cats or loyal, friendly dogs', Roy asserts. 'Marabou Storks run this place, and they are known to be nasty bastards' (p. 55). This neo-Darwinist fable of a cruel and inexorable natural world eventually prompts Roy's profoundly demoralising insight that 'it was you against the world, every cunt knew that: the Government said it' (p. 165). Initially, Welsh's rendition of the Marabou Stork as a symbolic encapsulation of patriarchal tyranny internalised, and to be exorcised, by the individual male works very well. Roy must 'HUNT THE STORK, TO GET CONTROL' (p. 11) over his life. Aptly, he perceives the stork as 'the personification of all this badness. If I kill the Stork I'll kill the badness in me. Then I'll be ready to come out of here, to wake up, to take my place in society' (p. 9). Also, within patriarchy men do tend to engage in expedient homosocial bonding at the same time as they remain emotionally detached from one another, just like the storks who 'although one or two social groupings could be evidenced . . . they were largely standing in isolation from each other' (p. 14). However, Welsh's representation becomes problematic when he appears to switch from illustrating Roy's situation to granting him mitigating circumstances for his behaviour. Can Roy possibly be absolved from all responsibility for his actions? Is he totally determined by the laws of nature that allegedly condition and inform human society? And, most crucially, is there no difference between humanity and the animal kingdom, both being 'purely a product of their environment' (p. 55)?

Marabou Stork Nightmares displays a number of striking resemblances to Alasdair Gray's *1982 Janine*. Caught up in the first-person narrator's attempts to retain authorial control over the self-perpetuating tradition-ality of typically masculine modes of self-representation, both novels unfold from a disempowered male's predicament of defeat and total incapacitation. Jock is shown to give in to the reassuring potency of masturbatory fantasies conjured from the mind-numbing stupor of an alcohol-induced delirium, while Roy finds himself in a coma after what is described as a euthanasian suicide attempt. To begin with, both narra-tives are marked by an acute denial of self-consciousness, deliberately silencing and shutting out both external and internal voices that would interfere with and ultimately shatter the self's delusive pose of untroubled recreation. Jock deflects from his real-life inadequacies by recurrently launching into self-aggrandising visions of pornographic domination. Roy embarks on a fantasy safari through Africa that casts him alternatively in the roles of explorer, heroic hunter, butch game-keeper and benevolent patron of simple-minded, child-like natives. What both novels ultimately reveal is the insidious inextricability of even the most resolutely escapist male-authored fantasies from the supra-individual genres of patriarchal self-(de)formation. Intent on awakening from the nightmare of traditional masculinity, both Roy and Jock ironically implicate themselves ever more intricately in the despotic master plots of imperialist adventure and pornographic sado-masochism respectively. However, unlike Jock's suicidal breakdown, which triggers a curative process of emancipatory reconstitution, Roy's thwarted attempt at radical self-(de)termination leaves him tragically divided between efforts at genuine self-exploration and deeply ingrained phallogocentric tendencies to obfuscate and thus evade the truth.

Symptomatically, commenting on his semi-conscious state of mind, Roy states that '*this* world's real enough to me and I'll stay down here out of the way, where they can't get to me, at least until I work it all out' (p. 17). However, what Roy knows only too well is that too much introspection would not allay but, on the contrary, severely aggravate his dilemma. Deep inside, Roy knows he is guilty of Kirsty's rape, yet he continues to protest his innocence, feigning incomprehension as to 'why whenever I thought of her I wanted to die' (p. 193). In what could be construed as a typically masculine manoeuvre, he strategically keeps himself in the dark about his own motives, obstructing his inward-gazing enquiry in the very process of setting it in motion. Genuine, honest self-reflection is diverted by assuming a pose of self-effacing heroic action that eclipses the need to delve any more deeply into the complexity of his psychological dilemma. 'Somehow . . . this has given me a sense of purpose', Roy declares. 'I know why I'm in here. I'm here to slay the Stork. *Why I have to do this I do not know*' (p. 17; my emphasis). Roy's resolution 'tae dae something, like tae sort ay prove tae myself that I've changed' (p. 250) lacks the fruitful indeterminacy of Jock's rehabilitation in *1982 Janine*. The problem is that even at the most cogent and articulate moment in his rebellion against normative pressure, Roy finally resorts to taking it like a man, preferring the conclusive logic of death to the utopian open-endedness of change:

> I had opened up my emotions and I couldn't go back into self-denial, into that lower form of existence, but I couldn't go forward until I'd settled my debt. For me it wasn't running away. That was what I had been doing all my fuckin life, running away from sensitivity, from feelings, from love. Running away because a fucking schemie, a nobody, shouldnae have these feelings because there's fucking naewhair for them tae go, naewhair for them tae be expressed and if you open up every cunt will tear you apart. So you shut them out; you build a shell, you hide, or you lash out at them and hurt them. You do this because you think if you're hurting them you can't be hurt. But it's bullshit, because you just hurt even mair until you learn to become an animal and if you can't fuckin well learn that properly you run. Sometimes you can't run though, you can't sidestep and you can't duck and weave, because sometimes it just all travels along with you, inside your fuckin skull. This wasn't about opting out. This was about the only resolution that made sense. Death was the way forward. (pp. 254–5)

Unlike Gray, Welsh fails to break up and start rewriting the death-bound master script of patriarchal masculinity which – according to Cixous's feminist envisioning in 'The Laugh of the Medusa' – would, as a first step, involve a radical unleashing of individual desire from its bondage in the discourse of binarist oppositioning. Gray seeks to re-introduce man to his own intrinsic gynandricity, to himself as 'the ensemble of the one and the other, not fixed in sequences of struggle and expulsion or some other form of death but infinitely dynamized by an incessant process of exchange from one subject to another' (Cixous 1976: 883). In contrast,

Welsh's nightmarish fatalism definitively stifles literature's utopian potentialities by incarcerating man once and for all within the exclusive, self-
centred limits of his patriarchal persona. Symptomatically, by ceaselessly
asserting himself as a man, Roy eventually arrives at a state of mind
not very dissimilar to the autism of his brother Elgin who, 'trapped in a
world of his own', embodies a kind of impervious self-containment
ardently envied and coveted by Roy. 'Perhaps Elgin had the right
idea', Roy ponders in his coma, 'perhaps it was all just psychic defence
. . . Now I have what he has, his place and detachment from it all'
(p. 30).

Similar to extreme cases of hypermasculine self-fashioning, the psy-
chiatric condition of autism is characterised by an abnormal form of
both mental and physical self-absorption, caused and considerably compounded by a debilitating lack of response to external stimuli and a
severely impaired ability to communicate with others. While often in the
possession of an outstanding intelligence or natural giftedness, many
autistics never learn to speak or express themselves coherently. Significantly, autism is commonly explained as an exaggerative strategy of self-
protection, manifesting itself most typically in the patient's delusion of
having grown a protective, impermeable shell that renders him (or her)
invulnerable to extraneous manipulation. Frances Tustin describes autism
as 'an adaptation that is extremely effective . . . for being in control over
what happens' (Tustin 1990: 19) and as a 'rigid overdevelopment of the
normal processes of shutting out of one's mind those affairs that cannot
be handled at the moment' (Tustin 1990: 43). The parallels between the
psychological affliction of autism and Roy's coma, from which he seems
so adamantly determined not to re-emerge, are conspicuous. Analogically speaking, these parallels disclose how under patriarchy the individual male's paranoid need to maintain a sense of emotional detachment
renders him particularly susceptible to systemic remote control by stifling
the expression of his singularity. Symptomatically, Elgin who, according
to Roy, has achieved a state of perfect invulnerability ends up utterly
disenfranchised in an institution not without irony called a 'VENTURE
FOR EXCEPTIONAL YOUNG MEN' (p. 205).

Together with Welsh's use of Africa as a central image, Elgin's unusual
first name introduces an unequivocally (post)colonial dimension into
the novel, within which Scottish masculinity features as both a badly
colonised and complicitous, instrumental presence. Roy's father represents an exemplary case, compensating for his own political disempowerment and marginalisation by keeping files on his 'asocial' neighbours and
christening his Alsatians 'Winston' and 'Maggie'. By dint of a facetious

pun on Elgin's mental illness, Welsh also alludes to the contentious issue of the Elgin Marbles, a group of Ancient Greek sculptures originally decorating the Parthenon in Athens and now on display in the British Museum in London, which over the years have become a symbol of English imperial arrogance and presumptuousness. The Elgin Marbles were lost to England in the early nineteenth century or, rather, they were deliberately removed by Thomas Bruce, Earl of Elgin, a Scotsman, and have been demanded back by Greece ever since, so far to no avail. Within the context of Welsh's novel, this historical circumstance appears to assume figurative significance. Serving and no doubt benefiting as indispensable helpmates in the construction and maintenance of the British Empire, Scottish men – and those of a lower social rank especially – have never won perfect equality with their allegedly super-ior English counterparts. Quasi-English colonisers abroad, their accul-turation at home has remained spurious and incomplete, a circumstance perhaps most poignantly illustrated in Welsh's novel by the mistrans-lation of the Strangs' family name into 'strange' rather than 'strong'. While living under the South African apartheid regime Scottish 'schemies' may pass for legitimate members of the master race. In Britain, how-ever, they represent a severely disadvantaged underclass, of which the men especially find themselves at risk of 'losing their marbles' to the constant taunts and provocations of systemic emasculation. Small won-der, then, that in terms of realistic opportunities for social advance-ment, Africa must strike Roy as a promised land offering virtually effortless heroic success, thus standing in exactly diametric opposition to Scotland:

> Edinburgh to me represented serfdom. I realised it was exactly the same situation as Johannesburg; the only difference was that the Kaffirs were white and called schemies or draftpaks . . . Edinburgh had the same politics as Johannesburg: it had the same politics as any city. Only we were on the other side. (p. 80)

When his suicide attempt fails, Roy seeks refuge in an African safari of the mind that, according to the novel's table of contents, takes the form of a spiritual quest leading Roy from the rediscovery of 'Lost Empires' and 'The City of Gold' on to 'The Trail of the Stork' and 'The Paths of Self-Deliverance'. Initially, though, 'this crazy high-speed journey through this strange land in this strange vehicle' (p. 3) serves not to explore but simply to celebrate the dark continent of Roy's masculine imaginary. Parodying the glamour of imperial Anglo-British masculinity, Welsh shows how a comatosed 1990s urban Scotsman of council estate origin is able to access colonial Africa as a state of virtual power, freedom and authority by having accurately memorised all the relevant props and scripts of imperial adventure. Significantly, while roaming the vast interior spaces of this illusory projection of a country, Roy never expresses himself in the Scottish vernacular but skilfully mimics the pseudo-aristocratic diction of traditional public-schoolboy adventure narratives, displayed perhaps most notoriously in the use of typical sociolectic expletives like 'wizard', 'gosh', 'horrid', 'beastly', and so forth. There are also manifold intertextual echoes from middle-class English children's literature of the Enid Blyton variety, further accentuated by the odd ubiquity of Merchant-Ivory picnic hampers that keep material-ising out of the hot air of the savannah.

Marabou Stork Nightmares illustrates how alluring nostalgic fantasies of untrammelled power and superiority, like that facilitated by a colonial Africa, are to many men as fictitious places of safety where a man's traditional privileges and centre-stage import appear to have stayed unchallenged and intact. Resuscitating a mode of manly self-fashioning that, albeit hopelessly obsolescent and quaint rather than imposing, remains irresistibly attractive, Roy's fantasies offer him a chance of exotic self-expansion from which in real life he could not possibly be any more categorically excluded. However, already Roy's choice of a travelling companion ought to alert Welsh's readers to the precarious instability of this heroic fantasy. Sandy Jamieson, a thinly disguised fictional double of the former football star Jimmy Sandison, 'the *enfant terrible* of British soccer' (p. 9), who fell from grace due to 'an obvious miscarriage of sporting justice' (p. 255), personifies the brittle fragility of all projections of ideal masculine perfection. Moreover, the two young men's homo-social bliss is irreparably marred by Roy's irrepressible memories of the abuse he suffered at the hands of Uncle Gordon in Africa as well as the numerous instances of sexual exploitation at home in which, more often than not, he himself featured as the perpetrator rather than the victim.

Roy's attempt to revive and bask in the glory of imperial heroism triggers nightmarish visions of evil corruption that serve to highlight the systematic colonial rape and betrayal of indigenous innocence and beauty. The imperial fantasy of Africa, casting white European men in the role of paternal guardians and protectors, is constantly undermined by the continent's stark reality as a site of ruthless exploitation. Memor-ably cited by Freud as a supposedly suitable image of the ultimate inscrutability of femininity and female sexuality, in *Marabou Stork Nightmares* the Dark Continent becomes emblematic of the irreconcilable contra-dictions and inconsistencies that at once constitute and destabilise the male psyche. Like Marlow in *Heart of Darkness*, Roy embarks on an exploration of his own unfathomable depth and darkness in the hope of experiencing some kind of meaningful, redemptive revelation only to find himself eventually confronted by pure apocalyptic horror. Welsh's representation of the heroic male psyche as both a lost empire and a dark continent, in which reality and fantasy overlap and delusively blur into one, characterises masculinity as an obscure, rudimentarily explored and speciously mapped *terra incognita* in urgent need of a radical conceptual overhaul.

As outlined above, Roy's dilemma resembles Jock's in *1982 Janine* in that both male characters' escapist indulgence in borrowed fictions of masculine prowess exacerbates rather than dissolves their systemic entrapment. The fantasies of individual male desire are forever subject to the ideological remote control of oppressive master plots. Accordingly, Roy's sense of having reached a point 'where they can't get to me: deep in the realms of my own consciousness' (p. 7) must be regarded as a sad illusion. Traumatised by memories of abuse, both suffered and inflicted, the innermost privacy of Roy's mind reflects and reproduces the nightmarish reality from which he is trying to escape. Intent on abseiling into a phantasmatic, alternative sphere of being, he in fact lowers himself into the Gothic substructures of his own irremediably scarred, systemically incarcerated psyche: 'I try to hide in my little cubby-hole in the darkened well, beyond Sandy and the horrible Storks, but still out of range of the loathsome reality in that sick world on the other side of the trapdoor above' (p. 157). At the beginning of the novel, Roy still feels confident that he is an independent agent fully aware of his motives and in total control of his course of action. 'I am driven to eradicate the scavenger-predator bird known as the Marabou Stork', he announces. 'I wish to drive this evil and ugly creature from the African continent' (p. 4). However, when it gradually dawns on him that the 'one large blighter . . . which I know somehow must perish by my own hand' (p. 4) is in fact himself, he comes to realise that 'I now have as little control down there as I did in the real world' (p. 157).

Opening up a striking parallel to Gray's typographically enhanced representation of Jock's reconstitutive crisis in 'The Ministry of Voices', Roy eventually hears 'other voices shouting [from] the periphery of my vision . . . it's Ozzy and Dempsy and Lexo and they're shouting that she's had enough' (p. 261). Here as in *1982 Janine*, the truth will out. However, unlike Jock, Roy is refused a chance to recapitulate on where he went wrong and start afresh. Roy's encounter with himself results in an inexorable, definitive verdict of guilty:

who do you fuckin hate Roy Strang you hate schemies Kaffirs poofs Weedgies Japs snobby cunts jambos scarfers English cunts women only you don't do you Roy Strang the only cunt you really hate is

Roy Strang.

cannae go aroond hatin fifty per cent ay
the population just because some dirty
auld cunt fucked ye up the erse as a
bairn, nae use that, eh.
(pp. 261–2)

Appropriating, rather than merely echoing, the central slogan of Edinburgh District Council's Zero Tolerance campaign, a feminist initiative intended to denounce and condemn violence against women, Welsh insists that 'THERE IS NEVER AN EXCUSE' (p. 262). Indicative perhaps of the impact exerted by patriarchal ideals on Welsh's own thinking, in *Marabou Stork Nightmares* this slogan comes to be understood not as a general awareness-raising deterrent but as Roy's unequivocal death sentence. Disconcertingly, Welsh re-asserts the masculine imperatives of action and revenge to the acute detriment of possible alternative responses facilitated, for example, by the faculties of forgiveness and rehabilitation that have traditionally been assigned to the feminine gender. Against this background, one finds it hard to shake off the impression that perhaps Roy is not so much punished for his violent masculine behaviour as for his feminine inability to cope with it and pull himself together. In a highly problematic manoeuvre, Welsh employs what is clearly marked as feminist justice to legitimate the killing of an impossibly emotional, almost hysterical man, a man who has also just begun to critically assess and meditate upon his masculine conditioning. Welsh's novel shows no real interest in Roy's possible regenerative reconstitution of himself as a man. Thus, rather uncomfortably, *Marabou Stork Nightmares* appears ultimately not to resist but to concur with the political reasoning behind John Major's recommendation, cited in the novel's epigraph, that sometimes it may be better, and safer, to cut a long story short.

Categorically debarred from refashioning himself as a Kristevan subject-in-the-making, Roy is silenced at the very moment his inward gaze genuinely catches sight of himself for the first time and zooms in to make 'SENSE OF THIS FUCKING CRAZY SHITE YOU'RE INVOLVED IN THIS TROPICAL LAND THIS COLONISED NATION OF YOUR DISEASED MIND Africa, my Africa . . .' (p. 253). Most depressingly, the ending of *Marabou Stork Nightmares* fails to introduce a constructive, emancipatory vision of how the vicious circle of violence and violation could be broken. Instead of challenging the phallocentric principle of exploitative domination, Welsh's novel confirms and consolidates its hegemonic power. The moment Kirsty takes her revenge on Roy and cuts off his penis is not a moment of feminist emancipation but a moment of acute patriarchal subjection. Stepping into the shadow of the phallus, the victim succumbs to the binarist logic of oppression and re-emerges as yet another victimiser. As Kirsty explains to Roy, she knows now that 'might is right' (p. 260) 'because you've made me just like you' (p. 259). Notably, Welsh's woman can only fight back and assert herself by learning how to act like a man.

By denying Kirsty her womanly difference, Welsh denies himself the opportunity to conceive of an alternative, feminine response to violence, a woman's way out of the clockwork orange that is patriarchy. He never truly investigates his own questioning of what Kirsty will do, and why: 'Will she show compassion or is she just the same as us? Is she what we made her?' (p. 227). Welsh also seems oblivious to the fact that within patriarchy terms like 'weakness' and 'strength' may ultimately connote entirely different kinds of behaviour and attitude to women and men, which is why Roy's eventual, rather muddled 'understanding' of Kirsty is so evidently warped by Welsh's appropriative, androcentric projection:

> I understand her.
> I understand her hurt, her pain, how it all just has to come out. It just goes round and round, the hurt. It takes an exceptionally strong person to just say: no more. It takes a weak one to keep it all to themselves, let it tear them apart without hurting anyone else.
> I'm not an exceptionally strong person.
> Nor is Kirsty. (p. 264)

Universalising the insidious dynamics of patriarchal power as some kind of irremediable, generic by-product of human nature, *Marabou Stork Nightmares* concludes with a total eradication of sexual difference. Woman is deprived of her potentially subversive heterogeneity and becomes a completely predictable mirror image of man. Violently driven out of the Dark Continent of her hitherto inscrutable alterity, she finds herself compelled either to become or – more ominously perhaps – to enter the colonised, systemically enclosed Africa of man.

12

·

The U-Turn of the Father

·

Ian McEwan's The Child in Time

K IERNAN RYAN DESCRIBES *The Child in Time* as 'a new kind of story about a new kind of experience, the liberation of men from masculinity' (Ryan 1994: 51). This 'pioneering venture' is triggered by the sudden disappearance of Kate, Stephen and Julie's three-year-old daughter, who vanishes without trace after being abducted on a trip to the local supermarket. The nuclear-family bliss of mother, father and child is irreparably shattered and superseded almost immediately by the ancient charade of man and woman misunderstanding and failing to communicate with each other, marooned as they are in their mutually exclusive, gender-specific spheres of being. In what could perhaps be construed as a typically masculine manoeuvre, Stephen responds to the acute emotional pain incurred by Kate's vanishing 'with admirable self-control' (p. 20) and 'composure' (p. 24), exhausting and 'anaesthetis[ing] himself with activity' (p. 23) in a pointless, if meticulously organised search for the lost child. Julie, on the other hand, 'stayed at home' (p. 23), sitting virtually motionless 'in her armchair, lost to deep private grief' (p. 24), an attitude interpreted by her husband as 'a feminine self-destructiveness, a wilful defeatism' (p. 24). Stephen and Julie's domestic set-up as a modern couple who, evidently inspired by the egalitarian principles of a pragmatic feminism, share the housework and childcare between them, is disclosed as the façade of a barely disguised *égoisme à deux*. Their ostensibly emancipated life style turns out to be not so far removed from the patriarchal dynamics of battle and strife that inform and ineluctably condition their existence within a societal framework depicted by McEwan as a Thatcherite dystopia. Tragedy does not so much drive a wedge between them as *release* the wedge of binarist oppositioning whose forceful impact had merely been suspended. 'The loss had driven them to the extremes of their personalities', it says in the novel. In consequence, 'they went their different ways . . . Their old intimacy, their habitual assumption that they were on the same side, was dead' (p. 24).

While Stephen continues to search for Kate, Julie withdraws to a cottage in the country to contemplate and come to terms with her loss in solitude and seclusion. Significantly, during Stephen's one and only visit to his wife's refuge, they make love and, unbeknown to Stephen, Julie becomes pregnant. In a creative manoeuvre reminiscent of Mary Shelley's confinement of her novel within an epistolary framework spanning nine months, McEwan unravels Stephen's desultory adventures as a disoriented, grief-stricken picaroon against the background of his wife's new pregnancy, thus enclosing 'all the sorrow, all the empty waiting. . . within meaningful time, within the richest unfolding conceivable' (p. 211). The main body of the novel delineates a protracted healing process – not only of Stephen individually, but of Stephen and Julie as a couple – which will eventually, at the birth of their new child, reunite them as mother and father. Unlike the other works discussed in this part, *The Child in Time* is not geared towards an escape from self-perpetuating circles of oppression; rather, it is designed to come full circle, to complete a cycle of fruitful, organic becoming. In this respect, McEwan's novel represents a critique of the classic male *Bildungsroman* in the tradition of which, after many a struggle and mishap, the protagonist is always granted full integration into society's symbolic order. Within the context of *The Child in Time*, this particular mode of presenting an often domophobically motivated escape as the only legitimate kind of both progressive and conclusive development becomes highly problematic and questionable.

McEwan intends to educate his protagonist out of the given traditional frame of *Bildung*, introducing him instead to a position of marginality which Julie is shown to have sought out unprompted, almost instinctively. Stephen's heroic quest for masculine self-fulfilment, which appears to depend on the prospect of rescuing his daughter from the clutches of whatever evil forces detain her, is deliberately thwarted. The fact that *The Child in Time* concentrates almost exclusively on Stephen's struggle, while more or less leaving the reader to guess at Julie's plight, does not indicate an androcentric bias on McEwan's part. On the contrary, McEwan aims to show that despite, or rather because of, all his resolute determination Stephen finds himself consistently on the wrong track, taking an unnecessarily long-winded and circuitous route to the site of semiotic revelation at the end of the novel, which is symptomatically identical with the site Julie arrived at via a short cut many months before him. Stephen's masculine progress is saved from petering out inconclusively by following Julie's example and making a complete U-turn 'home' (p. 212). The novel's concluding scene echoes the ending of the first chapter in that on both occasions Stephen digresses into prolonged distractive action before he eventually follows Julie's suit. Only once his wife has left the house and vacated her position of inward-gazing meditation does Stephen feel ready to sit down, reflect on what has happened, and start mourning. As he admits, 'everything before had been fantasy, a routine and frenetic mimicry of sorrow' (p. 26). Purely for the sake of keeping up an appearance of masculine propriety, man is reluctant to succumb to his emotions until it is (almost) too late. More importantly, man seems debarred from opening up to his feminine qualities as long as he finds himself in the company of woman. The imperative to behave oppositionally appears to prevail over the need to be true to himself.

Adam Mars-Jones seems mistaken when he refers to *The Child in Time* as perhaps 'the most sustained meditation on paternity in literature' (Mars-Jones 1990: 19). In fact, the main body of the novel details Stephen's experiences as a single man who, deprived of his wife and child, seems desperate to re-arrive at himself while rapidly regressing into boyhood. His erstwhile masculine stature defined by responsibility and emotional maturity crumbles under the impact of Kate's disappearance and Julie's gradual retreat into a spiritually self-contained interiority. Odyssean fantasies of manly freedom, churned out by the speciously rebellious, cult-heroic desire machines of masculine self-fashioning, begin to enthral him. Scornfully rejecting Julie's feminine example, Stephen yields to the irresistible magic of what he later identifies as 'images and arguments [that] paraded in front of him, a mocking, malicious, paranoid, contradictory, self-pitying crowd' (p. 136). It is here that he first starts seriously drifting off course:

> [Julie] was reading mystical or sacred texts . . . Her pencilled annotations crowded the margins . . . For his part he made first approaches to a serious drinking habit and indulged the books of his adolescence, reading of unencumbered, solitary men whose troubles were the world's. Hemingway, Chandler, Kerouac. He toyed with the idea of packing a light suitcase, taking a taxi out to the airport and choosing a destination, drifting about with his melancholy for a few months. (pp. 52–3)

The Child in Time presents paternity not as a bedrock essence of manly being but as a delicate process of maturation that crystallises and consolidates itself in the indispensable care of the feminine and maternal. In the absence of woman, Stephen's masculine composure disintegrates. His tennis instructor's comments on his attitude at play are curiously indicative of Stephen's disposition in general: 'You're passive. You're mentally enfeebled. You wait for things to happen, you stand there hoping they're going to go your way' (p. 157).

Stephen's life only re-aggregates on being given another chance at fatherhood by Julie and the new-born child with whom he is united shortly after indulging his 'boyhood dream' (p. 212) of catching a ride in the cab of a railway engine. Clearly, Stephen needs mothering. On moving out of the family flat, he comes to appreciate the 'brisk, maternal thoroughness' (p. 42) of Thelma, his friend Charles's wife, and even little Kate is said to have been 'quaintly protective towards her father' (p. 13). McEwan ultimately gives the impression that the great majority of men never grow up but remain boys merely playing at scientists and politicians, their actions and general behaviour orchestrated by a deep-rooted paranoid fear of never appearing quite manly enough to live up fully to what is expected of them by other boy-men. Evidently prepared to risk the outbreak of worldwide war, the American President, for example, is described as 'anxious to demonstrate that he was not the weakling in foreign policy that his opponents frequently claimed' (p. 35). Even more explicitly, Charles Darke, a renowned political strategist, is introduced as both Thelma's husband and 'her difficult child' (p. 40), a remark further accentuated by Stephen's startled observation that 'without the padding of a tailored jacket, [Charles's] shoulders appeared to be delicately *constructed*' (p. 41; my emphasis).

The setting of *The Child in Time* is a late twentieth-century, post-imperial Britain, politically hollowed out by the people's increasing disaffection with a totalitarianist Thatcherite regime and at the same time – to striking paradoxical effect – ideologically eroded by post-modernity's culture of self-doubt and unstoppable pluralist diversification. In such a climate of all-encompassing entropy, there is really nowhere to go for an old-fashioned, self-made public-school Englishman like Charles. All the arenas in which masculinity used to assert itself are closed off or have acquired a rather dubious reputation. Notably, according to Thelma, Charles's obsession with political power only ever served one purpose and that was 'to keep his weakness at bay' and compensate 'for what he took to be an excess of vulnerability' (p. 204). To eschew confrontation with both the ultimate meaninglessness of his work and the impending subversive dissolution of his meticulously crafted public persona, Charles withdraws into the solipsistic safety of a perfect children's-book fantasy of carefree, untroubled boyishness where, for a brief period of time, he succeeds in bringing time to a halt and preserving an irretrievably lost ideal. However, death is inevitable as Charles begins quite literally to freeze into place. His attempt to recapture a sense of imperial purity and innocence is a doomed, overly neat, calculated act: 'Once a business man and politician, now he was a successful prepubescent' (p. 109). Patriarchal conditioning is not a vest that can be cast aside so easily; it is a totalitarianist conspiracy connate rather than extraneous to the self, not only infiltrating but engendering the innermost core of man's being.

It seems to Stephen 'as if his friend . . . had diligently consulted the appropriate authorities to discover just what it was a certain kind of boy was likely to have in his pockets' (p. 113). Desperate to disappoint, truant and rebel, Charles merely comes to reiterate the very myth of boyish freedom and autonomy that originally induced him to become the man he now does not want to be. Whereas Jack Slay suggests that Charles's regression is 'an escape, a freedom from the pressures of politics, a freedom from the chaos of contemporary society' (Slay 1994: 212), his departure into a sphere of supposedly untrammelled adventure is in fact death-bound, crushing him instead of facilitating his emancipation. As with Jock and Roy's oneiric cultivation of irresistibly compelling alternatives to their quotidian selves, Charles's new life enmeshes him ever more inextricably in the mixture of contradictions and inconsistencies that together constitute the masculine gender. Keen to embody the impossibly pure, free, and indivisible essence of true masculine being, he yields to processes of binarist splitting and doubling that eventually result in an emergence of the self as an overly refined, residual distillate haunted by its origin in self-fashioning manoeuvres of extensive phobic repression. In consequence, both Charles's desires and experiences are at risk of becoming hopelessly stylised and inauthentic. As Thelma notes wisely, what Charles 'needs is quite at odds with what he does, what he's been doing'. At the same time, the internal life he denies is 'with him all the time, it consumes him, it makes him what he is' (p. 46).

McEwan insists that Charles's regression is not a rare, exceptional aberration but 'an extreme form of a general problem' (p. 204). Men appear to find it exceedingly difficult to reconcile their need for solid, definitive self-representations with the fundamentally unstable, vicissitudinary inconclusiveness of their *conditio humana*. The fluidity of time constitutes a particular problematic since it continually threatens to blur man's accustomed self-image out of focus. Unlike women, so McEwan suggests, men are conditioned to abhor and resist change because it necessitates constant, often radical readjustments that overtly undermine the logocentric monumentality of history and, more immediately, the narrative consistency of the masculine self. Hence why so many men appear to prefer the homeostatic timelessness of traditional myths and symbols to the notion of an ultimately unpredictable past/present/future continuum that not only endorses but proliferates endlessly reconfigurative change. Although patriarchal masculinity depends for its ongoing success on an idealisation of progressive achievement, it tends to cancel out the past in favour of an eternal present supposedly impervious to the destabilising impact of ontological flux. As McEwan reflects, 'past a certain age, men froze into place . . . They were who they thought they were', separating them incisively from women who 'upheld some other principle of selfhood in which being surpassed doing' (pp. 54–5). Whereas women's identities are mnemonically accumulative, with 'previous certainties . . . not jettisoned so much as encompassed' (p. 54), men's identities are resolutely selective: 'If it's untidy or doesn't fit, throw it out' (p. 135).

Unlike Julie, to whom time is a variable, yet holistic continuum comprising an organic unfolding and enveloping of experience, Stephen appears to have internalised what Thelma designates as 'the common-sense, everyday version of it as linear, regular, absolute, marching from left to right, from the past through the present to the future' (p. 117). A man's development moves along a linear trajectory of discrete, successive phases that eclipse and supersede rather than fruitfully interpermeate each other. Accordingly, Stephen's journey consists – at least initially – of a never-ending sequence of departures, of leaving behind and extricating himself from experience. Whereas Julie allows the traumatic shock of Kate's disappearance to hit, engulf and totally possess her, Stephen attempts to emerge from it before it has properly sunk in, purposely evading an emotional response that would break his pose of masculine resilience and effectively stop him dead in his track. From the beginning, however, while frantically preoccupied with working out a possible route of escape, Stephen seems fully aware of Julie being several curative steps ahead of him. As he confesses in a sudden panic about halfway through his narrative, 'he did not want to lose his place in her story' (p. 54). What happens to Julie and Stephen as a couple thus turns out to be not a mutual drifting apart but a case of one-sided desertion, with the allegedly active partner ironically being the one in danger of losing his way and being left behind. Only once Stephen has revised his course and started to move towards rather than away from Julie does his story open up to an experience of time as a multi-layered, epiphanically permeable phenomenon, designed to deepen rather than merely trigger and drive his quest for self-fulfilment.

In an intriguingly mystical encounter at the centre of the novel, Stephen finds himself transported back in time to his embryonic beginnings where he is called upon to give birth to himself. He comes to witness his parents in their youth, deliberating on whether or not it is the right time for him to be born, and establishes contact with Claire, his mother-to-be, assuring her of their mutual bond and thus encouraging her to carry her pregnancy to term. Importantly, the beginning of Claire's relationship with her unborn child coincides with her realisation that, in order to be able to start a new life together, man and woman must make a genuine effort at overcoming the deeply ingrained sexist dynamics of binarist oppositioning that rule and insidiously determine their every thought and emotion:

> [Claire] remembered her love and the adventure they were beginning together. It was not duplicity or cowardice she was witnessing here. This [Douglas, her fiancé] was a man summoning all his manly powers of reason and logic, all his considerable knowledge of current affairs because he was in a deep panic. How was he to know what it was to have a baby? . . . It was her mistake to believe that he or any man could be strong in all circumstances. She had broken her news in a passive spirit, expecting him to react just as she had, to take the matter in hand for her. And then she had been sulky, masochistic, self-pitying. Where Douglas had been weak, she had made herself weaker. And yet the truth was she was one step ahead, for she already loved the child, she knew something Douglas could not. (pp. 175–6)

In McEwan's novel, the loss and acquisition of children operates as a central leitmotif that, while accentuating the evident differences between men and women, also signals their essential compatibility and potential for mutual understanding, love and support. In particular, *The Child in Time* is concerned with the whereabouts of the lost female, or perhaps gynandric, child that originally inhabited every single adult self and whose gradual disappearance, or sudden forceful abduction, instigated the development of gender-specific individualities that now characterise and categorically separate the sexes. McEwan focuses his attention on the impact society's symbolic structures, educational practices and behavioural imperatives exert upon the child's individuation. It is in this context that Stephen's membership of an advisory government committee, summoned to decide on the content of a new Authorised Childcare Handbook, gains special significance.

McEwan launches a sarcastic attack on the pseudo-democratic politics of a patriarchal establishment that, while ostensibly prepared to negotiate its recommendatory guidelines, in actual fact continues to dictate its conservative agenda with unmitigated force. Not intellectuals, scientists and academics but representatives of the military, the aristocracy and the government determine how children ought in future to be raised. Boasting chapter headings like 'Security in Obedience' and 'Boys and Girls – vive la différence' (p. 161), the Handbook is eventually discovered to have been finalised and prepared for publication long before the committee has come to any definitive conclusions. Its author turns out to be Charles Darke, whose name in this context seems ominously indicative of the work's profoundly sinister implications. To inculcate in the child an early awareness of its gender-specific role and destiny within society appears as a top priority. The Handbook almost exclusively refers to the child as masculine, highlighting not only the second-sex status of girls (like Kate) but also the particular pressure on boys to identify themselves in opposition to their mothers as well as the female and feminine in general. Moreover, considering Stephen's dilemma in later life, it appears highly disingenuous of the Handbook's author to suggest that anybody could be 'prepared emotionally for the separations to come, separations which are an inevitable part of growing up' (p. 49), especially if these separations are not inevitable *per se* but represent a direct corollary of men's (and women's) systemic conditioning.

Symptomatically, the Handbook portrays childhood as 'a physically and mentally incapacitating condition, distorting emotions, perceptions and reason, from which growing up is the slow and difficult recovery' (p. 179). As it turns out, the Government is interested not so much in the care of children as their swift and efficient transformation into easily manipulable adults. The child's as yet untrammelled desires, its sexual ambiguity and physical conspiracy with the mother, constitute a subversive threat, an intolerable semiotic disruption, to the parametric symbolism of patriarchal rule. The battle that opens up in *The Child in Time* over the Childcare Handbook problematises the tensions between the individual's proprioceptive desire for autonomous, experiential self-authentication on the one hand and the system's *Bildung*-induced homogenisation of all its subjects on the other. Redolent of the scenario surrounding Jock's nervous breakdown in *1982 Janine*, in McEwan's novel a dissenting committee of voices is about to disrupt and clash irreconcilably with the monologic symbolism of a totalitarianist regime. Taking Gray and Carter's envisioning of the adult's essentially unified body of desire a crucial step further, McEwan locates the roots of this originary multi-genderedness in the innate semiotic potentialities of the child as an archetypal exemplification of the Kristevan *sujet en procès*. The rediscovery of the (female) child within themselves, so McEwan suggests, may enable men at last to resist the interpellative processes of patriarchal conditioning, defy the impact of systemic subjection, and thus develop into perfectly reconstructed contributors to a new 'magical citizenry' (p. 78).

Consciously or not, McEwan is undoubtedly inspired by what Kristeva theorises as the continuous conflictual interplay between symbolic fixity on the one hand and playful, semiotic disruption on the other. The semiotic constitutes an unruly, inherently ambivalent modality originating in the niches and gaps, the in-between and the beyond, of the strictly ordered into which it sporadically erupts 'to ensure the generative potential for new meaning' (Morris 1993: 145). Perhaps indicative of Stephen's own semiotic predisposition is his choice of a birthday present for his absent daughter, picked from amongst 'the more interesting toys [that] lay in between [the shop's gender-specific compartments], where imitation of adults gave way to purer fun' (p. 127). The present is a walkie-talkie set. The casually made-up, euphonic word evokes the playful, uncensored chatter of freely communicating children. However, in McEwan's representation, the toy appears also to possess a deeper, more subversive significance. It bears a promise of utopian infringement, a regenerative disruption, both undermining and reaching across the barren, symbolically obstructed no man's land between the mutually isolated sexes: 'On the packet a boy and a girl communicated delightedly across a small mountain range on what looked like the surface of the moon' (p. 128).

The Child in Time is perhaps best described as a contemporary *psycho-machia* involving Stephen in 'a conflict of the soul', torn between the symbolic and semiotic modes of being that vie for predominance over his temporarily suspended sense of self. Pam Morris's succinct definition of Kristeva's concepts provides us with an apt diagnosis of Stephen's critical dividedness between the equally irresistible choices of integrative masculine progress on the one hand and self-indulgent child-like regression on the other:

> the *symbolic* disposition is driven by an urge to master and control, through the act of defining, what is other and therefore potentially threatening to the self. On the other hand, the origins of the *semiotic* modality lie in the non-gendered libidinal drives of the pre-Oedipal phase so that its disposition is towards meaning as a continuum, with identification rather than separation from what is other. (1993: 145)

McEwan poignantly illustrates Stephen's internal conflict in his description of one particular committee meeting into which he introduces an anonymous guest speaker as a contrastive foil or *doppelgänger* to Stephen who, on this occasion, is shown to become painfully self-conscious at hearing himself argue 'like a politician, a Government Minister' (p. 81). The stranger's portrayal as ugly and ape-like is curiously free of pejorative connotations. On the contrary, it exudes an odd attractiveness and thus aptly reflects the spellbinding fervour of his speech that centres on an appeal to foster and cherish rather than categorically condemn the prepubescent child's semiotic resourcefulness. The speaker's voice is an originary, primal voice, the voice of humankind's preliterate, prehistoric child, a voice that appears to draw its inspiration directly from the complex, as yet unconditioned core of Stephen's representative, systemically complicitous persona. Notably, Stephen can only access, experience and retrieve the semiotic via a physical union with the other, in sexual intercourse, when he realises that 'this was exactly what you were meant to do' (p. 64). Now he is required to rediscover the other inside of himself and open up to his intrinsic gynandricity. As the stranger continues to speak, his plea develops into an eloquent analysis of Stephen's personal dilemma as well as patriarchal man's existential quandary in general. Problematising the 'harsh isolation which we like to explain away to ourselves as individuality' (p. 77), the speaker refers to the manifold processes of psychic splitting that cause men (and women) to become:

> deeply divided from ourselves, from nature and its myriad processes, from our universe . . . we have undernourished our capacity for emphatic and magical participation in creation, we are both alienated and stunted by abstraction, removed from the profound and immediate apprehension, which is the hallmark of a whole person, of the dancing interpenetration of the physical and the psychic, their ultimate inseparability. (p. 76)

Torn between the imperatives of progressive man-making on the one hand and his deep-rooted, irrepressible desire for a child-like union with the mother on the other, Stephen must initiate himself to a holistic mode of maturation that, rather than exclusively prioritising the acquisition of masculine traits, would also feminise him. Clearly, Stephen's quest for self-fulfilment would benefit greatly if he could allow himself to be inspired by Thelma's visionary project of feminising science, of rendering it 'softer, less arrogantly detached, more receptive' (p. 43). The aim of saving one's inner child from systemic abduction is not accomplished by identifying with it to the point of adult and child becoming virtually indistinguishable, but by assuming the role of its nurturant, both motherly and fatherly parent. Such a parent would embody what the committee's guest speaker designates as 'a whole person' (p. 76), at once attuned to the responsibilities necessitated by the order of the symbolic and semiotically empowered to resist its deformative influence of gender-specific conditioning. As Terry Eagleton points out, it is essential to understand that the semiotic can never be 'an *alternative* to the symbolic order, a language one could speak instead of "normal" discourse: it is rather a process *within* our conventional sign-systems, which questions and transgresses their limits' (Eagleton 1983: 190). In light of this statement, it seems crucial to acknowledge Kiernan Ryan's remark that in its final reconciliatory vision '*The Child in Time* is aware of the impossibility of leaping out of history into a purified space, uncontaminated by hierarchy, force, fear or envy' (Ryan 1994: 53).

The semiotic modality definitely comes to the fore at the end of McEwan's novel where Stephen and Julie deliver their new child together and emerge from the experience as a newly born couple. Stephen's hitherto inconclusively meandrous narrative reaches a point of arrival in the regenerative domain of the mother where the male logos must yield to the eruptive ur-language of woman's procreative body: 'His words of encouragement were cut off by a loud shout. She fought to inhale, and there was another, a prolonged hoot of astonishment . . . Again, his words were cut off' (p. 218). Both Stephen and Julie experience the moment of delivery as a moment of self-deliverance at which desire fulfils itself magically in the creation of a perfect physical bond beyond words that, for the time being, radically demolishes the symbolic self/(m)other binary. As McEwan writes, 'for moments they were beyond forming sentences and could only make noises of triumph and wonder, and say each other's names aloud' (p. 220). While all the divisive everyday processes of gender-specific becoming are momentarily arrested in a timeless celebration of pure being, differences dissolve in a miraculous manifestation of organic unity. Although eventually the modality of the symbolic re-introduces itself, and the couple reawakens to the importance of gender as they become curious about their baby's sex, it is hard to believe that Stephen and Julie's experiential immersion in the semiotic should not have significantly changed them in their attitude to each other as well as the world at large. There can be no doubt that if anything at all can motivate and empower them to undertake 'to heal everyone and everything, the Government, the country, the planet themselves' (p. 215), it will be the birth of this child.

So far McEwan's inspired vision of perfect gender unity and reconciliation, full of utopian promise and potential, has failed to elicit the critical acclaim it undoubtedly deserves. Marc Delrez, for instance, downright dismisses McEwan's representation of the couple's semiotic union as 'an ahistorical moment in which the protagonists cherish their own snugness and immunity from "a harsh world"' (Delrez 1995: 14). Male critics especially have displayed a keen interest in dismantling and systematically denigrating McEwan's well-intentioned effort, ascribing its perhaps inevitable conceptual weaknesses to what they suspect to be the author's politically dubious cultivation of an ultimately reactionary New Man agenda. Only Kiernan Ryan seems prepared to grant McEwan mitigating circumstances for the precarious, potentially contradictory ambiguities that jeopardise the political correctness of his final vision. Supported by D.J. Taylor's comment that a male writer's adaptation of feminist ideas and principles must of necessity represent 'a progress not without its inconsistencies and bruising encounters' (Taylor 1989: 57), Ryan explains that critical problems are only to be expected as ultimately 'the desire to transfigure masculinity cannot be disentangled from the deep-rooted feelings it seeks to abolish' (Ryan 1994: 53).

What appears to worry and incense McEwan's critics most is the circumstance that it is Stephen who delivers the child who, without his intervention, would most certainly have been stillborn, strangulated by its own umbilical cord. Disregarding the self-conscious authorial comment that Stephen 'was only the catcher, not the home, and his one thought was to return the child to its mother' (p. 219), Adam Mars-Jones, for example, suggests that *The Child in Time* may ultimately be little more than a surreptitious rewrite of the Frankenstein myth, enclosed in the fraudulent rhetoric of a male-appropriated feminism and hence propagating 'not a true indifference to gender, let alone a transcendence of it, but a temporary artificial blurring of identities, under cover of which the male, all the while loudly extolling the sanctity of her privileges, usurps the female' (Mars-Jones 1990: 33).

What Mars-Jones short-sightedly overlooks is the importance of *The Child in Time* as McEwan's attempt to conceive of a kind of *écriture masculine* whose greatest achievement would reside in its redirective insertion of the traditional male *Bildungsroman* into the semiotic matrix of a hitherto exclusively female experience. Stephen, the lost father, is shown to abandon his solipsistic quest for masculine self-fulfilment in order to return home where he assumes the role of midwife and partners Julie in her labour to give birth. Thus, within the familial sphere of the personal and private, Stephen's conduct mirrors Thelma's utopian undertaking to feminise the man-made structures and practices of science, a project intended to instigate a gradual overhaul of the symbolic order as a whole. Promisingly, Julie and Stephen's experience of semiotic empowerment manifests itself as a perfect fulfilment of all the conditions needed to facilitate the revolutionary change envisaged by Thelma:

> When science could begin to abandon the illusions of objectivity by taking seriously . . . the indivisibility of the entire universe, and when it could begin to take subjective experience into account, then the clever boy was on his way to becoming the wise woman. (p. 120)

McEwan's novel deliberately refrains from a heroic portrayal of Stephen as 'the clever boy'; instead, it casts him as a nervous neophyte about to be initiated into the arcane knowledge of 'the wise woman'. The ending of *The Child in Time* envisions neither a mutual assimilation or interpenetration of the sexes (as in *The Wasp Factory, The Passion of New Eve* and *1982 Janine*) nor violent, spuriously emancipatory acts of grasping and killing (as in *Marabou Stork Nightmares* or, going further back, *The Turn of the Screw*). McEwan suggests that gender is both destiny and a process of learning and tentative exploration, at once definitive, relational and mysteriously open-ended. To trace and understand its significance, we are requested to follow Julie's suit who, on asking the question '"A girl or a boy?" . . . reached down under the covers and *felt*' (p. 220; my emphasis), thus launching an attempt at interpellating the body of the child without violating it by symbolic inscription.

Part IV

Coming Out of *Bildung*:
A Case of Gay Subversion

Inspired by feminist strategies of emancipation, a few contemporary men have begun self-consciously to re-assess their given status as representatives of a standard norm whose systemic hegemony is safeguarded by an oppression of alterity in all its significatory manifestations. To resist and unlearn the sexist practices of masculine self-fashioning, these men often deliberately assume a position of societal marginality – traditionally occupied by women and other subordinate identities – from which they are able to 'come out' of patriarchy's totalitarianist frame of *Bildung* and rehabilitate their gender in new, less one-dimensionally specific configurations. As Joseph Bristow insists, 'coming out' in this sense is not achieved by confessing and bewailing one's guilt and unwitting complicity in systemic violence and oppression. To 'come out' is 'to claim a sexual-political identity', not 'to reveal some shameful fact of one's being but to partake in a community of interests' (Bristow 1992: 75). According to Diana Fuss, 'coming out' involves a subversion of the symbolic inside/out binary that traditionally demarcates masculinity from femininity or, in more general terms, the monolithic standard from its margin of categorically ostracised others. Such a resolute demolition of phallogocentric certainties would cause the former centre gradually to disintegrate to be ultimately superseded by what used to inhabit 'the exteriority of the negative' (Fuss 1991: 4).

Ironically, heterosexual masculinity of the patriarchal mould is already 'out'; it is outdated and outmoded, finding itself ever more vociferously cornered by the manifold processes of minoritarian 'coming out' that characterise our postmodern era of pluralist diversification. At the same time as 'the ministry of voices' of erstwhile marginalised, subordinate identities begins to gather force in 'a movement into a metaphysics of presence, speech, and cultural visibility' (Fuss 1991: 4), patriarchal masculinity loses its hegemonic foothold. As Fuss's explication of the gay meaning of 'out' suggests, only if heterosexual men 'come out' and embrace their counterdiscursive identification as a minority as yet oblivious of its own minoritarian status, can they begin to participate in the newly reassembling communal forum of a turbulently, often tumultuously, reconfiguring symbolic sphere that promises to reconstitute contemporary society:

> To be out, in common gay parlance, is precisely to be no longer out; to be out is to be finally outside of exteriority and all the exclusions and deprivations such outsiderhood imposes. Or, put another way, to be out is really to be in – inside the realm of the visible, the speakable, the culturally intelligible. (Fuss 1991: 4)

not female?

It is in this respect that heterosexual men might benefit from allowing themselves to be inspired not only by feminist but also gay male strategies of emancipation. While no doubt bearing its own critical difficulties and hence being far from representing an exemplary *non plus ultra*, gay men's often playfully appropriative conflation of masculinity and femininity could serve as a useful paradigm for heterosexual men who are keen to re-imagine their gender role in order to instigate a proliferation of new, post-patriarchal masculinities. According to Harry Brod and Michael Kaufman, 'gay men are socially situated in such a way that they have particularly noteworthy insights into the social construction of masculinities across the board' (Brod and Kaufman 1994: 6). As born and/or self-fashioned 'traitors to the cause' of patriarchal gender politics (Segal 1990: 135–67), the lives of gay men – whether in the closet or 'out' – testify to the fact that gender, as we know it, is neither natural nor originary, and 'that hegemonic heterosexuality is itself a constant and repeated effort to imitate its own idealizations' (Butler 1993: 125). Invariably, as Harold Beaver explains, 'the homosexual codes are counter-codes' (Beaver 1981–82: 100). Whereas closeted gay men's performative expertise in maintaining their straight camouflage indirectly draws attention to traditional masculinity as an artificial, author(is)ed script, the emergence of gay men who are 'out' overtly disrupts the monologic text of strictly oppositional, mutually exclusive gender identities and relations.

From the moment he first acknowledges his difference, the gay male cannot but experience himself as an inveterate misfit to the gender moulds of patriarchal *Bildung*. At once encaged in and excluded from the common code, he becomes a restive subject-in-the-making endlessly searching for suitable models of self-authentication. The utopian position of marginality, circuitously arrived at by Gray and McEwan's protagonists, is the gay male's original point of departure. As Jacob Stockinger suggests, 'for the homosexual, marginality is both the price of his stigma and the escape from that stigma; he is both condemned to it and saved by it' (Stockinger 1978: 143).

13

·

Of Ceremonies

·

Neil Bartlett's Ready to Catch Him Should He Fall

F OCUSING ON THE INTEGRATION of Boy into the curiously arcane life
style of an imagined gay community, Neil Bartlett's debut novel *Ready
to Catch Him Should He Fall* constitutes a highly self-conscious appropriation of the classic *Bildungsroman*. It presents itself as a kind of subcultural
talking (and reading) cure that transforms what is in reality a tale of
systemic confinement and oppression into a counterdiscursive fantasy of
liberation. Clearly, the story of Boy's successful maturation is intended to
fulfil the speaker and his audience's long-cherished dream of gay communal emancipation. The novel intriguingly contains the man-making
trajectory of the masculine quest narrative – usually geared towards a
youth's complicitous initiation into patriarchal society's system of power
relations – within the romantic format of what would traditionally be
regarded as a tale of perfect feminine socialisation. Although it begins as
a promiscuous sexual odyssey, Boy's accession to manhood is ultimately
designed to transport him into courtship, engagement and marriage with
another man (named Older). Boy's maturation is considered complete
only once he has become both a son and a lover, a husband and a wife
and, most importantly perhaps, both a mother and a father who, as a
newly qualified master of ceremonies, begins to facilitate the communal
initiation of men even younger and less experienced than himself.

Unlike the great majority of traditional male quest narratives, Bartlett's
novel starts with an arrival, a homecoming, rather than an escapist or
domophobic departure. The hardest and most hazardous stage in Boy's
quest for self-authentication seems mastered when, exhausted and without having been able to ask anyone for directions, he finally arrives at
The Bar, 'a very strange place' which the narrator describes as 'a

destination' (p. 19). The Bar is where the gay community lives. As indicated by its name, it represents not only a place, but also a boundary at once debarring and sheltering the men from the world outside. Its designation oscillates between that of a marginalised, real-life location and that of a totally fictitious, impossible place, an '*ou*-topia', characterising it simultaneously as a self-contained communal closet and a seminal revolutionary cell. As the narrator explains, 'there was no name painted up over the door. We just left it blank most of the time, because The Bar was always changing its name' (p. 21). According to Stockinger's list of typical 'homotextual' traits, the ambivalent anonymity of The Bar would identify it as representative of 'the most frequent type of homotextual space [which] is the closed and withdrawn place that is transformed from stigmatizing into redeeming space' (Stockinger 1978: 143). Boy's entrance into The Bar must be read as a gesture of disintegrative detachment from society's conformative frame of *Bildung*. Notably, by depriving him of suitable models of manly identification, conventional *Bildung* could have ruined Boy's prospects of maturation and in effect condemned him to lifelong adolescence. Boy's 'immaturity' and allegedly deliberate eschewal of social responsibility (as a family man) would then most certainly have been cited as proof of his innate homosexual inadequacy rather than patriarchy's failure to accommodate all of its members' needs and desires, irrespective of their gender or sexual orientation.

The Bar's namelessness also signals its importance as a site of undeclared, as yet symbolically uncharted desire, thus hinting at the gay community's potential for powerful semiotic disruption which, on coming out, promises both to subvert and reinvigorate the prevalent societal order with a sudden influx of innovative, hitherto unprecedented modes of signification. As Bartlett suggests, despite – or perhaps because of – their categorical exclusion from the grand symbols and narratives of patriarchal masculinity, the gay men in The Bar know not only how these symbols and narratives operate and what they mean, but also how they can be appropriated and effectively deconstructed. This double knowledge of the systemically othered manifests itself, for example, in the gay men's improvised fashioning of The Bar into a ludic(rous) homely centre of imperialist adventure:

> The bells didn't work and I don't know who put the names there, they've just always been there. The first bell was labelled *San Francisco*; the second *El Dorado*; and the third *Timbuctoo*. Underneath the third bell someone had also written, using a biro on the paint of the wall, ETIOPHIA. (p. 22)

In the camp ambience of The Bar, the domophobic myth of exotic masculine self-expansion is replaced by experimental, inward-gazing strategies of invariably tentative individuation enacted as part of a theatrical hide-and-seek of desire, sex, love and communal belonging. Different places and times are travelled and momentarily conquered in fanciful flights of an extravagant imagination. 'And suddenly we'd all be in Amsterdam or Paris or something like somebody's idea of America for the evening', the narrator throws in, 'or else it would still be our own dear city, but from very definitely another era' (p. 27).

As it begins quite literally to infringe upon the significatory centre of homeostatic heterosexual normality, The Bar's hidden potentialities as a semiotic fulcrum of notorious gender appropriation become increasingly evident. Bartlett's sumptuous implementation of camp which, according to Susan Sontag, 'sees everything in quotation marks' and expertly stylises 'Being-as-Playing-a-Role' (Sontag 1967: 280), threatens to topple the inside/out binary of heterosexual centre and homosexual margin. Clearly, should the new significatory energies hatched in The Bar ever come to spill out into the open and disseminate, the erstwhile margin-alised enclave would rapidly turn into a vortex of groundbreaking societal change. Exposed as only one possible, strictly censored variation from a vast repertoire of as yet to be tried and tested gender identities, the supposedly natural standard would then swap places with what has traditionally been viewed as derivative and parasitic, demonstrating 'that the qualities predicated of "homosexuality" (as a dependent term) are in fact a condition of "heterosexuality"; that "heterosexuality", far from possessing a privileged status, must itself be treated as a dependent term' (Beaver 1981–82: 115).

In *The Epistemology of the Closet*, Eve Kosofsky Sedgwick observes that certain 'ignorances, far from being pieces of the originary dark, are produced by and correspond to particular knowledges and circulate as part of particular regimes of truth' (Sedgwick 1994: 8). Naturally, any knowledge of the heterosexual standard's ultimate dependency on its ostracised homosexual other must be hidden and suppressed in order not to jeopardise the former's authoritative legitimacy. The symbolic order of heterosexual patriarchy is not derived from an originary source of natural authenticity but clusters with paranoid tenacity around an absent centre upheld by an assumption of deliberate, systematic ignorance. Accordingly, in *Ready to Catch Him Should He Fall*, Boy makes what is probably his most important discovery when he sees through the repre-sentational fraudulence and biased, heterosexist design of the society in which he lives: 'He worked out where The Bar was on his maps, and checked his perspective against the actual view – from where he saw the city it looked like The Bar was right in the middle of it, not hidden away at all like it was on the map' (p. 43). That Boy should come to behold the full extent of the multifarious obfuscatory strategies deployed by patriarchal *Bildung* to frame everybody's perception of reality represents a constitutive part of his process of 'coming out'. Confirming Thomas Yingling's assertion that 'for the homosexual the "problem of homosexuality" is in fact the problem of signs' (Yingling 1990: 34), Boy's subcultural education is to transform him into a discerning (proof)reader and versatile interpreter of heterosexual signification whose symbolic inscriptions he must learn to challenge, manipulate and resist.

On entering The Bar, Boy becomes a novice about to be initiated to the political counterdiscourse of camp. His tutors are older gay men who expertly 'proliferate a protean, and never normative, range of fantasies in social dramas of their own choosing' (Beaver 1981–82: 106). Bartlett's novel must in itself be understood as a camp artifact subversively inspired by 'a suppressed and denied oppositional critique [of compulsory heterosexuality] embodied in the signifying practices that processually constitute queer identities' (Meyer 1994: 1). From the outset, *Ready to Catch Him Should He Fall* incorporates much more than a semi-autobiographical, testimonial account; it represents an allegory of resistance intent on appropriating the regulatory conventions of romantic heterosexual love by exposing them as a theatrical script of variable roles. As the narrator's preliminary remarks indicate, the novel aims at a visionary reconstellation of given cultural stereotypes, enquiring if ultimately the whole constitutes more or less than a mere summing up of its individual parts:

> that 'Great Romance of Our Times', as it became known amongst us, had not yet begun, its theme tune had not yet been composed on Gary's piano, its scenario was not yet subject of our daily gossip and speculation, we were not yet auditioning for a place in the credits – The Friend, The Admirer, Blonde Man in Bar, Second Guest at Dinner Party. (p. 14)

What motivates the gay men in their pursuit of camp as a life style is the desire for an establishment of 'our own rules' (p. 30), a flexible, intrinsically utopian establishment that would allow for sudden shifts in attitude and perception as well as the tentative (p)robing of ever new gender identities. Eager to create a sphere where 'you could live just how you wanted' (p. 30), the men in The Bar seem resolved to quarry the monolith of patriarchal *Bildung* as if it were a self-service reservoir of stylistic possibilities rather than an authoritative catalogue of normative standards. Bartlett's narrator indignantly dismisses the accusation of indulging in deliberate inauthenticity and pure make-believe. 'Playing like we played wasn't lying at all', he insists, 'it was nothing to do with lying' (p. 26). Indeed, within the conceptual framework of camp, lies do not exist, only possible truths that have not as yet been formulated and blatant falsities in need of radical exposure. All expression and behaviour is performative artifice, meaningful only in relation to its immediate context.

As Boy approaches The Bar for the first time, he briefly halts to admire a display of silk flowers in a next-door shop window which, in retrospect, appears to serve as an epiphanic moment signposting the developments to come. Pertinently foreshadowing the nature of Boy's imminent encounter with the men in The Bar, the flowers are described as 'all artificial, but so good that they were better and fresher than the real thing, and certainly more expensive' (p. 19). Once inside The Bar, Boy's learning process begins and, while it does not fundamentally differ from the experiences of any other trainee or apprentice in its emphasis on 'application, study, repetition, diligent imitation and sincere admiration of his peers' (p. 33), it seems more faithful to the original *telos* of education than conventional *Bildung*. Etymologically speaking, education designates a combination of directive guidance and free, organic growth. The young person is led out of childhood to familiarise him/herself with the responsibilities of adult being. As problematised by McEwan in *The Child in Time*, patriarchal *Bildung* aims to regulate and manipulate the child's maturation so that it must inevitably result in a conclusive manifestation of definitive, often one-dimensional self-formation. In contrast, Boy is encouraged to 'come out' and orient himself as a dynamic *sujet en procès*. Rather than being interpellated into a fixed framework of naturalised signs, the lessons he is taught are intended to prompt an intimately personal investigation into the inherently arbitrary and ambivalent nature of signification itself.

In effect, Boy learns to become free to be himself. Within Bartlett's no doubt highly idealised gay community, identity never deteriorates into an entitative strai(gh)tjacket constructed through either feminine or masculine interpellation, but continues to mould and remould itself at different moments in different contexts, remaining defiantly open to sudden proprioceptive whims and mood swings: 'Sometimes [Boy] thought that he needed to feel like a woman, a younger woman or at least The Other Woman; certainly he needed to feel like The Young Man' (p. 37). Clearly, Boy is unaccustomed to so much freedom. For instance, on reading a book given to him by Madame, the proprietor of The Bar, it is said that 'he did not know who he was supposed to be – the child-wife, the monstrous heroine, the burner of men's bodies, the woman of independent means, the beloved or expensive son' (p. 80). Only gradually does he come to realise that identity need not ever be conclusive and unequivocal but is free to express itself in a turbulent welter of wildly unspecific desire: 'I want to be like this . . . I want to be like that . . . I want to be this, I want to be that' (pp. 39–40). Boy discovers himself to be inhabited by a polyphonic chorus of diverse identities that are inclined to interpermeate unpredictably as when, for example, 'his white-powdered female face and livid red lips were suddenly split open by a masculine grin of triumph' (p. 162). However, while facilitating his individual emancipation, Boy's semiotic experiments do not automatically make him a man and fully initiated member of the gay community, which is something he achieves only much later by marrying Older. As the narrator comments, although 'he wanted so much to be one of us . . . Boy would never, of course, have used the word *us* at this time. And there's lots of men won't use the word *us*, still' (p. 38).

To establish and sustain themselves as a subculture in opposition to the order of patriarchy, gay men must invent their own rituals and symbols of integration. *Ready to Catch Him Should He Fall* tells not only the story of an individual 'coming out' but indirectly addresses the complicated issue of communal gay unification and resistance. The union of Boy and Older, described by the narrator as 'our mascots, our perfect pair, the sign of all our hopes' (p. 127), mobilises and unites all the men in The Bar in a subversive interrogation of heterosexual privilege. Significantly, the moment at which the gay lovers decide to get married and appear to slough off their glamorous difference to become 'a regular couple, just like an ordinary couple' (p. 184), is also the moment that sees their counterdiscursive potential at its peak. As soon as Boy and Older 'go normal' – notably without relinquishing their revolutionary capacity as stigmatised misfits and categorical outsiders – the normative order finds itself at risk of irreparably caving in on itself. As Judith Butler points out,

> [i]f subversion is possible, it will be a subversion from within the terms of the law, through the possibilities that emerge when the law turns against itself and spawns unexpected permutations of itself. The culturally constructed body will then be liberated, neither to its 'natural' past, nor to its original pleasures, but to an open future of cultural possibilities. (Butler 1990: 93)

Opening up an interesting parallel to Evelyn's transformation in Carter's *The Passion of New Eve*, in 'Robing the Bride' (pp. 186–203) Boy is made to experience both the depression and exhilaration that inform a variety of different patriarchally engendered roles. Heterosexuality is effectively parodied when, after an evening out, Older, 'the man', goes straight to bed while Boy, 'the woman', spends over half an hour disrobing and demasquerading himself, thereby unveiling traditional femininity not only as an unnatural, performative act but also as a passive suffering of self-deformative subjugation. Boy 'felt all the particular pains that you feel after a night in drag', the narrator informs us, 'the calves of his legs ached, his face aching too from all the smiling, the cuts on his legs hurt, his feet were almost numb with pain from the shoes' (p. 199). Only a few moments later, one finds masculinity and femininity deliberately confused and reshuffled when Older and Boy experimentally swap roles, with 'the man' snuggling up to 'the woman' and Older doing, 'in fact, what Boy usually did' (p. 199). Eventually, the chapter concludes with Older's radical challenge of the originary authenticity of any individual identity donned and impersonated by Boy. 'Which outfit do you prefer?', he asks. 'Or would you rather go just as yourself tonight?' (p. 200).

However, in 'Robing the Bride' it is not only Boy's strength and determination that are put to a series of tests in preparation of his marriage into the gay community but also, more importantly, the gay community itself – its solidarity, wisdom and integrity. It is almost as if a secret colony were petitioning for the acknowledgement of their communal independence by symbolically staging their first wedding on unknown ground, mimicking, yet also considerably appropriating, the hoary ceremonial conventions of a culture that continues to persecute and expel them. Since gay progress towards self-fulfilment has categorically been obstructed by heterosexual traditions, the gay couple's self-assertive 'publishing [of] the banns' (pp. 174–85) symbolises a communal moment of emancipatory resistance which disclose(t)s the subculture's banishment from society's institutionalised rites of passage. Successfully rallying the men in The Bar as a community, Boy and Older's marriage 'in the face of considerable opposition' (p. 206) signals that 'the revolution's come' (p. 185). The ritualised role-plays Boy undergoes in 'Robing the Bride' have clearly been designed for him especially. However, Boy's marriage to Older also lays the foundation to a new, subversive tradition open to all those of a similar persuasion who may eventually decide on following in his footsteps. As the narrator emphasises, this wedding must not be dismissed as an extravagant performance of gay self-indulgence but had better be acknowledged as a serious political manifestation of counterdiscursive desire:

not for always, but just for once in my life I wanted to live out my love for a man like they did. I suppose you think I mean I want to walk down the aisle in white with my friends watching, but that's not it, that's not what this feeling is to do with. Or not all of it, because of course I would love to do that. But that's easy to laugh at. What I want is to hold his hand in public. And what I want then is to hold his hand in front of the television for several evenings a week, and if you don't understand that, if you don't know what that feeling is, if you don't know why it's like that then you know nothing, nothing, nothing. (p. 113)

As Beaver explains, 'only partners in marriage . . . can undermine that institution. Only those who have entered on a contract can break it' (Beaver 1981–82: 99). However, it does not appear to be Bartlett's intention to demolish what is possibly the most powerful societal strategy of sanctioning and privileging heterosexual normality. Rather, his approach is both iconoclastic and conciliatory.

The generally rehabilitative tone of 'Couple' – the novel's central part – is highlighted by its epigraph taken from 'Of Ceremonies: Why some be abolished and some retained', a section in *The Book of Common Prayer*: 'Neither dark nor dumb ceremonies, but . . . so set forth that every man may understand what they do mean, and to what use they do serve' (p. 97). Clearly, rather than simply aiming to upset the institution of marriage, Bartlett intends to reinvigorate it, endowing it with new semiotic significance propagated by society's marginalised and oppressed in centuries of silence and seclusion. In *Ready to Catch Him Should He Fall*, homosexuality as an 'almost permanently radical experience of alterity and liminality' subversively infiltrates the ideological centre to appropriate and claim for itself 'the domestication and naturalization that make heterosexuality seem the only adult sexuality compatible with love' (Yingling 1990: 30). However, Bartlett refrains from proffering gay experience as an alternative life style that, due to its forever-newborn status and constant significatory flux, naturally surmounts the calcified patterns of heterosexual behaviour. Rather, the challenging counter-discourse of effective gay mimicry is meant to induce patriarchal society to purge itself of its gamut of ignorances that ultimately prevent it from recognising its own artificial make-up. Momentarily paralysing society's homophobic machinery of categorically abjecting what in fact represents a constitutive part of itself, Boy and Older's engagement quite literally unleashes a storm. To similar effect, their first love-making as a married couple is shown to conjure ghostly apparitions from the suppressed history of homosexuality that now come to materialise and take shape in the very midst of the city, so that anyone walking home late that night could have looked up at the bedroom window at four a.m., and seen an inexplicable sight: framed by a bedroom window on the fifth floor, lit by a single candle flame, a silent crowd of fifty or sixty smiling, naked men, pressed close together, fifty or sixty of them together in a single council flat bedroom. (p. 219)

The tale of Boy's maturation within the sheltered confines of The Bar is interspersed with reports of violent homophobic attacks on gay men in the city. While it would be truistic to agree with Gregory Herek that 'homophobia serves to deny one's own homoerotic attractions and "feminine" characteristics' (Herek 1987: 77), his criticism of the term as a problematic misnomer is certainly of the utmost significance. As Herek explains, the misleading '-phobia' suffix suggests that homophobic behaviour is inherently irrational and motivated by a deep-rooted per-sonal fear or horror when, in fact, 'homophobia is tenacious partly because it is very functional' (Herek 1987: 69), not only for its individual perpetrator but also, more importantly, for society in general.

Homophobia forms a constitutive mechanism of patriarchal condi-tioning, designed to police the sexual conduct of all men and women, who must suppress their gynandric disposition and identify with the given gender binary lest their sexual orientation appear dubious and thus become subject to processes of societal penalisation and ostracism. In a remarkable scene describing the attempt of a homophobic assault on Boy and Older, Bartlett both uncovers and defeats the widely held belief 'that male homosexuality derives from and expresses something "feminine" in men – the absence of appropriate levels of masculinity' (Segal 1990: 135). Older is shown to fight back like a man, utterly perplexing the young assailants who back away on realising 'that these two men who they had assumed would be afraid were not afraid, or seemed not to be' (p. 297). Walking openly hand in hand through the city, the union of Boy and Older represents a celebration of rebellious desire that is 'perfect, perfect, perfect' (p. 301) in its exemplary elision of the conflictual inside/out binaries of masculinity and femininity, hetero-sexuality and homosexuality or, more generally speaking, sameness and difference. This is the beginning of a revolutionary movement of libera-tion. Significantly, Boy and Older's 'coming out' as a couple prompts the narrator to imagine 'the night they changed the law and we danced all night, spilling out of The Bar and dancing our way into the street, and nobody stopped us' (p. 311).

However, the ubiquitous constraints of patriarchal law are not all that easily exploded and shrugged off. With increasing persistence, the presence of a mysterious father figure is shown to intrude upon the narrative of gay emancipation, initially via letters, then in person. The exact origin and identity of the old man, whom Boy calls 'Father' and eventually invites to move in with him and Older, remain obscure. In fact, his influence on both Boy and the newly wed lovers as a couple seems of purely symbolic significance. Father represents an encumbering traditional legacy, the burden of the old order, which Boy and Older must learn to negotiate and accommodate within the framework of their new, unprecedented domestic set-up. Older's theory that Father may be homosexual himself appears erroneous since the latter displays no solidarity with the gay cause, referring to men of Boy's kind as 'you people' (p. 100) and commenting on the day of the great storm, which is also the day of Boy and Older's engagement, as 'a sad day for all of us' (p. 173). Also, more evidently perhaps, Father is placed in diametric opposition to 'Mother', The Bar's proprietor, who asserts unequivocally that 'these Fathers are low-down and miserable fuckers to a man' (p. 227). Father's arrival threatens to open up an alienating rift between Boy and Older's pretended family on the one hand and the men in The Bar on the other. His presence not only exerts a considerable strain on the lovers' personal relationship; it also incapacitates them as pioneering revolutionaries, causing the communal gay project of finding a foothold and creating a home base within society seriously to flag.

Significantly, the gay project of 'coming out' and emerging from an oppressive background of symbolic allocation is problematically entwined with a fervent desire to belong, to find 'some home to go back to' (p. 237). As the narrator explains, 'The Bar is just one big orphans' home anyway, and that's why we use all of those words all the time to each other, Mother, Daddy, Baby, Sister' (p. 235). In the final section of the novel, Bartlett shows the symbolic orders of patriarchy and gay counterculture in an allegorical clinch over the issue of who owns the right to found and run families and homes. Testifying to Bartlett's general optimism, it is Father, already weakened by loneliness and old age, who loses the struggle, falls ill, and eventually dies in the care of Boy, who has nursed him as a mother would nurse her ailing child. As a result of his death, the law seems ready to change. Patriarchy dwindles and subsides in reverse proportion to the gay couple's consolidation of their virtual normality. However, the reader's jubilation and sense of triumph are short-lived. While one of its ultimately blameless and innocent representatives has passed away, the system continues to perpetuate itself: on the day of Father's funeral there is another homophobic attack. As the narrator reflects, 'what is the sense of those two things happening at the same time . . . those two ceremonies, just what is the sense in that, just when . . .' (p. 291) – one is tempted to proceed – the rule of binaries seemed toppled.

Whereas it appears relatively easy for the gay community to replace the societal institution of marriage with a viable counterdiscursive equivalent, finding a suitable substitute for the initially absent, then intrusive father presents itself as a rather more problematic and daunting enterprise. Mourning not so much Father's death as 'the life he led' (p. 289), Boy realises that systemic homophobia is responsible for depriving gay men of adequate fathering, and this appears to be a circumstance that is hard, if not impossible, to remedy, even if one is as passionately determined as Boy who cries that 'if [Father] wasn't to blame then who was to blame, who was it, oh I want to hurt them, I want to hurt them, I want to hurt them' (p. 289). While 'Mother' is readily associated with home and familial communality, the love/hate of the father inscribes itself as an agonising, deep-structural lack in the lives of many gay men. According to Bartlett's narrator, gay men's sexual desire is conspicuously pervaded by 'father and son fantasies that no one admits to but everybody has' (p. 235), and about Boy it is said on one occasion that he was 'the way that sons always are, the way they always expect to be taken care of' (p. 42). Promisingly, if however not without giving rise to its own inherent difficulties, Boy's father complex appears to be in the process of happily resolving itself in his love for Older who is shown to 'play both Father and Lover to Boy in a single evening' (p. 164).

In *Ready to Catch Him Should He Fall*, sexual desire and self-fulfilment succeed and eventually come to eclipse the patriarchal imperative of filial obedience, replacing the inexorable law of the father with the lovers' mutual bond of boundless, unconditional solicitude. While this is no doubt conceptually attractive, it also problematically enmeshes male homosexual love in the potentially abusive dynamics of traditional masculine power. Despite Boy's protestations that Older would never do anything to hurt him, his frequently bruised and battered appearance tells a different story, suggesting – at a first cursory glance – that the lovers' allegedly perfect relationship is seriously marred by practices of violent, sado-masochistic sex. However, as a less prejudiced and more open-minded enquiry reveals, Boy and Older's almost relentlessly passionate love-making is definitely not a private re-enactment of the politics of 'fucking' that ruin people's lives in Gray's *1982 Janine* and Welsh's *Marabou Stork Nightmares*. Even Lynne Segal's observation that 'many gay men are convinced that the ability to express needs for power, punishment, and so on through sexual play actually limits any need to express it in other ways' (Segal 1990: 153), seems to fall short of the full significance of Bartlett's lovers' extreme physical passion. The violent sex they engage in appears to incorporate the symbolic expression of a love too radically different to speak its name, a love beyond adequate means of conventional signification, an uncompromising love that annihilates the self in an interpenetrative, climactic union with its other. This is the kind of love addressed by Mother in her song: 'All of me,/Why not?/ Take all of me;/Can't you see?/I'm/No good,/Without you' (p. 312).

In Boy and Older's terms, 'fucking' comes to signify both a total semiotic dissolution and mutual orgasmic authentication of two selves in communion with each other. Far from re-inscribing the hierarchical oppositions that foster and sustain traditional male power, Boy and Older's love-making is radically egalitarian in that it undoes all the bars of significatory difference that separate the domineeringly active self at the top from its passively enduring other at the bottom. Accordingly, Older's passionate declaration of love gives voice to both his control and his dependency, his dominance as well as his total emotional surrender:

> You're my boy, you're my body, you're my woman, you're my pussy; you're my dog with a bone, you're my bruised and broken darling, you're the song in my heart, you're my sky at night, you're my little brother, you're my river through the city, you're the bird in the bush, you're my lover in my arms, you're my daddy home from work. You're my fucker, fucker, fucker, fucker what are you? (p. 216)

Ultimately, by portraying Boy as someone who retains, and continues to develop, his gynandric disposition beyond the conclusive, gender-specific devices of patriarchal emplotment, Bartlett powerfully contests Derek Duncan's categorical assertion that, 'in the "coming out" novel, the traditionally masculine quest for self-determination can be said to resolve itself by means of a feminine ending' (Duncan 1994: 158). Skilfully conflating the narrative conventions of masculine and feminine plot trajectories, Bartlett exploits the counterdiscursive resourcefulness of a deliberate aesthetic cultivation of 'effeminacy' to render his protagonist at once a perfectly domesticated heroine and a rebellious, self-affirmative hero. The ending of *Ready to Catch Him Should He Fall* presents us with the ironic paradox of a fully integrated couple of outcasts who have entered the system's significatory nexus by the backdoor of subcultural appropriation, thus effectively planting their subversive desire at the very heart of patriarchy's symbolic exclusivity.

Bibliography

Achebe, Chinua (1977), 'An Image of Africa', *Massachusetts Review* 18, pp. 782–94.

Adler, Alfred (1928), *Understanding Human Nature*, London: Allen and Unwin.

Baldick, Chris (1987), *In Frankenstein's Shadow. Myth, Monstrosity, and Nineteenth Century Writing*, Oxford: Clarendon Press.

Banerjee, A. (1993), 'A Modern Hamlet: Jimmy Porter in *Look Back in Anger*,' *Hamlet Studies* 15: 1–2, pp. 81–92.

Banks, Iain (1990), *The Wasp Factory*, London: Abacus. (First published in 1984.)

Bartlett, Neil (1992), *Ready to Catch Him Should He Fall*, London: Penguin. (First published in 1990.)

Beaver, Harold (1981–82), 'Homosexual Signs (In Memory of Roland Barthes)', *Critical Inquiry* 8, pp. 99–119.

Berger, Maurice, Wallis, Brian and Watson, Simon (eds) (1995), *Constructing Masculinity*, New York and London: Routledge.

Bewell, Alan (1988), 'An Issue of Monstrous Desire: *Frankenstein* and Obstetrics', *Yale Journal of Criticism* 2, pp. 105–28.

Bhabha, Homi K. (1994), *The Location of Culture*, London and New York: Routledge.

Bode, Rita (1994), '"They . . . Should Be Out Of It": The Women of *Heart of Darkness*', *Conradiana* 26: 1, pp. 20–34.

Boone, Joseph A. and Cadden, Michael (eds) (1990), *Engendering Men. The Question of Male Feminist Criticism*, New York and London: Routledge.

Botting, Fred (ed.) (1995), *Frankenstein*, Basingstoke: Macmillan.

Boyd, S.J. (1991), 'Black Arts: *1982 Janine* and *Something Leather*', in Crawford and Nairn, pp. 108–23.

Braine, John (1989), *Room at the Top*, London: Mandarin. (First published in 1957.)

Bristow, Joseph (1992), 'Men after Feminism: Sexual Politics Twenty Years on', in Porter, pp. 57–79.

Bristow, Joseph and Broughton, Trev Lynn (eds) (1997), *The Infernal Desires of Angela Carter. Fiction, Femininity, Feminism*, London and New York: Longman.

y (1987a), 'A Case for Men's Studies', in Kimmel (1987), pp. 263–77.

ry (ed.) (1987b), *The Making of Masculinities: The New Men's Studies*, Allen and Unwin.

rry and Kaufman, Michael (eds) (1994), *Theorizing Masculinities*, nd Oaks: Sage.

Broughton, Lynda (1991), 'Portrait of the Subject as a Young Man: The Construction of Masculinity Ironized in "Male" Fiction', in Shaw and Stockwell, pp. 135–45.

Burgess, Anthony (1972), *A Clockwork Orange*, Harmondsworth: Penguin. (First published in 1962.)

Butler, Judith (1993), *Bodies that Matter. On the Discursive Limits of 'Sex'*, New York and London: Routledge.

Butler, Judith (1990), *Gender Trouble. Feminism and the Subversion of Identity*, New York and London: Routledge.

Byers, Thomas (1995), 'Terminating the Postmodern: Masculinity and Pomophobia', *Modern Fiction Studies* 41: 1, pp. 5–33.

Cairns, David and Richards, Richards (1988), 'No Good Brave Causes? The Alienated Intellectual and the End of Empire', *Literature and History* 14: 2, pp. 194–206.

Carey, John (ed.) (1986), *William Golding: The Man and His Books. A Tribute on His 75th Birthday*, London and Boston: Faber & Faber.

Carter, Angela (1982), *The Passion of New Eve*. London: Virago. (First published in 1977.)

Carter, Angela (1979), *The Sadeian Woman. An Exercise in Cultural History*, London: Virago.

Chanter, Tina (1997), 'Can the Phallus Stand, or Should It Be Stood Up?', in Dufresne, pp. 43–65.

Chapman, Rowena and Rutherford, Jonathan (eds) (1988), *Male Order. Unwrapping Masculinity*, London: Lawrence and Wishart.

Cixous, Hélène (1976), 'The Laugh of the Medusa', *Signs* 1: 4, pp. 875–93.

Cixous, Hélène and Clément, Catherine (1986), *The Newly Born Woman*, trans. by B. Wing, Minneapolis and London: University of Minnesota Press.

Claridge, Laura and Langland, Elizabeth (eds) (1990), *Out of Bounds. Male Writing and Gender(ed) Criticsm*, Amherst: University of Massachusetts Press.

Cockburn, Cynthia (1991), *In the Way of Women. Men's Resistance to Sex Equality in Organizations*, Basingstoke: Macmillan.

Cohen, David (1990), *Being a Man*, London: Routledge.

Conley, Verena Andermatt (1984), *Hélène Cixous: Writing the Feminine*, Lincoln, Nebraska and London: University of Nebraska Press.

Connell, R.W. (1995), *Masculinities*, Cambridge: Polity Press.

Conrad, Joseph (1996), *Heart of Darkness*, ed. by R.C. Murfin, second edition, Boston and New York: Bedford Books of St Martin's Press. (First published in 1902.)

Cornwall, Andrea and Lindisfarne, Nancy (eds) (1994), *Dislocating Masculinity. Comparative Ethnographies*, New York and London: Routledge.

Cottom, Daniel (1981), '*Frankenstein* and the Monster of Representation', *Sub-Stance* 28, pp. 60–71.

Crawford, Robert and Nairn, Thom (eds) (1991), *The Arts of Alasdair Gray*, Edinburgh: Edinburgh University Press.

Crew, Louie (ed.) (1978), *The Gay Academic*, Palm Springs, CA: ETC Publications.

Culler, Jonathan (1983), *On Deconstruction. Theory and Criticism after Structuralism*, London: Routledge.

Daly, Mary (1973), *Beyond God the Father*, Boston: Beacon.

Dawson, Graham (1994), *Soldier Heroes. British Adventure, Empire and the Imagining of Masculinities*, London and New York: Routledge.

Delrez, Marc (1995), 'Escape into Innocence: Ian McEwan and the Nightmare of History', *Ariel* 26: 2, pp. 7–23.

Dixon, Graham A. (1994), 'Still Looking Back: The Deconstruction of the Angry Young Man in *Look Back in Anger* and *Déjàvu*', *Modern Drama* 37: 3, pp. 521–9.

Dollimore, Jonathan (1983), 'The Challenge of Sexuality', in Sinfield (1983), pp. 51–85.

Dufresne, Todd (ed.) (1997), *Returns of the 'French Freud'. Freud, Lacan and Beyond*, New York and London: Routledge.

Duncan, Derek (1994), 'AIDS to Narration. Writing Beyond Gender', in Ledger et al, pp. 156–69.

Eagleton, Terry (1983), *Literary Theory. An Introduction*, Oxford: Blackwell.

Easlea, Brian (1983), *Fathering the Unthinkable. Masculinity, Scientists and the Nuclear Arms Race*, London: Pluto Press.

Edwards, Paul (1995), 'Time, Romanticism, Modernism and Moderation in Ian McEwan's *The Child in Time*', *English* 44: 178, pp. 41–55.

Egan, Robert G. (1989), '*Anger* and the Actor: Another Look Back', *Modern Drama* 32, pp. 413–24.

Ehrenreich, Barbara (1995), 'The Decline of Patriarchy', in Berger et al. (1995), pp. 284–90.

Felman, Shoshona (1995), '"The Grasp With Which I Recovered Him": A Child Is Killed in *The Turn of the Screw*', in James, pp. 193–206.

Fitting, Peter (1985), '"So We All Became Mothers": New Roles for Men in Recent Utopian Fiction', *Science Fiction Studies* 12, pp. 156–83.

Flannigan-Saint-Aubin, Arthur (1994), 'The Male Body and Literary Metaphors for Masculinity', in Brod and Kaufman (1994), pp. 239–58.

Fletcher, John and Benjamin, Andrew (eds) (1990), *Abjection, Melancholia and Love*, London: Routledge.

Freeman, Alan (1996), 'Ourselves as Others: *Marabou Stork Nightmares*', *Edinburgh Review* 95, pp. 135–41.

Fuss, Diana (ed.) (1991), *Inside/Out. Lesbian Theories, Gay Theories*, New York and London: Routledge.

Fussell, Edwin (1980), 'The Ontology of *The Turn of the Screw*', *Journal of Modern Literature* 8, pp. 118–28.

Gagnon, Madeleine (1981), [excerpt from] 'Corps I', in Marks and Courtivron, pp. 179–80.

Giddings, Robert (ed.) (1991), *Literature and Imperialism*, Basingstoke: Macmillan.

Gilbert, Sandra M. and Gubar, Susan (1979), *The Madwoman in the Attic. The Woman Writer and the Nineteenth-Century Literary Imagination*, New Haven: Yale University Press.

Golding, William (1958), *Lord of the Flies*, London: Faber & Faber. (First published in 1954.)

Goonetilleke, D.C.R.A. (1991), 'Ironies of Progress: Joseph Conrad and Imperialism in Africa', in Giddings, pp. 75–111.

Gray, Alasdair (1985), *1982 Janine*, Harmondsworth: Penguin. (First published in 1984.)

Grosz, Elizabeth (1990), 'The Body of Signification', in Fletcher and Benjamin: pp. 80–103.

Gutterman, David (1994), 'Postmodernism and the Interrogation of Masculinity', in Brod and Kaufman, pp. 219–38.

Hagan, Kay Leigh (ed.) (1992), *Women Respond to the Men's Movement*, San Francisco: Pandora.

Harrison, William M. (1995), 'The Power of Work in the Novels of Alasdair Gray', *Review of Contemporary Fiction* 15: 2, pp. 162–9.

Hatlen, Burton (1983), 'Milton, Mary Shelley, and Patriarchy', *Bucknell Review* 28, pp. 19–47.

Hawlin, Stefan (1995), 'The Savages in the Forest: Decolonising William Golding', *Critical Survey* 7: 2, pp. 125–35.

Hearn, Jeff (1996), 'Is Masculinity Dead? A Critique of the Concept of Masculinity/Masculinities', in Mac an Ghaill, pp. 202–17.

Herek, Gregory M. (1987), 'On Heterosexual Masculinity. Some Psychical Consequences of the Social Construction of Gender and Sexuality', in Kimmel, pp. 68–82.

Hodges, Devon (1983), '*Frankenstein* and the Feminine Subversion of the Novel', *Tulsa Studies in Women's Literature* 2: 2, pp. 155–64.

Hogle, Jerrold (1980), 'Otherness in *Frankenstein*: The Confinement/Autonomy of Fabrication', *Structuralist Review* 2, pp. 20–48.

Jardine, Alice and Smith, Paul (eds) (1987), *Men in Feminism*, New York and London: Routledge.

James, Henry (1995), *The Turn of the Screw*, ed. by P.G. Beidler, Boston and New York: Bedford Books of St Martin's Press. (First published in 1898.)

Johnson, Barbara (1982), 'My Monster/My Self', *Diacritics* 12: 2, pp. 2–10.

Johnson, Heather (1997), 'Unexpected Geometries: Transgressive Symbolism and the Transsexual Subject in Angela Carter's *The Passion of New Eve*', in Bristow and Broughton, pp. 166–83.

Johnson, Heather (1994), 'Textualizing the Double-Gendered Body: Forms of the Grotesque in *The Passion of New Eve*', *Review of Contemporary Fiction* 14: 3, pp. 43–8.

Jones, Ann Rosalind (1986), 'Writing the Body. Towards an Understanding of *l'Écriture Féminine*', in Showalter (1986), pp. 361–77.

Justad, Mark J. (1996), 'A Transvaluation of Phallic Masculinity: Writing with and through the Male Body', *Journal of Men's Studies* 4: 4, pp. 355–74.

Kaur, Bhagwan (1990), '*Look Back In Anger*: A Feminist Approach', *Punjab University RES Bulletin* 21: 1, pp. 71–80.

Keenan, Sally (1997), 'Angela Carter's *The Sadeian Woman*: Feminism as Treason', in Bristow and Broughton, pp. 132–48.

Kimmel, Michael. (ed.) (1987), *Changing Men. New Directions in Research on Men and Masculinity*, Newsbury Park: Sage.

Kristeva, Julia (1982), *Powers of Horror. An Essay on Abjection*, trans. by L.S. Roudiez, New York: Columbia University Press.

Kristeva, Julia (1981), [excerpt from] 'Oscillation between Power and Denial. An Interview with X. Gauthier', in Marks and Courtivron, pp. 165–7.

Laing, R.D. (1965), *The Divided Self*, Harmondworth: Penguin.

Leavis, F.R. (1963), *The Great Tradition*, New York: New York University Press.

Ledger, Sally, McDonagh, J. and Spencer, J. (eds) (1994), *Political Gender. Texts and Contexts*, New York: Harvester.

Ledwon, Lenora (1993), 'The Passion of the Phallus and Angela Carter's *The Passion of New Eve*', *Journal of the Fantastic in the Arts* 5: 4, pp. 26–41.

Lewis, Peter M. (1991), 'Mummy, Matron and the Maids. Feminine Presence and Absence in Male Institutions, 1934–63', in Roper and Tosh, pp. 168–89.

London, Bette (1993), 'Mary Shelley, *Frankenstein*, and the Spectacle of Masculinity', *PMLA* 108: 2, pp. 253–67.

London, Bette (1989), 'Reading Race and Gender in Conrad's Dark Continent', *Criticism* 31, pp. 235–52.

Lumsden, Alison (1993), 'Innovation and Reaction in the Fiction of Alasdair Gray', in Wallace and Stevenson, pp. 115–26.

Mac an Ghaill, Mártín (1996), *Understanding Masculinities. Social Relations and Cultural Arenas*, Buckingham and Philadelphia: Open University Press.

Magrs, Paul (1997), 'Boys Keep Swinging: Angela Carter and the Subject of Men', in Bristow and Broughton, pp. 184–97.

Makinen, Merja (1997), 'Sexual and Textual Transgression in *The Sadeian Woman* and *The Passion of New Eve*', in Bristow and Broughton, pp. 149–65.

Marks, Elaine and Courtivron, Isabelle de (eds) (1981), *New French Feminisms. An Anthology*, New York: Harvester Wheatsheaf.

Mars-Jones, Adam (1990), *Venus Envy*, London: Chatto and Windus.

McEwan, Ian (1988), *The Child in Time*, London: Picador. (First published in 1987.)

McEwan, Ian (1986), 'Schoolboys', in Carey, pp. 157–60.

McLeod, John (1998), 'Men against Masculinity: The Fiction of Ian McEwan', in Rowland et al., pp. 218–45.

McMaster, Graham (1988), 'Henry James and India: A Historical Reading of *The Turn of the Screw*', *Clio* 18: 1, pp. 23–40.

Meyer, Moe (ed.) (1994), *The Politics and Poetics of Camp*, London and New York: Routledge.

Middleton, Peter (1990), *The Inward Gaze. Masculinity and Subjectivity in Modern Culture*, London and New York: Routledge.

Miles, Rosalind (1992), *The Rites of Man. Love, Sex and Death in the Making of the Male*, London: Paladin.

Moers, Ellen (1977), *Literary Women*, Garden City: Doubleday.

Moi, Toril (ed.) (1986), *The Kristeva Reader*, New York and London: Routledge.

Moi, Toril (1985), *Sexual/Textual Politics: Feminist Literary Theory*, New York and London: Routledge.

Morgan, David H.J. (1992), *Discovering Men*, London and New York: Routledge.

Morgan, Thaïs (ed.) (1994), *Men Writing the Feminine: Literature, Theory, and the Question of Gender*, Albany, NY: SUNY Press.

Morris, Pam (1993), *Literature and Feminism. An Introduction*, Oxford: Blackwell.

Morrison, Blake (1997), *As If*, London: Granta.

Murphy, Peter F. (1994), *Fictions of Masculinity. Crossing Cultures, Crossing Sexualities*, New York and London: New York University Press.

Nairn, Thom (1993), 'Iain Banks and the Fiction Factory', in Wallace and Stevenson, pp. 127–35.

Newman, Beth (1995), 'Narratives of Seduction and the Seductions of Narrative: The Frame Structure of *Frankenstein*', in Botting, pp. 166–90.

O'Hara, J.D. (1966), 'Mute Choirboys and Angelic Pigs. The Fable in *Lord of the Flies*', *Texas Studies in Literature and Language* 7, pp. 411–20.

Orr, Mary (1998), 'Defining a New "Ecu-Menicism"? European Identities in the Masculine', *Forum for Modern Language Studies* 34: 3, pp. 209–13.

Orwell, George (1989), *Nineteen Eighty-Four*, London: Penguin.

Osborne, John (1993), *Look Back in Anger and Other Plays*, London: Faber & Faber.

Parrinder, Patrick (1981), 'Updating Orwell? Burgess's Future Fictions', *Encounter* 56: 1, pp. 45–53.

Piercy, Marge (1979), *Woman on the Edge of Time*, London: Women's Press.

Porter, David (ed.) (1992), *Between Men and Feminism*, London and New York: Routledge.

Ray, Philip E. (1981), 'Alex Before and After: A New Approach to Burgess' *A Clockwork Orange*', *Modern Fiction Studies* 27: 3, pp. 479–87.

Reilly, Patrick (1992), *Lord of the Flies. Fathers and Sons*, New York: Twayne.

Rimmon-Kenan, Shlomith (ed.) (1987), *Discourse in Psychoanalysis and Literature*, London and New York: Methuen.

Robbins, Bruce (1984), 'Shooting Off James's Blanks: Theory, Politics, and *The Turn of the Screw*', *Henry James Review* 5: 3, pp. 192–9.

Roger, Angela (1996), 'Ian McEwan's Portrayal of Women', *Forum for Modern Language Studies* 32: 1, pp. 11–26.

Roper, Michael and Tosh, John (eds) (1991), *Manful Assertions. Masculinities in Britain since 1800*, London and New York: Routledge.

Rosen, David (1993), *The Changing Fictions of Masculinity*, Urbana and Chicago: University of Illinois Press.

Rosenfield, Claire (1961), '"Men of a Smaller Growth": A Psychological Analysis of William Golding's *Lord of the Flies*', *Literature and Psychology* 11, pp. 93–101.

Rowland, Antony, Liggins, Emma and Uskalis, Eriks (eds) (1998), *Signs of Masculinity: Men in Literature 1700 to the Present*, Amsterdam: Rodopi.

Rutherford, Jonathan (1992), *Men's Silences. Predicaments in Masculinity*, London and New York: Routledge.

Ryan, Kiernan (1994), *Ian McEwan*, Plymouth: Northcote House.

Schmidt, Ricarda (1989), 'The Journey of the Subject in Angela Carter's Fiction', *Textual Practice* 3: 1, pp. 56–75.

Schoene, Berthold (1995), 'Angry Young Masculinity and the Rhetoric of Homophobia and Misogyny in the Scottish Novels of Alan Sharp', in Whyte (1995), pp. 85–106.

Schwenger, Peter (1984), *Phallic Critiques. Masculinity and Twentieth-Century Literature*, London: Routledge and Kegan Paul.

Scullion, Adrienne (1995), 'Feminine Pleasures and Masculine Indignities. Gender and Community in Scottish Drama', in Whyte (1995), pp. 169–204.

Sedgwick, Eve Kosofsky (1994), *Epistemology of the Closet*, London: Penguin.

Sedgwick, Eve Kosofsky (1985), *Between Men. English Literature and Male Homosocial Desire*, New York: Columbia University Press.

Segal, Lynne (1990), *Slow Motion. Changing Masculinities, Changing Men*, London: Virago.

Sharpless, Geoffrey (1994), 'Clockwork Education: The Persistence of the Arnoldian Ideal', *Postmodern Culture* 4: 3.

Shaw, Peter and Stockwell, Peter (eds) (1991), *Subjectivity and Literature from the Romantics to the Present Day*, London and New York: Pinters.

Shelley, Mary (1992), *Frankenstein, or The Modern Prometheus*, edited by J.M. Smith, Boston and New York: Bedford Books of St Martin's Press. (First published in 1818.)

Showalter, Elaine (1990), *Sexual Anarchy. Gender and Culture at the Fin de Siècle*, New York: Viking.

Showalter, Elaine (1987), 'Critical Cross-Dressing; Male Feminists and the Woman of the Year', in Jardine and Smith, pp. 116–32.

Showalter, Elaine (ed.) (1986), *The New Feminist Criticism: Essays on Women, Literature, and Theory*, London: Virago.

Sillitoe, Alan (1994), *Saturday Night and Sunday Morning*, London: Flamingo.

Silverman, Kaja (1992), *Male Subjectivity at the Margins*, New York and London: Routledge.

Sinfield, Alan (1992), '*Macbeth*: History, Ideology and Intellectuals', in Wilson and Dutton, pp. 167–80.

Sinfield, Alan (ed.) (1983), *Society and Literature 1945–1970*, London: Methuen.

Slay, Jack (1994), 'Vandalizing Time: Ian McEwan's *The Child in Time*', *Critique* 35: 4, pp. 205–18.

Smith, G. Gregory (1919), *Scottish Literature: Character and Influence*, London: Macmillan.

Smith, Johanna M. (1992), '"Cooped Up": Feminine Domesticity in *Frankenstein*', in Shelley, pp. 270–85.

Sontag, Susan (1967), 'Notes on "Camp"', *Against Interpretation and Other Essays*, London: Eyre and Spottiswoode, pp. 275–92.

Spector, Judith A. (1981), 'Science Fiction and the Sex War: A Womb of One's Own', *Literature and Psychology* 31: 1, pp. 21–32.

Spence, Donald (1987), 'Narrative Recursion', in Rimmon-Kenan, pp. 188–210.

Stenhouse, David (1996), 'A Wholly Healthy Scotland: A Reichian Reading of *1982 Janine*', *Edinburgh Review* 95, pp. 113–34.

Stockinger, Jacob (1978), 'Homotextuality: A Proposal', in Crew, pp. 135–51.

Straus, Nina P. (1987), 'The Exclusion of the Intended from Secret Sharing in Conrad's *Heart of Darkness*', *Novel* 20, pp. 123–37.

Sullivan, Andrew (1995), *Virtually Normal. An Argument about Homosexuality*, London: Picador.

Sullivan, Zohreh T. (1981), 'Enclosure, Darkness, and the Body: Conrad's Landscape', *Centennial Review* 25, pp. 59–79.

Taylor, D.J. (1989), *A Vain Conceit: British Fiction in the 1980s*, London: Bloomsbury.

Tustin, Frances (1990), *The Protective Shell in Children and Adults*, London: Karnac Books.

Wagner, Hans-Peter (1994), 'Learning to Read the Female Body: On the Function of Manet's *Olympia* in John Braine's *Room at the Top*', *Zeitschrift für Anglistik und Amerikanistik* 42, pp. 38–53.

Wallace, Gavin and Stevenson, Randall (eds) (1993), *The Scottish Novel Since the Seventies. New Visions, Old Dreams*, Edinburgh: Edinburgh University Press.

Walton, Priscilla L. (1992), *The Disruption of the Feminine in Henry James*, Toronto: University of Toronto Press.

Wandor, Michelene (1987), *Look Back in Gender. Sexuality and the Family in Post-War British Drama*, London and New York: Methuen.

Welsh, Irvine (1995), *Marabou Stork Nightmares*, London: Jonathan Cape.

Whyte, Christopher (1998), 'Masculinities in Contemporary Scottish Fiction', *Forum for Modern Language Studies* 34: 3, pp. 274–85.

Whyte, Christopher (ed.) (1995), *Gendering the Nation. Studies in Modern Scottish Literature*, Edinburgh: Edinburgh University Press.

Wilcox, Helen, McWatters, Keith, Thompson, Ann and Williams, Linda R. (eds) (1990), *The Body and the Text. Hélène Cixous, Reading and Teaching*, New York: Harvester Wheatsheaf.

Wilson, Richard and Dutton, Richard (eds) (1992), *New Historicism and Renaissance Drama*, London and New York: Longman.

Woolf, Virginia (1993), *A Room of One's Own* and *Three Guineas*, London: Penguin.

Yingling, Thomas (1990), *Hart Crane and the Homosexual Text. New Thresholds, New Anatomies*, Chicago and London: University of Chicago Press.

Index

abjection, definition of, 11
acceptance, unconditional maternal, 44
accomplishment, obedience to patriarchal
    jurisdiction as, 38
Achebe, Chinua, 21, 29
Achilles, 87
action, 85
    fear and, 58
adolescent male violence, as inevitable, 69
Africa, 151, 153, 154, 155
    as Europe's other, 22, 27, 28, 29
alcohol, 131, 149
alliances, of convenience, 59
alter ego, superman-type, 19
alterity, nature and, 110
altruistic imperial heroism, 27
America, 118–19, 126
American Dream, 68
androgyny, 101
Angry Young Man, 48, 49, 66, 69, 76,
    77–88, 89–98
apartheid, 152
As If (Morrison), *Marabou Stork Nightmares*
    and, 147
authority, males opposing, 78
autism, 25, 110, 125, 151
autonomy, 41, 42
    delusion of individual, 82

Banks, Iain, 101, 103–16

Bartlett, Neil, 175–86
Beaver, Harold, 182
behavioural imperatives, 35
behavioural norms, ambiguity of, 51
Bhabha, Homi, 101
Bildung, xii, 3, 114, 158, 164, 173–8
Bildungsroman, 74, 158, 168, 175
binarisms, gender, 6, 23, 35
binarist oppositioning, 30, 83, 112, 150,
    156, 157–8, 163
birth-myth, 5
The Book of Common Prayer, 182
Braine, John, 48, 89–98
Brando, Marlon, 68
Bristow, Joseph, xi, 173
British Empire, collapse of, 77
Brod, Harry, ix, 3, 102, 174
Bulger, James, 147
Burgess, Anthony, 47, 66–76
Butler, Judith, viii, 82, 104, 114, 124, 129,
    144, 180
Byers, Thomas, 11, 87

Cairns, David, 80, 82
Caledonian antisyzygy, 105
Cameron, James, 87
camp, 177, 178, 179
Carter, Angela, 101, 117–29, 134–5, 136,
    180–1

195